POLITICAL PHILOSOPHY AND RHETORIC

POLITICAL PHILOSOPHY AND RHETORIC

A study of
the origins of American party politics

JOHN ZVESPER

Lecturer in Politics, University of East Anglia

CAMBRIDGE UNIVERSITY PRESS

Cambridge

London · New York · Melbourne

Published by the Syndics of the Cambridge University Press
The Pitt Building, Trumpington Street, Cambridge CB2 1RP
Bentley House, 200 Euston Road, London NW1 2DB
32 East 57th Street, New York, NY 10022, USA
296 Beaconsfield Parade, Middle Park, Melbourne 3206, Australia

First published 1977

Printed in Great Britain at the
University Press, Cambridge

Library of Congress Cataloguing in Publication Data

Zvesper. John, 1948–

Political philosophy and rhetoric.

(Cambridge studies in the history and theory of politics)

Includes index.

1. Political parties – United States – History. I. Title.
JK2260.Z93 329'.02 76-11097
ISBN 0 521 21323 1

CONTENTS

PREFACE

This book appears in a series of 'studies in the history and theory of politics.' Although it may seem more historical than theoretical, it differs from many history books by being less fascinated by evolution and accident than by nature and design. While the historian may find it 'useful,' it is hoped that it will not be useless to the theorist: the interested spectator, who tries to gain more clarity than the actors possess, without discarding the advantages of their viewpoints in order to seek more certainty than the subject permits.

This work had its origins in dialogues with students and teachers in the Claremont Colleges. Of those who helped it along by criticism and encouragement, Dr J. R. Pole of Churchill College was especially persevering. The National Science Foundation provided financial support. Angela Zvesper liberally gave support and assistance of innumerable kinds.

London J.Z.
Washington's Birthday, 1976

Quoique le désir d'acquérir des biens de ce monde soit la passion dominante des Américains, il y a des moments de relâche où leur âme semble briser tout à coup les liens matériels qui la retiennent et s'échapper impétueusement vers le ciel.

Tocqueville, *Democracy in America*, Volume II, Part II, Chapter 12

PROLOGUE

I

Party government and
party politics

The nature of American party government

In studying the nature of American government, political scientists frequently point to the lasting significance of the political understanding and undertaking of the 'framers' of the federal Constitution of 1787. Historical inquiries are considered appropriate to this scientific study, for the current shape of the object of study, the American polity, can be well understood as a development of the regime which was founded and formed by the famous men who were members of the Philadelphia Convention. Knowledge of their intentions is rightly considered to be a firm foundation for understanding American politics. And not only the legal forms of the Constitution have endured. Indeed, some of them have been amended. However, when taken together with the work placed before the first Congress under the new Constitution by Alexander Hamilton, the political arrangements of the Federalists were such a comprehensive and durable achievement that they can with some reason be seen as the 'embryo' of American 'civilization' and an important contribution to 'the American philosophy.'[1] But important parts of American civilization are alien to Federalist intentions and accomplishments. And American political thought has been full of conflicts and divisions on issues which find characteristically Federalist notions on one side only; 'the American philosophy' is complex. So if we wish to consider the origins of the American polity in order to uncover something of its nature, we should study not only Federalism but also the successful alternative which quickly appeared and left its mark on the regime: Jeffersonian Republicanism. For the Republicans founded their party in order to oppose essential parts of the Federalist project.

When political scientists do look at the founding of American party politics, they usually see not such a formative antithesis, but a slight

3

modification and perfection of the Federalists' Constitution. The appearance of political parties in America in the years immediately following the ratification of the Constitution is seen as a development which confirms the indispensability of informal, quasi-private parties for the operation of the formal, public institutions of the Constitution. They see past the apparently irreconcilable opposition between Federalism and Republicanism, to the practical result, the pragmatic adjustment, which was a step or at least a drift in the direction of party government as it exists today. The first parties are not so much studied for any light that they might throw on the nature of the American polity as they are celebrated as the first example of institutions which proved to be both more and less necessary than the first partisans themselves supposed. The first partisans had healthy instincts, but they were too hesitant to use parties and too eager when they did use them. Parties were and are necessary not as emergency devices to remove threats to the safety of the Republic, nor as agents of progress, but as everyday methods of governing in a mass democracy. Americans need and accept parties not primarily as designers and implementers of programs, but for the population and lubrication of the constitutionally separate parts of government, for structuring and moderating the conflict of interest groups, and – perhaps – for improving the participation of citizens in government. According to this view, American party government has been truest to itself when it has appeared as a professional, pragmatic, patronage-oriented, cautious, 'accommodationist two-party system,'[2] in which the 'issue-oriented party' is the undesirable exception which causes the system to disintegrate.[3] Conflicts of principle like those which, unfortunately, marked the beginning of party politics in the 1790s are seen as events that hinder the growth of party government as a harmonizing system, even if they do have the advantage (if it is an advantage) of advancing the participatory, democratic thrust of party government.[4]

Advocates of this way of understanding the character of American party government are confronted by the paradox that 'a politics of interest is made possible by the fact that the American party system occasionally collapses under the onslaught of a politics of principle.' An occasional breakdown of the system seems to be necessary for its sustenance, for 'party allegiances exist today because in the past certain traumatic events precipitated a debate and a meaningful choice.'[5] Defenders of a moderate 'politics of interest' must admit the necessity of occasional implacable disagreements. The understanding of American party government would not lead to such a paradoxical stance as

this if the original and recurring 'politics of principle' could be comprehended as aspects of parties and of the system themselves, instead of
being seen as an *ad hoc* remedy for an otherwise theoretically perfect
system. Parties which completely forgot their principled origins might
cease to be useful tools of pragmatic politics, because they might cease
to be.

The suggestion that partisan principles are continuously important
to American party government – in times of consensus as well as in times
of conflict – should not be astonishing, for not only American but all
modern party government had its origins in the attempt to make
politics conform to certain kinds of principles. Modern government is
everywhere party government. The existence and encouragement of
party or parties is a part of the public constitution in modern regimes
– a part of the way in which government is seen and allowed to work.
The singularity or plurality of party is often used to distinguish among
the variety of modern regimes, but party is a more or less respectable
pursuit in all of them. The desirability of a single party or a system of
two or more parties is publicly defended. This is a remarkable departure
from the ways of Western politics for all but the last two centuries. Before
the eighteenth century, party was generally thought of either as an
emergency device, which might properly be used by public-spirited
politicians in private; or as a tolerable pursuit of private ends, but hardly
a laudable, public-spirited activity. This latter opinion persists today, not
only in two- or multi-party regimes, but also in one-party regimes, where
the party is after all distinguished from the government; nowhere is
party completely public in the way that a constitution is. But, in all
modern regimes, party is more public, and more closely associated with
the common good, than the tolerable but unrespectable party of less
recent times. Modern parties are publicly respectable parties, and they
can be that because they have a principled side to their character. Even
Edmund Burke's famous defense of the respectability of parties, which
was directed against the idea and the practice of a party of abstract
principle, had recourse to the idea of parties of principles derived from
history.[6] Modern parties depend on publicized principles and programs
which restrict the sphere of discretionary statesmanship. They resemble
the parties which politicians employed before party became respectable
and gentlemanly, in that they claim to be directed to the public good.
But they are different in that they define themselves publicly, and
therefore constrain those who lend them their support. Thus, statesmen
sometimes find it necessary to alter their party allegiance. They do not
thereby testify to the soundness of the apology for a plural party system

made by the opponents of a 'politics of principle,' for a statesman's party allegiance need not be less wholehearted for being altered; it could well be more. In fact, by lending their support to a party, for however long a term – and with however high a rate of interest – they testify to the power of party principles in modern politics. A sensible alteration of party allegiance makes the sufficiency of party principles questionable, but it merely confirms their power.

The least that can be said about American parties in this respect is that they are by nature potentially programmatic, even if they are actually so only infrequently. Examination of the intense conflicts that accompany the origins of the great American parties would make this potential more intelligible. But it might also be asked how far this potential affects the everyday character of parties and their overall impact on the American regime.

Depreciation or neglect of this principled side of American parties can lead to the neglect of important differences between American and British party government. In Britain, where party was first publicly advocated in opposition to a programmatic party of abstract principle, party government can be traced more directly than in America to 'the rise of legitimate opposition.'[7] But in the United States, party was first made publicly respectable by a particular party – the Jeffersonian Republicans – who were themselves attached to a program based on abstract principle. It is true that they did not intend a permanent establishment of the practice of party, but it is equally true that later American politicians who reintroduced party returned as well to a principled posture similar to that of the Republicans. Consequently, the defense of party in America was for several decades in the hands of those who denied equal legitimacy to any other party. Moreover, while a system of parties has become, with the recurrence of party and the disillusionment with party, a fixture of the American regime, and approved as such by its students, a system of legitimate opposition has yet to be politically established. The American two-party system is truly a capacious one-party system. The pressures sustaining the duality of parties in American national politics are numerous; the Presidential focus of American politics and the absence of proportional representation figure prominently among them. But one of the most important reasons for the existence and encouragement of two parties in America can be seen in the 'theory of critical elections.'[8] According to this theory, each of the great majority parties in American politics – the Jeffersonian Republicans from 1801 to the 1820s, the Jacksonian Democrats from the 1830s to the 1850s, the Republicans from the 1860s to the 1930s, and the

Democrats from the 1930s to the present – each of these parties, although born in intense conflict, has yet been so victorious that it has been able to enforce its own principles as a consensus. These parties have dominated the American political scene so much that party government has been in an important sense one-party government. This is true not simply in terms of the success or failure of partisan office-seeking, although the statistics here are impressive enough: to mention only the most impressive figure, in 1976, after 183 years of party politics, the minority parties – that is, the major parties in opposition to Jefferson's, Jackson's, Lincoln's and Franklin Roosevelt's parties – will have controlled simultaneously the House of Representatives, Senate and Presidency for a total of fifteen years; while the corresponding figure for the majority parties is 110 years. More important is the fact that these minority parties survive as well as they do by reshaping themselves in the image of their more formidable opponents. David H. Fischer has shown how the Federalists after their defeat at the turn of the century tried to imitate the electoral style of the Republicans.[9] The Whigs were most successful when they took their cue from the Democrats, denied their Federalist inclinations and nominated for President military heroes; even then their victories might more properly be attributed to the Democrats' misfortunes in economic affairs (in 1840) and intra-party divisions (in 1848). From the Civil War to 1932, 'The Democratic Party,' Adlai Stevenson once remarked, 'had the dubious distinction of wandering in the desert for a longer time than the children of Israel after their flight from Egypt.'[10] The oases provided by Cleveland's and Wilson's victories depended on divisions in the Republican ranks (the desertion of Mugwumps in 1884, discontented farmers in 1892, Progressives in 1912, and neutralists and some Progressives in 1916). These were 'deviating' rather than critical realigning elections;[11] they did not signal the arrival of a new party system. The same can be said of the Eisenhower and Nixon victories in the current party system, inaugurated by the Roosevelt Revolution of 1932, which was a critical realigning election. Again, the electoral hegemony of the majority party in each system is less significant than its enforcement of a policy and a rhetoric, and the pressures on the minority party to offer an 'echo' rather than a 'choice.' The national enforcement of the policy decision made by the election of 1860 was assisted by a conflict of arms; the consequence was a general acceptance of an end of the expansion of slavery, and a beginning of the expansion of nationally-encouraged industry. Neither major party could effectively oppose these policies; at the same time, both were able to bid for the support of reformers, and to speak for 'the response to

industrialism.' The decades between the Civil War and the New Deal
were a Republican regime not only because the Republicans were able
to win most of the electoral battles, but also because they had in any case
already won the decisive battle, the one which determined the principle
of the regime. In the 1930s there was another decisive battle – not
between the old armies, however. As in the 1790s and the 1850s, an
essentially new political party was created – the New Deal Democrats –
and this party successfully defined the new principle of consensus. At
first, the Republicans clung to opposite principles, but they soon came
to respect the new regime; as early as 1936, new-model Republicans
emerged, sympathetic to the goals of the interventionist welfare state.
By 1940 this conformity to the principle of the new Democratic party
extended to the Republican Presidential nominating convention, where
– except in 1964 – it has ruled ever since. A new Republican party took
its place alongside the new Democratic party.[12]

The reasons for the two-party system thus vary with the presence or
absence of conflict over leading principles. When a new principle is to
be introduced, it requires a party to advance it. This new party can be
composed of elements of old ones, but the principle to which they adhere
is a new formula which binds all the elements together and defines the
new compound. The opposition party, which can contain many elements
of the former majority party, will become the new minority party,
defined at first by a principle opposed to the new one, but at last, after
being clearly defeated in one or more critical elections, by the victorious
new principle. In this way, the 'two-party system' has been an instrument
of the 'politics of principle,' not only in the obvious case when principled
conflicts between parties have been the order of the day, but also when
these conflicts have been resolved and one party's principles have
become common ground of both parties. This is not to deny that the
'politics of interest' has played an important role in the party system.
Especially in times of uncritical elections, major American parties have
appeared as uneasy coalitions of interest groups. Indeed, this role has
been no less important when principles have been disputed than when
they have been settled; the presence of a 'politics of interest' does not
guarantee pacific moderation. But neither does such moderation require
the absence of a 'politics of principle'; it only requires that the 'principle'
be an object of consensus. Recognition of the importance of principle
in American party politics does not imply acquiescence in traumatic
party strife.

Additional reassurance on this last point can be produced by arguing
that even when principles have been disputed rather than agreed by

American parties, the disputes have not concerned fundamentals. Although modern governments are avowedly party governments, they also claim to be impartial governments, representing the people rather than ruling them. Accordingly, under whatever party regime, American government is supposed to be limited government, restricted from the realm of society by being restrained from the comprehensive direction of men's lives, which would be partial to a particular way of life. The best means to maintain this liberal kind of government has been disputed – and decided by critical elections – but such liberty has been accepted as the proper end by all the major parties. Partisan controversies have therefore concerned the best way to secure impartiality. This may seem paradoxical, but it is historically reasonable, for modern party government did not arise until impartiality had been advanced as the end of government. Recoiling from the devastations of partisan Christian politics in the sixteenth and seventeenth centuries, men came to accept the modern idea that partisanship regarding the proper way of life need not be the primary concern of politics, which could be fully occupied with the necessary means to life. Once the settlement of politico-theological partisanship was effected in this way, political parties could be considered tolerable, if petty.[13] It is true that the respectability granted to modern parties in the eighteenth and nineteenth centuries required the reintroduction of principles into parties. But it also required the maintenance of that fundamental modern principle, political impartiality. Modern parties advance public-spirited principles of government, but they do not reintroduce the superseded notion of ruling. If they did, they could not present themselves as parties; they would have to claim comprehensiveness and impartiality. As it is, they claim partiality, but their underlying impartiality is evident. They often promote interference in the way people live, but this interference is justified by scientific or historical arguments that it tends to the self-realization of people; it 'forces them to be free.' It is not justified as forcing or teaching them to be good men, as defined by the regime, in the traditional manner of ancient and medieval polities. Modern parties do not return to the traditional definition of man as a naturally political creature, whose rulers are determined through the use of his natural power of argument about good and bad.[14] American parties are no exception.

The study of American government must include a study of the origins of American party government, in order to understand more completely the founding of the regime. In addition, the origins of American party politics must be studied, in order to comprehend the phenomenon of critical elections in general, and particularly the origins of the cycle of American party alignment;[15] to be able to judge how much the principled aspect of parties is employed in their uncritical operation; and to understand some of the possibilities of partisanship after the impartial, apolitical aspirations of modern politics are taken into account.

The origins of American party politics

In studying the origins of American party politics, historians have suggested several valuable ways of understanding the conflict between Federalists and Republicans. Each way reveals part of the truth about party government.

Sometimes an international focus is adopted. Most historians have not gone as far along this route as a few contemporaries did, in reducing the Federalists to a British party and the Republicans to a French party. There are two kinds of difficulties with such a reduction. First, it simply does not fit the facts. The parties had plenty to quarrel about aside from international affairs. Foreign labels played a greater role in exacerbating already existing partisanship than in causing it in the first place. The first partisan election campaign took place in 1792, before the issues between the parties were complicated by the disputes over foreign policy which followed the outbreak in 1793 of war between France and the First Coalition. And when these disputes did come to the fore, the parties could perhaps be more truthfully described as anti-French and anti-British, than as pro-British and pro-French. The British and French governments were aware that they were dealing with Americans, proud of their independence and anxious to reap the benefits of neutrality. Secondly, in so far as it is true that the Federalists leaned toward Britain and the Republicans toward France, there remains the question of the reasons for these tendencies. Were they economic? social? ideological? strategic? accidental? Whatever they were, these causes rather than their effects would be the more essential features of the party conflict.

Many historians suggest that the heat of this party conflict was essentially accidental, a product of unwarranted and even imaginary friction. Each party is seen to have harbored unreasonable suspicions of the other's motives. It is suggested that the truth about the division between Federalism and Republicanism can be seen more clearly if, instead of thinking about it 'as a contest of abstractions, we regard it as one between two shifting groups of men who, differing upon practical problems as they arose, came to suspect the views and purposes of those in the opposite camp and to regard their own pursuit of power and their determination to defeat their opponents as the supreme consideration.'[16] The decade preceding Jefferson's election in 1800 is interpreted as an 'age of passion' in which negligible or at most negotiable differences of opinion were exaggerated out of all proportion in the minds of the partisans, so much so that they became obstacles that prevented Americans from seeing their shared political assumptions. The unnecessarily desperate and acerbic political conflict of the 1790s was caused by the American consensus being forgotten or mislaid. Happily, it was eventually recalled or rediscovered, and in retrospect the benefits of the conflict between Federalists and Republicans can be highlighted, even if these first partisans must be chided for their immature hostility to organized political parties. One of these benefits was their unintended demonstration of the tolerableness of organized opposition. Equally unintended was another major benefit: the advancement of democracy. Neither Federalists nor Republicans were democrats, but their competition for votes helped to democratize American politics. This historical interpretation is intended to support the case for the 'accommodationist two-party system.' It argues that there were no foundations for serious partisan conflict in the 1790s. It is not surprising that much of the history written from this point of view is directed against the work of the progressive historians, who assert the substantial nature of these foundations, in two different accounts.

One of these accounts is the idealistic interpretation of the conflict between Federalists and Republicans as an epic confrontation between aristocracy and democracy. Jefferson's victory is enthusiastically attributed to the 'democratic temper' of the country.[17] The contention that the Jeffersonian Republicans were democrats has been as effectively challenged as the contention that the Federalists were aristocrats or monarchists. However, this pro-Republican interpretation does have the advantage of reflecting some of the idealism which was undeniably more Republican than Federalist.

This is an advantage which the self-proclaimed realists among the progressives felt able to do without. Their mood was one of 'honest realism,' which was thought to be 'putting away the naïve myths that passed for history and substituting homely authentic fact.'[18] The most famous and influential of these realists, Charles Beard, argued that the main issue between Federalists and Republicans was whether capitalistic or agrarian interests should prevail in America. What is more, he insisted that the parties *presented* themselves as mere agents of these economic interest groups: Hamilton's hard-headed, realistic program revealed his 'penetrating wisdom' as a statesman; and the Republicans' political and economic ideology was important not for its attempts at moral justification of the party, but for its identification of the Republicans as the agrarian party. Like James Madison in *The Federalist*, Beard treated all economic interests as morally equal.[19] Beard's emphasis on economic reality and his dismissal of the claims of political rhetoric are current in more recent histories of the 1790s; there are more post-Beardians than anti-Beardians. It is recognized that 'the social sources of party were far more complex and less homogeneous than Beard suggested'; ethnic, religious, residential and diverse occupational factors have been added to Beard's analysis of the class basis of Federalists and Republicans.[20] These qualifications of Beard's thesis blunt his explanation of the sharpness of the partisan conflicts, and can therefore support the case for accommodationist parties. However, they do not question the soundness of Beard's adoption of a class analysis of parties, and his dismissal of 'unrealistic' partisan rhetoric. That this premise is questionable can be indicated by contrasting Beard's praise for Alexander Hamilton's realism with Hamilton's own judgement of the shortcomings of his statesmanship and his party. In 1792, when first confronted by the challenge of the Republican party, Hamilton exclaimed, 'Were ever men more ingenious to torment themselves with phantoms?' And ten years later, reflecting on the Federalists' defeat, he concluded, 'Men are rather reasoning than reasonable animals, for the most part governed by the impulse of passion.'[21] Hamilton discovered that the cold, calculating 'realism' of Federalism was insufficient; perhaps the success of Republicanism owed something to its warm idealism. The exploration of this possibility would require more serious attention than the class analysis gives to the principles of the parties.

Recent historians of early American political ideology have turned their attention to the first parties in America. But they have persuaded Federalism and Republicanism to sit together for a single portrait against a New World background only by making them sit so close as to become indistinguishable. Consensus on an 'American science of politics,' developed by Federalists but usable by other parties, seems to foreclose the possibility of fundamental ideological differences between American parties, whose conflicts must therefore be explained mainly in terms of sociology.[22] Or, if ideology was important in the conflict between Federalists and Republicans, this was only because of a temporary aberration: pessimistic Federalists had lost faith in the American science of politics, and Revolutionary ideology had to be reasserted by the Republicans in order to cast out this Federalist heresy.[23] The possibility of conflict within the American science of politics is not investigated.

The reason for this seems to be that this science and American partisan ideologies are defined in narrowly political terms. Differences of opinion on the form and structure of government are assumed to be the significant differences, and opinions on the kind of life promoted by governmental policies, along with the theoretical foundations of these opinions, are neglected.[24] This is to follow the genius but not the intricacies of modern representative government, which does legislate in the moral and even the sacred realm, if only to reduce the need for comprehensive legislation in these realms. It is not surprising that modern political science, compelled to deal with such matters, has failed in its attempt to be uncontroversial. It would be surprising to find that the American science of politics was immune to controversy; its purity of modernity, its low level of contamination by Old World doctrines, should make this science display modern controversy very clearly. This book explores the thesis that this kind of controversy characterized the origins of American party politics, and that the conflict between Federalism and Republicanism concerned 'ideas about the proper origins, extent, and ends of civil government,' as well as 'ideas about its proper structure.'[25] It suggests that the principles of the partisan divisions in America in the 1790s can be understood as a reflection of the difficulties which appeared in modern political philosophy (or modern political science, an equivalent term) after its initial success. Modern political philosophy, as it was developed in England in the middle of the seventeenth century, set out to give peaceful political society a firm, solid foundation in a 'realistic' appraisal of human nature. This liberal Hobbesian project (reflected in Federalism) ignored or tried to suppress the more aspiring elements in humanity, aspirations that seemed intrinsically to claim the right to rule rather than merely to be represented. But human aspirations proved to be irrepressible, and modern idealism (reflected in Republicanism) thus came to rival modern realism in its practical effects. This idealism did not return to the traditional idealistic position, which contemplated ruling rather than representation. The rivalry between realism and idealism was a battle between moderns, not a quarrel between ancients and moderns. The division between Federalism and Republicanism reflects this rivalry and illustrates some of the possibilities of theoretical and practical conflicts within modern liberalism. Political doctrines congenial to modern idealism were expressed in the English and Scottish responses to Hobbes and Locke, but the soul of this idealism was epitomized by the moral teachings of Jean-Jacques Rousseau. Rousseau's moral philosophy reached different conclusions from his political philosophy: the good man was not a very good citizen. This kind of tension between morality and politics came to be expressed in politics by the idealistic rhetoric employed by realistic regimes. This can be seen happening in America, in the Revolution of 1800.

The political scientists of the Federalist party developed, in sober whiggish fashion, a realistic republicanism for America. Federalist political science accepted the primary assumption of modern political philosophy, that government and civil society were necessary correctives to the warlike state of nature. Man was not naturally political, but government was made necessary by his self-interested nature. It was made possible, on the other hand, by the existence of men whose ambitions were political rather than economic, men motivated by what Hamilton called 'the love of fame, the ruling passion of the noblest minds.'[26] With such men in government, the conflicts of economic interests in society could be regulated and directed to the common good, civilized peace, while men outside government need rarely lift their eyes above their selfish pursuits.

Spokesmen for the Republican party developed an idealistic republicanism as an alternative to this Federalist vision. They argued that the state of nature was not so terrible. Men were not naturally political; the realists' desire to end rule by natural or supernatural right was not unhealthy. But men were naturally social. The natural harmony of selfish interests, together with the operation of a natural moral sense, made government less urgent than Federalists imagined. Politicians needed to do little more than remove the impediments to the growth of the good side of humanity, and men outside government should be allowed and encouraged to do much more than merely pursue their narrow, selfish interests. While Federalists looked for men of virtue in politics, Republicans expected men's moral sense to flourish in society, their selfish passions subdued and limited.

The two distinct images of the state of nature reflected conflicting perceptions of human nature and, accordingly, of the form and purpose of human associations. Although these two different sets of political principles were not the only alternatives expressed by Americans in the 1790s, these were the principles in the light of which many of the leading men saw and judged the new government. The influence of these principles on politics was supported by many who did not agree with them. In this way, they were ruling principles, *political* principles which were carried by other beliefs as well as by less thoughtful interests.

In the chapters that follow, these principles are analyzed, and the widespread and remarkably consistent expression of them by partisans of the 1790s is exhibited. Connections are drawn between theoretical and practical differences, to show how Americans' different expectations of their new government led to partisan competition within that government. Along the way, suggestions are made as to how the principles and rhetoric of the two parties might be intelligibly related to the class composition of the parties.

The major theme of this study is the tension between the practical aims and the rhetorical necessities of modern political philosophy. Republicans were opponents not only (with Federalists) of the mixture of Christianity and politics, but also of elaborate, expensive government and complicated economic policies: those not so pious frauds of modern politicians (including Federalists) which the Republicans considered to be the modern equivalent of priestly tyranny. But it may be suggested that Republicans owed the success of their partisanship to their rhetoric, and that the psychological effects of this rhetoric resembled those of religion. The origins of American party politics can be seen as the origins of American political religion. This religion is seen less consistently in the effective policies than in the effective rhetoric of American parties. The rhetoric of American political religion appears throughout American politics, but it is particularly striking in and essential to the electoral strategies of the most successful political parties: not only (as might be expected) of the Jacksonian revivals of Jeffersonianism in the nineteenth century, but also (and more significantly) of those winners of critical elections who have carried anti-Jeffersonian ideas into American government. The Republican party of the 1850s, which advanced many of the projects of the former Whig opponents of Jackson, did not do so solely by advocating them. There were other, more idealistic issues that proved more decisively politic. And Lincoln's charge that the government was engaged in a conspiracy against the liberties of the people echoed the Republican rhetoric of Jefferson and Jackson.[27] The Democratic party of the 1930s prospered on the expression of moral indignation at the 'economic royalists' and the 'money-changers,' who were castigated in Roosevelt's First Inaugural Address as 'self-seekers' with 'no vision' who had failed to solve business problems because they had not adopted 'social values more noble than mere monetary profit.' Roosevelt even called for a redistribution of population back to the land, to correct 'the overbalance of population in our industrial centers.' This was not as eloquent as Jefferson's vision of agrarian virtue. It lacked that clear articulation of its assumptions about human nature which had been expressed in the eighteenth century. Nevertheless, in accordance with Democratic rhetoric, the imposing government apparatus erected by the New Deal was publicly most successfully justified not as an elitist regulatory system, but as a tribune of the 'forgotten man at the bottom of the economic pyramid.'[28] *The* American political parties – especially in their origins – have followed the Jeffersonian precedent by paying homage to popular virtue, indirectly expressing in rhetoric the anxieties and doubts that Americans have felt about the realities of their civilization.

PART I
THE FEDERALIST PROJECT

2
The Federalist science of politics

Revolutionary realism

The republican ideals of many Americans were somewhat tempered by a certain realism in the 1770s, as they came to terms with the demands of durable state governments. And it is well known that a 'hard, clear realism in political thought' reached fulfillment 'in the formation of the national government' and achieved 'its classic expression in *The Federalist*'[1] (the famous articles composed by Alexander Hamilton, James Madison and John Jay for publication in the New York press, under the pseudonym 'Publius'). But the realism of *The Federalist* and the national Constitutional movement was only one of the legitimate descendants of the realism that Americans had embraced in the 1770s.

The realism of the later Revolutionary years meant turning away from a preoccupation with the constitutional balancing of grandly conflicting social orders, to a concern with controlling the lesser but more pressing conflicts within the single social order remaining in their political vision and vocabulary after the repudiation of royalty and nobility. This single social order was internally ordered, but its orderedness was the result of a social deference that, however persistent in American society, had no roots in the political thought that was made dominant in and by the successful Revolution.[2] Political control of conflicts in society was therefore not to be based openly on a political recognition of the orders of wealth and birth; for example, after 1776, American senates were justified more successfully as a second body representative of (not to say instructed by) 'the people' than as an embodiment of 'the better sort' of people.[3]

The upper social classes in the new American states did not vanish simply because they were effectively denied a place in political rhetoric. Neither were the social elite kept out or even turned out of political office. But they were given no special political privileges on the Old World

model, no titles, no estates. Their political privileges were publicly
justifiable only in terms of their property,[4] and in terms of the talents
that their property enabled them to cultivate.[5] Their retreat to the refuge
of property had the weakness of the promiscuity of property: property
is today of some import in American politics, habits of social deference
in the eighteenth century fashion are now rare. The revolution of
American political rhetoric that accompanied the War of Independence
meant that social distinctions had to be translated before being turned
into political power, and they lost longevity if not vitality in translation.
Yet, the refuge of property served well enough to foreclose the possibility, if it ever existed, that the restriction of the American political
world to egalitarianism portended an immediate democratic social
revolution.[6]

This limited but limiting restriction of politics to an enlarged 'democracy' gained impetus in the 1780s from the nationalists' desire to escape
the influence of the states and therefore of the great families of the
states.[7] The success of this restriction lies behind the characterization
of American politics as a tradition of liberalism, or as a pure creature
of the 'Age of Equality.' But the establishment of American politics on
the egalitarian creed roundly proclaimed by the Declaration of Independence not only failed to break down social distinctions; it also failed
to preclude the possibility of profound political dissension. It simply set
the stage and furnished a lively vocabulary for such dissension. This
dissension was political: it was not determined by social distinctions, and
it could have existed even if they had been corroded or destroyed.
Revolutionary realism left room for differences within the American
science of politics.[8]

The gradually predominating concern with the control of a single-
order society, while it was a 'fresh, direct comprehension of political
reality'[9] in post-Revolutionary America, could and did receive both a
realistic and an idealistic response. Whereas some sought this control
by means of governments, others came to rely on the self-control of
society, coupled with a little government as an instrument of society. The
ideal of a society of independent and virtuous men who would neither
wish nor be compelled to look to government for guidance and regulation, and of a government that was weak enough to remain dependent
on the will of this society, became the alternative to the Federalist
scheme of a clearly governed society of extremely ordinary mortals.
And who can say that this alternative, harking back as it did to one of
the major themes of Revolutionary ideology, the inability of human
nature to withstand the corrupting influence of power, was not closer

in spirit to the dream of the Revolutionary *élan* than was the 'worldly wisdom' of this Federalist scheme?[10] However, Federalist realism prevailed for a time.

Federalist realism

The eighteenth-century British opposition theorists whose thinking informed American Revolutionary ideology were wholly pessimistic regarding the possibility of virtue remaining intact as well as in power. This pessimism left them with nothing but 'fear for the future';[11] their fear could have been allayed by the theories of *The Federalist*. 'The science of politics...like most other sciences has received great improvement.'[12] Therefore *The Federalist* could claim to solve the problem of government in such a way as to dispose of the old opposition between power and liberty. It did so not by removing the corrupting influences of power, but by a 'policy of supplying by opposite and rival interests, the defect of better motives.' By this policy, pessimism regarding human nature could be accompanied by optimism regarding the success of powerful political arrangements that would preserve and propagate liberty instead of threatening it. *The Federalist* promised to show that the new Constitution would afford preservation 'to liberty, and to property,' in spite of and even because of the 'energy' of the government it established. There was no question of leaving society to control itself: 'Nothing is more certain than the indispensable necessity of government.' The greater multiplicity of economic interests would make the enlarged area of the union of the states more amenable to government, for the jostling of a wide variety of interest groups would ensure that no single interest became so overbearing in the society that it could become the single interest to which politicians were bound to cater. But the very fact that if given a chance an interest group would be oppressive and heedless of minority rights made a government with the power 'to break and control' such 'violence' rather more than less necessary. It was the unrealiability of 'better motives' that made a self-regulating society an unrealistic dream. For 'what is government itself, but the greatest of all reflections on human nature? If men were angels, no government would be necessary.' The classic definition of man as a political animal required amendment. Man was not naturally political; it was only man's imperfections that made politics necessary. James Wilson expounded a variation on this Federalist theme in a lecture at Philadelphia in 1791: 'Government is, indeed, highly necessary; but it is necessary to a *fallen* State. Had Man continued *innocent*,

Society, without the Aids of Government, would have shed its *benign influence* even over the *Bowers of Paradise.*'[13] Conviction of man's original sinfulness can engender pious pride and the passion for redemption of oneself and others, and lead to crusades and the burning of heretics. Republicans would display more crusading spirit than the enlightened scientists of Federalism did. Federalists acted less on the conviction of man's original sinfulness than on the assumption of his original lack of goodness, a hypothesis which frees the passion for self-preservation – for life, liberty and property. It was as hard for some Republicans to admit this bourgeois passion as it would have been to confess their irredeemable sinfulness. However, the 'knowledge of human nature' claimed by 'Publius' led him not to flinch at men's 'ambitious, vindictive, and rapacious' qualities, but to utilize these qualities in giving a solid social basis to politics, by accepting and even encouraging a multiplication of what he called 'factions' and 'parties,' or what are today called 'interest groups.'[14]

But what of 'government itself'? *The Federalist's* unblinking view of human nature was carried into its solution to the problem of power and liberty. 'Publius' did not depend on the vain hope that 'enlightened statesmen will be able to adjust these clashing interests, and render them all subservient to the public good.' For that would have been to expect moral virtue to have effect on men in power, when it could not even be expected to have much effect on the motives of men uncontaminated by power. It was as fruitless to look for 'angels...to govern men' as it was to expect men to be angelically exempt from the necessity of government. 'The regulation of these various and interfering interests' nevertheless formed 'the principal task of modern legislation.' 'Publius' wished to promote the establishment of a government sufficiently powerful to perform this task, without depending on the moral or religious motives of political officers to prompt them to the faithful performance of this task and to keep them from promoting their personal interests by means of their power. He reckoned to do this by taking 'the most effectual precautions for keeping them virtuous...' These precautions were the partial separation of the functional powers of the government so that each could effectively monitor the others, and the other famous institutional devices for scrutinizing and checking the improper uses of power. The clashing interests within government were perhaps expected to be more automatically productive of public good than the clashing interests of society; but the little society of governors also had an overseer, in the form of elections, to ensure that private vices conduced to public benefits.[15] If governments in general are the greatest of reflections on human nature, the government promoted by *The Federalist* was no exception.

The Federalist attitude to the place of popular virtue in politics was summarized by William Vans Murray in 1787 in his *Political Sketches*, where he observed (in opposition to Montesquieu and Mably) that if virtue 'be of so delicate a nature, as to suffer extinction by the prevalence of those luxurious habits to which all national improvements lead...it certainly is a principle of too whimsical nature to be relied on.'[16] Modern political philosophers, from Machiavelli to Montesquieu, had stressed that the durability of a republic depended on the maintenance of popular virtue. This 'republican virtue' was very different from the moral virtue that concerned ancient political philosophers. As John Adams discerned:

> It is not the classical virtue which we see personified in the choice of Hercules, and which the ancient philosophers summed up in four words, – prudence, justice, temperance and fortitude. It is not Christian virtue, so much more sublime, which is summarily comprehended in universal benevolence. What is it then? According to Montesquieu, it should seem to be merely a negative quality; the absence only of ambition and avarice.[17]

Montesquieu had written: 'Virtue in a republic is a very simple thing: it is a love of the republic; it is a sensation, and not a consequence of acquired knowledge, a sensation that may be felt by the meanest as well as by the highest person in the state.'[18] Even this passionate virtue of patriotism – to say nothing of classical moral virtue – was found to be unreliable by many American politicians in the 1780s. That is why Madison rejected as 'impracticable' what he thought was the one decent method of removing the cause of factions: 'giving to every citizen the same opinions, the same passions, and the same interests.'[19] Republican virtue, the unselfish passion of patriotism, was not seen to overcome the selfish passions of interestedness and avarice in Americans. Hamilton preached this Federalist gospel to the New York ratifying convention: 'Men will pursue their interests. It is as easy to change human nature, as to oppose the strong current of the selfish passions.'[20] 'Interest,' taken 'in the popular sense,' Madison believed, referred to 'the immediate augmentation of property and wealth.'[21] This kind of interestedness replaced the virtue of patriotism as the politically relevant passion in the Federalist science of politics. If the passion of republican virtue, which entailed the absence of popular luxury, was unreliable, the passion of avarice, the source of 'the most common and durable' cause of factions, was another matter. Acquisitiveness destroyed republican virtue, but by doing so it showed its strength and therefore its ability to serve as a more dependable substitute for republican virtue in a large commercial society.[22]

The importance of economic interests in politics formed the basis of the Federalist rejection of the ambassadorial theory of representation. Antifederalists argued that the representatives of an enlarged republic would be out of touch with the sentiments and interests of their constituents. Federalists argued that a certain distance between representatives and constituents was in fact necessary to the accurate representation of interests. The people's interests were to be strictly attended to, but the opinions of the people 'may be uninformed or misinformed, and consequently their measures may be repugnant to their own interests.'[23] If a representative merely reflected the feelings of the people, he might reflect feelings unaligned with popular interests. Feelings 'not formed upon these interests,' reasoned one Federalist, 'ought not to be represented, for they must be either evil or mistaken feelings. It would hardly appear beneficial to carry into the government the irregular passions, caprices and fanciful wishes of the people.' Before popular feelings could be justly represented, their connection with the regular passions of interests had to be established.[24]

Even after interests had been sorted out from whims, some independence was demanded of the representative. For this independence, Federalist political science depended on another kind of politically relevant passion, one that was connected more directly than economic interest with a certain notion of virtue. The precautions of 'Publius' for keeping governors virtuous presupposed that they had some virtue to keep. The interest-group sociology that James Madison elaborated in *The Federalist* (Nos. 10 and 51) was not fully extended by either Madison or Hamilton to the operations of government. Hamilton judged that in Congress 'it will rarely happen that the advancement of the public service will be the primary object either of party victories, or of party negotiations.'[25] Society would become more governable by the 'enlargement of the orbit' of government mentioned by Hamilton[26] and elaborated by Madison. But the device of mutual moderation of interests would be as insufficient on the floors of Congress as in the executive and judicial departments. In politics, Madison as well as Hamilton showed an interest in harnessing 'pride and vanity,' or 'the love of fame, the ruling passion of the noblest minds.'[27] *The Federalist* recognized the existence of men whose passion was not economic interest but political ambition, and it needed such men for its political arrangements. It needed men who would do more than simply reflect the multiplicity of interests in society, men who were capable not only of reflecting upon effective ways to regulate those interests, but also of seeing and pursuing the common interests of the whole society. And these men had to be 'virtuous' or public-spirited, so they would do these things their 'talents' made them capable of doing. As modern liberals, Federalists were faced with the difficulty of including political men in an apolitical theory of politics. Plato's Socrates supposed that the proper rulers (philosophers) would have to be compelled to rule; modern political philosophers have the problem of persuading someone (or *anyone*) to act as the sovereign. Perhaps this is a less difficult problem. To 'Publius,' at any rate, the necessity of political men did not demand anything like classical or Christian virtue. The talents of politicians in *The Federalist* were like the *virtù* of Machiavelli's glory-seeking prince; and their virtue or public-spiritedness was mainly a function of their passion for fame. That American colonial political oracle (and disciple of Machiavelli), *Cato's Letters*, expressed the tradition from which *The Federalist's* 'virtuous' politicians were drawn:

> when we call any Man disinterested, we should intend no more by it, than that the Turn of his Mind is towards the Publick, and that he has placed his own personal Glory and Pleasure in serving it, To serve his Country is his private Pleasure, Mankind is his Mistress, and he does Good to them by gratifying himself.[28]

The honor held out to politicians by *The Federalist* as an incentive to 'virtue' was primarily a means to pleasure, not to the inter-subjective confirmation of good character.[29] That this 'virtue' of politicians was thought necessary but not sufficient, was indicated by Hamilton's turning, in the same paragraph where he insisted on the existence of a 'portion of virtue and honor among mankind,' to remark on the Constitutional provisions for the prevention of corruption.[30] It is true that these 'auxiliary precautions' of the Constitutional mechanism were less characteristic of Federalism than the expansion of the scope that Federalists allowed to government: federalism had been a compromise forced on the nationalists, bicameralism and an independent judiciary had been directed against the popular legislative power, and the most important aspect of the Constitution was its strengthening of the executive, the modern residue of *the* classical ruling office. Still, this executive was monarchical only in a residual, attenuated sense, for he was to preside over a limited government; the virtue required in the executive – and *a fortiori* in officers of the other branches – was correspondingly less demanding.[31]

This limited but definite boosting of government and politicians appears in Hamilton's writing as early as 1782:

> We may preach till we are tired of the theme, the necessity of disinterestedness in republics, without making a single proselyte. The virtuous declaimer will neither persuade himself nor any other person to be content with a double mess of porridge, instead of a reasonable stipend for his services. We might as soon reconcile ourselves to the Spartan community of goods and wives, to their iron coin, their long beards, or their black broth. There is a total dissimulation in the circumstances, as well as the manners, of society among us; and it is as ridiculous to seek for models in the simple ages of Greece and Rome, as it would be to go in quest of them among the Hottentots and Laplanders.[32]

Hamilton raises doubts about the reliability of the disinterestedness of public servants. Yet he was arguing for the regulation of trade by the national government and against the 'delusion' that taxes are unnecessary; and he was rejecting the austere, virtuous republic as an ideal for Americans. Moreover it remained true that 'stern virtue,' though 'the growth of few soils,'[33] would be looked for in public servants more than in the public. The limited idealism of Federalism looked to government, not to the governed. A kind of intensive republican virtue was required in governors, not in the governed. As Caleb Blood argued in 1792, 'The nature of a republican government' demanded that 'virtue should be considered as a necessary qualification for a civil ruler.' Blood referred to Montesquieu's famous connection of republicanism and virtue, but he restricted 'virtue in the people' to 'three things': 'forming a Constitution that is a proper basis for a virtuous government,' 'choosing virtuous rulers to administer upon it,' and 'a cheerful submission to their righteous administration.'[34]

The realistic or pessimistic basis of the Federalists' optimism over their political solutions is clearly visible in both the private and the public writings of James Madison from 1787 to 1789. His adherence to Federalism in these years was not forgotten by his political rivals; it was one of the springboards of James Monroe's Presidential candidacy in 1808.[35]

In the Virginia ratifying convention Madison was compelled to answer Patrick Henry's standard opposition whig accusation that whereas popular licentiousness seldom led to the loss of liberty, the tyranny of rulers always did. Madison urged that, 'on a candid examination of history, we shall find that turbulence, violence, and the abuse of power, by the majority trampling on the rights of the minority have produced factions and commotions which, in republics, have more frequently than any other cause, produced despotism.'[36] To Thomas Jefferson, in Paris, he allowed that there was a theoretical possibility of oppression by 'those entrusted with the administration,' a danger that government might set up 'an interest adverse to that of the entire Society.' But, he insisted, there was little danger of encroachment in that direction in the United States:

> In our Government the real power lies in the majority of the community, and the invasion of private rights is chiefly to be apprehended, not from acts of Government contrary to the sense of its constituents, but from acts in which the Government is the mere instrument of the major number of their constituents. This is a truth of great importance, but not yet sufficiently attended to: it is probably more strongly impressed on my mind by facts, and reflections suggested by them, than on yours which has contemplated abuses of power issuing from a very different quarter.[37]

Assumptions similar to those behind the case for energetic national government backed Madison's conviction that a bill of rights had only marginal utility:

> It has been remarked that there is a tendency in all governments to an augmentation of power at the expence of liberty. But the remark as usually understood does not appear to me well founded. Power when it has attained a certain degree of energy and independence goes on generally to further degrees. But when below that degree, the direct tendency is to further degrees of relaxation, until the abuses of liberty beget a sudden transition to an undue degree of power. With this explanation the remark may be true; and in the latter sense only is it in my opinion applicable to the Governments in America.[38]

Perhaps men in power were not reliably virtuous, but neither were ordinary men. The speech which has been singled out to show that the Madison of 1788 was following the tradition of republicanism in relying on a rigorously virtuous populace shows rather the opposite. Defending the new Constitution before the Virginia convention, he mused:

> I have observed, that gentlemen suppose, that the general legislature will do every mischief they possibly can, and that they will omit to do every thing good which they are authorized to do. If this were a reasonable supposition, their objection would be good. I consider it reasonable to conclude, that they will as readily do their duty, as

deviate from it: nor do I go on the grounds mentioned by the gentlemen on the other side – that we are to place unlimited confidence in them, and expect nothing but the most exalted integrity and sublime virtue. But I go on this great republican principle, that the people will have virtue and intelligence to select men of virtue and wisdom. Is there no virtue among us? If there be not, we are in a wretched situation. No theoretical checks – no form of government can render us secure. To suppose that any form of government will secure liberty or happiness without any virtue in the people is a chimerical idea. If there be sufficient virtue and intelligence in the community, it will be exercised in the selection of these men. So that we do not depend on their virtue or put confidence in our rulers, but in the people who are to choose them.[39]

Considering the circumstances of this speech, it is a remarkably open statement of the modicum of virtue required of 'the people.' Not even the representatives of the people were to be expected to act on principles of 'exalted integrity and sublime virtue,' Madison was happy to admit. As for the people, Madison 'confidently' – was it not, rather, modestly? – expected them to have sufficient judgement to choose able men to represent them. Madison's outlook on the virtue of the people resembles Caleb Blood's view. His remarks actually parallel his co-author Hamilton's arguments in *The Federalist*, and no one has ever suggested that these or indeed any of Hamilton's arguments display an unwarranted abundance of confidence in 'the people.'[40] The popular 'virtue' that Madison required was not even related to the 'form of government.' The emphasis of Madison's argument was not on the virtues of the people, though his rhetoric allows anyone looking for such an emphasis to see it in his words. His assumptions were the same as those made in his 'Publius' essays: one 'must first enable the government to control the governed, and in the next place oblige it to control itself.'[41] The problem of control was paramount because of the unreliability of virtue, or self-control, both in the people and, in a more qualified sense, in their representative rulers.

In 1790, at the beginning of the road that was to take him from Federalism to Republicanism, Madison contemplated the Federalist political outlook:

The evils suffered and feared from weakness in Government, and licentiousness in the people, have turned the attention more towards the means of strengthening the former than of narrowing its extent in the minds of the latter.[42]

Revolutionary realism had been merely a perception of the novelty of the American political situation. It became Federalist realism only by the addition of a particular judgement of American society, and a realistic psychology, a specific perception of human nature in politics. Men who shared the Federalist view of the political situation could nevertheless think that this psychological view was dim in more ways than one. A different view of human nature accompanied their vision of different possibilities in the same political reality.

Federalist rhetoric

The realistic psychology that permeated the argument of *The Federalist* informed its rhetorical strategy as well as its theoretical vision, and it established the characteristic strengths and weaknesses of this strategy, which were shared by Americans of 'the Federalist persuasion,'[43] and which influenced their political successes and failures.

One of the most successful pieces of Federalist rhetoric was the outright theft of the *cachet* 'Federalism.' The so-called Antifederalists justly complained of the theft; even 'Publius' had to admit that the new Constitution was 'in strictness neither a national nor a federal constitution, but a composition of both.'[44] The label 'Federalism' was not as neutral as the candid formula of 'Publius.' Nor was it as accurate as the label suggested by Elbridge Gerry. Somewhat in the spirit of the nationalists' transgression, Gerry took Madison to task on the floor of the first House of Representatives, saying that since the division between Federalism and Antifederalism had really been between those in favor of and those opposed to ratification of the new Constitution without previous amendment, it had been more appropriate to call the two sides 'rats' and 'anti-rats.'[45] The nationalists of the 1780s were generally prudent enough to see that an avowal of nationalism was not politic. Their tactic in this instance was perhaps the most successful element of their rhetorical strategy, yet it was, in the nature of the case, limited, by time if nothing else, for the Federalist label could (and did) soon lose its national respectability.

John Miller has pointed out that Federalists failed to claim the mantle of libertarianism. In the Confederal period, 'some states had enacted laws which, besides invalidating the vested rights of creditors, had struck against the freedom of speech and the civil rights of unpopular religious minorities. Thus the Federalists were presented with an opportunity to stand forth as the defenders of minority rights in general.'[46] But they did not rise to this challenge. The violations of civil liberties in the

Confederal period they construed as the result of overly responsive governments; they did not blame governments themselves for illiberal policies. Although the mantle of libertarianism was to become soiled when the Jeffersonians wore it into office, it served well in opposition, and it became a durable element of American political rhetoric.[47]

Related to this Federalist shortcoming was the most general weakness of Federalist rhetoricians: their tendency to presume success in their justification of the Constitution before the tribunal of American republicanism. The realistic persuasion of Federalism thus inspired in Federalists an unrealistic confidence. The first qualification for political rhetoric in America after 1776 was that it be republican.[48] Federalism could claim most of the qualities that Americans associated with republicanism, but not all of them, and the missing elements were significant.

The federal Constitution did not establish any hereditary forms of government. That fact alone was enough for it to meet a loose but commonplace criterion of republicanism. Some prominent Federalists claimed, moreover, to have established a specifically democratic republic. In the 1780s, even if they entertained aristocratic opinions in private, 'political figures were more and more forced, in public discussions, to concede to the popular and egalitarian ideology of the Revolution.'[49] In 1787 some of the elite developed a democratic republicanism that was more to their taste, because it promised to avoid the 'inconveniences' previously associated with the democratic form of government. John Marshall, in the Virginia ratifying convention, called the proposed Constitution a 'well-regulated democracy.'[50] But the claim to democracy, while enabling *The Federalist* to make forceful appeals on the basis of the broad suffrage allowed by the Constitution, was not deemed as important or as universally appealing as the claim to republicanism. Madison was aware that only a *democratic* republic would do for America, and that it was '*essential* to such a government that it be derived from the great body of the society, not from an inconsiderable proportion, or a favored class of it.' But he also went so far as to contrast 'a republic,' which he defined simply as 'a government in which the scheme of representation takes place,' with 'a democracy,' and to insist that the 'true distinction' between the representative governments of the ancient world and those of America lay '*in the total exclusion of the people, in their collective capacity,* from any share in the latter.'[51] The assumption that 'the democracy' was the only order that could be successfully defended as the basis of American politics led to *The Federalist's* schemes for refining and re-refining this democracy in an attempt to make it safe for the world. *The Federalist's* 'republic' was perhaps, as Madison claimed, 'unmixed' with monarchy and aristocracy, but Madison had to assert that it was not simply democratic either. It appears that what Hamilton called – perhaps coining the phrase – 'representative democracy,' and publicly defended as 'republican government,' he privately regarded as mixed government, one that combined democratic, aristocratic and monarchical principles.[52] The democratic aspect of republicanism – the question of direct 'government by the people' – was not an inflexible element of Federalism.

However, the Federalists' flexibility in this respect was not unique, for they shared the rhetorical problem in making non-democratic politics acceptable to 'the democracy' with many Antifederalists, and later with Jeffersonians. The distinguishing aspect of Federalist republicanism was not its claim to compatibility with democracy, but its failure to claim compatibility with popular virtue – and, what is more, its insistence on basing policies on the assumption that popular virtue, where it existed at all, was so imbecilic that one could depend on interestedness to overcome it wherever the two failed to conspire. The 'virtue' of the people in Federalism – and, too often to be tactful, in Federalist rhetoric – was merely their ability to choose talented agents to safeguard their interests, and their diligent private pursuit of these interests. The traditional American whig was more pessimistic than the American Federalist over the possibility of the enduring goodness of men *in power*; unlike the Federalist, however, the whig cherished the notion that people *in liberty* could be and remain virtuous, even if their virtue was nothing more than passionate patriotism. Federalists were more inclined to presume the disinterestedness of men in power.

'Publius' did notice that some of the people showed that they were 'virtuous and disinterested' by applauding 'the integrity and moderation of the judiciary.'[53] The judiciary was meant to be the depository of constitutionalism; it was to embody the idea of republicanism as the rule of law. This idea was the broadest meaning of the political irrelevance of social orders in America. John Adams, who well appreciated the existence of those orders, was convinced that it was the 'true and only true definition' of a republic: a polity 'in which all men, rich and poor, magistrates and subjects, officers and people, masters and servants, the first citizens and the last, are equally subject to the law.'[54] This constitutionalism persists today, and it is partly to the credit of Federalism that it does. However, there are rhetorical limitations to republicanism as constitutionalism, for all sides can claim allegiance to the rules of the game, and at the same time disagree on who is to make the rules, and on the purpose of the rules made. Thomas Paine, no sober legalist, could argue that 'The government of a free country, properly speaking, is not in the persons, but in the laws.' But this opinion is best understood in the light of his view that the term '*republic*...is wholly characteristical of the purport, matter, or object for which government ought to be instituted, and on which it is to be employed.'[55] Both Federalists and Jeffersonians found occasion to appeal to constitutionalism, but they both found occasion as well to appeal from constitutionalism to the justice of controversial measures. Even in *The Federalist* Hamilton pointed out the significance of the fact that republics, as well as monarchies, are 'administered by men.' Whether or not the judiciary was a mere machine with 'neither FORCE nor WILL,' administrators were not always the impartial umpires required by a rule of law.[56] And besides the importance of the identity of administrators, there was the question of whether administrators should disregard rules when they judged that scrupulous fidelity to them would be harmful. Both Hamilton and Jefferson acted in ways that denied the sufficiency of the rule of law. They justified their formal deviations by reference to the justice of their purposes. Since they did not agree on the substance of just ends, their parallel appeals from the formalism of the rule of law pointed in different if not opposite directions. Jefferson appealed to the 'very highest interests' of the nation to justify his Louisiana Purchase, which he thought was unconstitutional.[57] Hamilton likewise appealed to 'the substantial interests of society' when he suggested that 'a strict adherence to ordinary rules' would be 'over-scrupulous' in the case of the proposed manipulation of the New York elections in 1800.[58] These episodes illustrate the weaknesses of both Federalist and Republican rhetoric: the former unable to win needed votes, the latter unable to conform to necessary policies. (The Republicans labored under a logical rather than a rhetorical weakness; in fact, it was a rhetorical strength – rhetoric being, as Aristotle says, the antistrophe of dialectic.) They also indicate that deviations from constitutionalism were required by both Federalism and Republicanism. Hamilton and Jefferson did not abandon the idea of the rule of law and the modern expansion of this idea, the notion of impartial representative government, in which discretionary statesmanship is justifiable only as a necessity.[59] But their appeals were connected with substantive questions of policy, even if the policy was only the means to the formal impartial end. These questions were objects of controversy and occasions for rhetoric that required more than a dry constitutionalism.

The rhetorical appeals of *The Federalist* were consistent with its motivation theory. 'Publius' addressed 'the important question, whether

societies of men are really capable or not of establishing good government from reflection and choice.'[60] But the arguments he then proceeded to offer for his readers' reflection very often presupposed that
reason was the slave not indeed of the passions, but of one particular
kind of passion: the cool and reasonable passion of immediate and
personal interests, which he thought were stronger motives than true
and common interests. His belief that men could be expected to divide
into 'parties' along the lines of their personal interests, and that the most
common and durable source of these parties in the civilized nations of
the modern world had been and would continue to be 'the various and
unequal distribution of property'[61] led him to promote his political
opinions by appealing to these interests as much as to the intrinsic merits
of his opinions.[62] No doubt these appeals were extremely effective.[63] But
his expectation of the way in which modern parties would form also
impoverished his rhetoric by leading him to neglect the non-economic
bases of party formation. In his theory, the unreliability of moral and
religious motives is turned to good effect, by reducing the motives that
will require the attention of government to the reliable motives of
economic interests. But it soon became evident that this reduction itself
was unreliable.

Writing to Jefferson in October 1787, Madison referred to diverse
economic interests as the basis of 'natural distinctions' among men;
other, 'artificial' distinctions were 'founded on accidental differences in
political, religious, and other opinions, or an attachment to the persons
of leading individuals.' Madison continued, 'However erroneous or
ridiculous these grounds of dissention and faction may appear to the
enlightened Statesman, or the benevolent philosopher, the bulk of
mankind who are neither Statesmen nor Philosophers, will continue to
view them in a different light.'[64] However, when he came to write *The
Federalist*, No. 10, Madison seemed convinced that these 'accidental
differences' could be expected to give way to the 'natural' ones, so that
government need only be concerned with the latter. Perhaps this was
because he had stopped reading John Adams, and begun to read David
Hume, who had suggested that, the 'passion for public good' being a
principle 'too disinterested, and too difficult to support, it is requisite
to govern men by other passions, and to animate them with a spirit of
avarice and industry, art and luxury.' This view supported Hume's
advocacy of a comprehensive commercial policy. His remarks appear
in Essay II, i ('Of Commerce'), and they may have had as great a role
as the large republic theory of Essay II, xvi ('The Idea of a Perfect
Commonwealth') in Madison's composition of *The Federalist*, No. 10.[65]

In fact, even before his letter to Jefferson, Madison had suggested, in the Philadelphia Convention, that economic 'interest' was the most important source of partisanship in the United States.[66]

Madison's anticipation of the continuing prominence of economic interests in American politics was the basis of Charles Beard's claim that Madison and not Marx was his mentor.[67] Understandably dazzled by the beauty of his system, 'Publius' forgot himself; he forgot his own partisanship, which was as political as it was economic, for he had been compelled to argue about the principles of his political opinions, and to show their conformity with republicanism. In this way he had re-defined republicanism to demonstrate how it could be compatible with a large territory and petty men. 'Publius' overlooked the possibility that republicanism might be redefined once more – with the particular assistance of James Madison.

The realism and rhetoric of John Adams

One Federalist who did not depend on the peaceful tendencies of the growth of economic interests was John Adams, the first Federalist Vice-President and the last Federalist President. His views are illuminat-ing because they provide a systematic contrast to his contemporaries' more orthodox Federalist views. His rhetorical posture, based on his views, offers a complementary counterpoint. In his penetrating political thought, it has been noticed, 'Economic problems arise only because of a defective political organization. Hence there is no need for detailed inquiry into economic problems as such.'[68] His political psychology recognized the natural and persistent quality of what Madison called the 'artificial' sources of political motivations. While Madison's political art attempted to make these sources yield to that single though diverse 'natural' source, economic interest, John Adams never lost sight of their political relevance. Therefore he appreciated the necessity of a political rhetoric that appealed to something besides mere rational interest. He saw that there were considerations that were 'nonsense to the philoso-pher' but ever relevant to politicians, because ever present in the springs of human behavior. In short, he saw the inevitability of political myths. However, he did not see the necessity of novel political myths in the novel political situation of the United States. A new political mythology was needed for a new world.

Adams shared the Federalist view that by 1787 the American people had demonstrated that they could not live up to the ideal of republican virtue, that noblest 'passion in the minds of the people,' which was generally believed necessary for republican government. But Adams was wilfully honest, and he said in public what other Federalists were tactful enough to say only in private – namely that the federal Constitution established a mixed government or 'monarchical republic.' The Constitution established a relatively strong unitary executive, but this office was called 'President,' not only as a reflection of the modesty of modern pretensions to rule, but also in deference to American republicanism. Adams might have agreed with William Cobbett's assessment of the federal Constitution:

> The many of all countries stand in need of a monarch, at once to keep them in obedience to itself, and to protect them from the tyranny and rapacity of the aspiring, rich and avaricious few. The people of America wanted such a protector, but the delusion of the times would not have permitted him to be called a *monarch*.[69]

But Adams does not seem to have thought that this delusion would endure. He believed that the Federalist abandonment of the reliance on republican virtue entailed a change to a mixed government, which he conceived would rest on the social orders that he saw still flourishing among Americans, undiminished by their single-order political vocabulary. He knew that this belief would be unpopular. 'This Book,' he said of his elaborate statement of this belief, 'will make me unpopular.'[70] But his tactlessness had a solid foundation, for his prediction of the Americans' inevitable adoption of monarchical and aristocratic forms was based on his psychological analysis of human passions. His honesty was wilful, but it was not consciously perverse.

Faced with the rejection of his ideas about the new American politics, he presented their psychological basis in his 'Discourses on Davila.' (It was these 'Discourses' that provoked Jefferson's phrase 'political heresies,' in his famous unintentional preface to the American edition of Paine's *Rights of Man*, Part One.) Here Adams explained the natural laws which 'go a great way in explaining every phenomenon that occurs in the history of government,' and which made certain the eventual vindication of his conviction that American government was not as exceptional as he and others had imagined. After all, 'The vegetable and animal kingdoms, and those heavenly bodies whose existence and movements we are as yet only permitted faintly to perceive, do not appear to be governed by laws more uniform and certain than those which regulate the moral and political world.'[71] Adams' certainty in psychology made him certain and tenacious of his politics.

Among all the 'passions, appetites,... propensities' and the 'variety of faculties' natural to man, none was 'more essential or remarkable, than the *passion for distinction.*' This desire for esteem provided 'a balance for the selfish affections,' and made men 'social' even 'in their primitive conditions.' It did this more certainly than natural benevolence or sympathy, because it was a more powerful part of the human soul: men enjoy congratulating success more than sympathizing with distress. Unlike rational economic interests, the object of the passion for distinction had no reasonable apology; it was no less powerful for that:

> On a selfish system, what are the thoughts, passions, and sentiments of mankind to us?
> 'What's fame? A fancied life in others' breath!'
> What is it to us what shall be said of us after we are dead? Or in Asia, Africa, or Europe while we live? There is no greater possible delusion. Yet the impulse is irresistible.

Adams was convinced that 'There are no men who are not ambitious of distinguishing themselves and growing considerable among those with whom they converse.' He acknowledged that men sought attention and approbation in various ways: 'not a few' through crimes and vices; 'more' through neither virtues nor vices, but by common-sense means, 'frivolous' things like riches; and 'a few' through admiration, hence 'your patriots and heroes, and most of the great benefactors to mankind.'[72] This last method of distinction resembled the search for honor, but it was 'a passion still, and therefore, like all other human desires, unlimited and insatiable.'[73] The 'virtue' of distinguished men was no more automatically conducive to good policy than the neutral morals of ordinary men. All of these strong passions therefore needed a 'check' in the 'form of government.'[74]

Adams refused to admit *The Federalist's* argument that men of talent and public spirit could be sifted from all classes in a scheme of representation, for he saw that it was all too easy for 'acquired talents' to be confused with – or even less valued than – the more usual acquirements of well-bred Americans. Perhaps 'real merit should govern the world,' but representative democracy was no way to arrange that it do so. Adams dared to suggest that there was a greater probability that a senator would possess wisdom and integrity if he owed his office to hereditary descent than if he were elected by a nation of thirty million, as in France.[75] This was an opinion he held tenaciously. In 1804 he wrote to a correspondent: '...you consider rank and wealth as anti-republican principles of precedence. Is this correct?... in every republican government...the more democratic the government, the more universal has been the practice of selecting political officers from the most ancient and respectable families.' And a decade later his response to Jefferson's remarks on natural aristocracy took the same tack: the people could not be expected to discriminate the talented and virtuous from the rich and well-born.[76] Even enlightenment and education could not be expected to diminish the fashion for titles and distinction, for 'there is no connection in the mind between science and passion, by which the former can extinguish or diminish the latter.'[77] Though the rich and powerful be ever so miserable in fact, people will admire their state. Adams quoted Adam Smith's observation of man's penchant for deferring to the inclinations and passions of his social superiors, as if they felt pains more intensely. He concluded: 'That kings are the servants of the people...is the doctrine of reason and philosophy; but it is not the doctrine of nature.'[78]

Because the deference paid by the lower to the upper classes was not reasonable, the best political arrangement was not representative democracy, but a mixed government, in which the different parts reflected the different social orders. The proper balance of these parts would ensure that no class ruled another, but that laws ruled all. Like Harrington, Adams departed from Machiavelli by insisting that the partisan warfare of classes could be 'restrained.' He supposed that without political balance a dual class rivalry would continue 'till one is swallowed up or annihilated, and the other becomes absolute master. As all this is a necessary consequence and effect of the emulation which nature has implanted in our bosoms,' he added, 'it is wonderful that mankind have so long been ignorant of the remedy, when a third party for an umpire is one so easy and obvious.' This idea of 'triple balance' was 'so established by Providence in the constitution of nature, that order without it can never be brought out of anarchy and confusion. The laws, therefore, should establish this equilibrium as the dictate of nature and the ordinance of Providence.'[79]

Adams believed that the laws not only should but also could establish this equilibrium in the new American national government. He did not propose *hereditary* monarchy and aristocracy for America, at least not immediately[80] – but 'the idea of hereditary descent is not an essential ingredient in the definition of monarchy or aristocracy.'[81] Nor was his mixed regime fundamentally classical, for it was based on the modern premise that 'there is but one element of government, and that is, THE PEOPLE.'[82] But his principles were nevertheless so inappropriate to Federalist America that the suggestions he made on the basis of his political and psychological theories were soundly defeated, and the theories themselves found few seconders. Adams' political theories, and the rhetorical principles he based on them, were more comprehensive than the theories and rhetoric characterized by *The Federalist*, because they paid more attention to the inevitability of irrationality in politics.[83] In this way his psychology was at least as 'realistic' as *The Federalist's*. But the more comprehensive Federalist realism became, the less success it had in practice. 'Publius,' whatever his private views, had not imagined that anything but strict republicanism would ever be publicly defensible, or 'reconcilable with the people of America; with the fundamental principles of the revolution; or with that honorable determination which animates every votary of freedom, to rest all our political experiments on the capacity of mankind for self-government.'[84] Although Jefferson might write (in 1787) to Adams that the Presidency 'seems a bad edition of the Polish king,'[85] he would not publicize such a comparison. And if Jefferson, as President, could be said to have strengthened the Presidency in order to make it stand against the aristocracy as Adams had envisaged, he did so not by making the office more monarchical, but by making it a tribune of the people. Federalists insisted that the President be elected directly or indirectly by the people,[86] but only to avoid his being dependent on the popular legislative branch, not to make him an agent of the people; the indirection of the electoral college reflects this intention. By 1802, Hamilton recognized the rhetorical error of Federalism: the diffusion of correct principles was not sufficient, he decided, for 'men are rather reasoning than reasonable animals, for the most part governed by the impulse of passion.'[87] Adams had known this all along. But the firmness of his belief that the myths that generated monarchy and aristocracy were necessary effects of human passions led him to think that monarchy and aristocracy would perforce reassert themselves in America, and to imagine that his predictions, if never granted popularity, would at least be given credit for their accuracy. Adams failed to see the potential for anti-monarchist monarchism in America, a potential which was realized by Federalists more orthodox than Adams as well as by Jeffersonian Republicans.

3

The confidence of unchallenged Federalism

Before they were challenged by the Republicans in 1792, and even afterwards, the Federalists did not fully comprise a political party in the modern sense. This is true primarily not on account of their lack of organizational skills, nor because they were undemocratic, but rather because their public organization was neither expected nor intended to outlast the secure establishment of the new central government. After this government had been launched, parties as interest groups would thrive, and Federalists tried to arrange for the interests in society to support an independent government, but *political* parties, with long-term policy programs and a corresponding organization of indefinite duration, were unforeseen and would be undesirable in the Federalist understanding of politics. The Federalists did not seek public legitimacy for continuing partisanship after the ratification of the Constitution. This legitimacy would have required the kind of limits and guides to statesmanship inherent in a publicized party program, and Federalists sought to expand rather than to limit the role of politicians in government. Post-ratification partisan organization might be part of the private constitution; for example, in the Philadelphia Convention, James Madison depended on some kind of interstate political cooperation in the future nomination of Presidential candidates, to insure that the contest would not be regularly decided by the House of Representatives.[1] But the desirable and respectable political party did not appear in the public constitution in the Federalist scheme. Hamilton anticipated the nuisance of a 'party in opposition' in Congress, but they would be opposed to 'the majority,' not to the majority party.[2] The Jeffersonian Republicans were thus the first modern party in America, the first party to establish the public respectability of party. However, the Federalists did have a comprehensive political project based on their science of politics. Since

39

the Republican party first appeared in opposition to this project, the Federalist project must be understood 'in order to understand the origins of modern party politics in America.

The Federalist science of politics was perhaps most clearly and widely expressed in the years between the ratification of the Federalists' new Constitution and the first broad, partisan challenge to their administration in 1792. It is in these years, when Federalists could still feel the unity and morale of their battle against Antifederalism, but were also full of the generosity that attends success, that they best realized and revealed their principles. Before, they had been constrained by the exigencies of battle. Afterwards, facing schism, challenge and finally defeat, those who remained Federalists became less optimistic and less generous in both word and deed. To understand the Federalists' bitter disillusionment with American government and society, their initial confidence and idealism must be appreciated.[3] In the full flush of victory, although they remained sober and 'realistic,' they were also confident and liberal. Their adherence to one version of the American science of politics is therefore most evident in speeches made in this period, which was felt to be even more secure than a honeymoon, for it seemed that there was not even the prospect of a new opposition to the ascendancy of sensible politicians. This Federalist idealism was voiced less in the Houses of Congress, which had their little quarrels, than on occasions like election day sermons (preached to legislatures before they elected state officers), Fourth of July orations, charges to grand juries and speeches to fraternal societies. But it also found ample expression in the policies of the new government, as they were defined in the system of legislation proposed by Alexander Hamilton. And although Federalists lacked some of the reforming zeal characteristic of American political parties, they did articulate a moral vision intimately related to their political theories and their practical policies.[4]

Human nature and the art of civilization

On July 4, 1776, out of 'a decent respect for the opinions of mankind,' the United States of America alluded to the self-evident truth that all men possess as 'unalienable Rights,...Life, Liberty and the pursuit of Happiness.' Government is to be limited to securing men's natural rights, for men are naturally equal, so no man should claim the natural or supernatural right to rule another. Civil government is not natural. As was declared in 1776, it must be 'instituted among Men,' and its 'just powers' must be derived 'from the consent of the governed.' On this basis, only impartial, apolitical representation, not partial, political ruling, is naturally right. The natural equality of men is reflected in civil society, wherein 'civil liberty consists not in a right to every man to do just as he pleases – but it consists in an equal right to all the citizens to have, enjoy and to do, in peace, security, and without molestation, whatever the equal and constitutional laws of the country admit to be consistent with the public good.'[5] Equal, constitutional laws are impartial laws. As Edward Gray remarked, 'To be neuter, or the friend of real liberty, was dangerous' in ancient Greece and Rome; Federalists, as well as Republicans, hoped that such impartial, non-factional government would prevail in modern America. The alternative, according to Federalists, was party government: faction, in the shape of democracy.

> A people subject to little or no constitutional rule, do not govern themselves. They are deceived, if they suppose they do. Faction rules them, and assumes to itself their honourable name, it calls itself the people.[6]

Gray's constitutionalist republicanism, like John Adams', was directed against the traditional kind of ruling. He alleged that party had no share in the Declaration of Independence, which merely 'spoke the united sentiments of the people.' Gray did not notice the divisive effects of the Declaration; he identified the American Patriots – just as he claimed any faction would identify itself – with 'the people.' Jefferson, in his well-known disavowal of originality in the composition of the Declaration, would specify that it was all 'American Whigs' who had 'thought alike' on the subject of Anglo-American relations in the 1770s.[7] But in 1790 he probably would have approved Gray's benign rhetorical neglect of Loyalism, just as he would soon come to hope that anti-republican Federalism, temporary aberration that it was, would be treated with a salutary forgetfulness. And there is an important sense in which these poor memories are justified: modern partisans – Loyalists and Patriots, Federalists and Republicans – can agree on the theory of limited, impartial government yet disagree on the means best suited to securing it. There is fundamental agreement concerning the end: 'that men can be free, and yet tranquil.'[8] This was recognized by the contemporary critics of the idea of limited government, who complained that statesmen were seeking only to keep people quiet under government, rather than to form good characters and make men better; liberty seemed more precious than virtue.[9] Allegiance to the idea of limited, liberal government demanded that men overcome the doubts both of those 'who have reprobated what they are pleased to call the inquisitive sauciness of the people,' and of others, who have ventured to suggest that the people 'ought to be governed against their wills, and without their choice, by men, to be sure, much wiser than themselves;' notwithstanding 'their boasted love of liberty,' the 'Grecian and Roman nations' were not acquainted with 'the true principles' of liberty:

> no longer shall we look to antient histories for principles and systems of pure freedom. The close of the eighteenth century, in which we live, shall teach mankind to be truly free.[10]

Unlike the member of a classical 'simple democracy,' where everyone was ruler, soldier and citizen, the 'private citizen' of a modern liberal republic need contribute 'only his due proportion to the support of government.' The private citizen has 'a most desirable situation in a society that enjoys the benefit of a free government;' he 'is protected in the full enjoyment of his liberty and property, and hath nothing to do but attend to his own domestic business.'[11]

In a Fourth of July oration in 1791, Edward Bangs suggested that one reason America could expect 'tranquility and true liberty,' as opposed to the persistent 'eddies of faction' in both ancient and modern polities, was that discovery of Revolutionary realism, and theme of many later commentators on American politics:

> we had among us no hereditary claims to particular privileges; no proud nobility, or haughty ecclesiastical orders, to compromise with: no different ranks or grades in society; but all stood together, as we now stand, upon the same extended plain of free citizenship.

The relatively equal conventions in America (slavery forgotten) made it easier to secure natural equalities. The accepted practice of political deference to 'men of wealth and learning' in America was not tantamount to an aristocratic government by an hereditary nobility, for learning was not hereditary, and the lineal descent of wealth would not be a danger until men could 'find out some method to prevent the children from squandering what their fathers earned,' and 'prevent an industrious poor from rising their superiors.' Bangs claimed that a number of examples of both rags-to-riches and riches-to-rags could be observed among his audience. And he pointed to specific differences between aristocratic English and republican American practices: the equal division of intestate estates, and the 'very moderate circumstances' necessary for a man to be able to avail his son of all the honors and advantages of an academic education. Poverty itself, thus 'properly encouraged' by equal opportunity, was 'the parent of exertion.'[12] The 'aristocracy' of America was as evident in Democratic Societies as in high offices of state, for it was based on personal influence, which could be increased by individual effort.[13] The new American Constitution was 'calculated to encourage genius, and bring merit to view from the obscure walks of life.' 'Titles and birth' gave 'no claim to rank or precedence'; instead, 'a capacity for business, with learning, eloquence, and virtue,' were the 'surest ways to rise to honor and preferment.'[14]

Federalists and Republicans might concur in their allegiance to impartiality and in their judgement of American social homogeneity. However, their partisan differences were colored by their inclination to different versions of the first principles of government. The natural rights to 'Life, Liberty and the Pursuit of Happiness' can be justified by reference to the correlative natural 'Passions that encline men to Peace': 'Feare of Death; Desire of such things as are necessary to commodious living; and a Hope by their Industry to obtain them.'[15] That is how Thomas Hobbes might have justified them – in spite of Thomas Jefferson's objections – on the basis of his doctrine that 'meer Nature' places mankind in the 'ill condition' of 'warre of every man against every man.' This doctrine has probably never been pronounced in American political rhetoric so much or so appropriately as it was by Federalists. Federalist politics was grounded in the conviction that there is a certain 'ferocity natural to the human mind'; in a state of nature, as examples in both ancient Europe and modern America demonstrated, 'mankind are in a state of hostility, and wage war as uniformly as the beasts of the forest engage.'[16] This doctrine could be associated with Christian theology; but even to the clergyman who explained it to the Massachusetts legislature in 1789, human government rather than divine grace presented itself as the solution:

In order to obtain the benefits of society, civil rule is essentially requisite. Those lusts of men, from whence come wars and fightings, are so prevalent in this apostate world, that they are obliged to form compacts and combinations, for mutual assistance and support.[17]

And worldly assumptions and conclusions were certainly uppermost in Federalist political science and policy. The young Alexander Hamilton once meditated on the devastating effects of a hurricane he had witnessed, and called on man to 'See thy wretched helpless state, and learn to know thyself. Learn to know thy best support. Despise thyself, and adore thy God.'[18] However, he became a political administrator rather than a minister of God, and his policies were related to the secular conclusions drawn from the 'ill condition' of man by 'meer Nature.' He and other Federalists were convinced of the necessity for 'the restraints of government,' because of this natural 'political infirmity of mankind.'[19] It is because of 'that state of individual imbecility in which man is supposed to have existed, previous to the formation of the social compact,' that government must be 'instituted for the common security of the natural rights of every individual.'[20] Believing that the proper 'design of government is to protect the life and property of the subject,' Federalists judged that, in the circumstances of postwar America, government must pay particular attention to the protection of the young nation's commerce from the threats it faced abroad, for without commerce, 'from whence are we to be supplied with the various exotic productions, which are not merely conducive to the enjoyment, but to the preservation of life?'[21] As well as reviving America's commerce, the government instituted by the new Constitution had to foster the establishment of 'credit and character,'[22] another faltering security to property rights. The energetic activity of government was made necessary by the inability of men by nature (unassisted by government) to secure the rights which they possessed by nature. This general truth was confirmed when Federalists looked at American society and government.

Enterprising society

During and after the Revolutionary War, many Americans who became Federalists reassessed the promise of American life. The Federalist design for America was based on the judgement that the American people did not exhibit many signs of republican virtue. This judgement, which was a retreat from Revolutionary idealism, became a hallmark of Federalism in the 1780s.[23] In Revolutionary days, even Alexander Hamilton had found useful the rhetoric that censured government for squandering taxes on 'ministerial tools and court sycophants,'[24] but Federalists saw no useful place for such rhetoric in the political system established in 1789, for they had lost whatever they had ever truly had of faith in Americans' republican virtues. The Federalist project assumed that self-interested acquisitiveness, not Spartan patriotism, was the strongest characteristic of American society, and therefore the necessary basis of American civilization. When Federalists praised certain popular virtues and condemned the opposite vices, they sounded less like traditional republicans than like John Locke extolling 'the Industrious and Rational' over 'the Quarrelsome and Contentious.'[25] Their notion of popular virtue was what Aléxis de Tocqueville was to call 'virtuous materialism' (matérialisme honnête).[26] The accentuation of economic virtues in Federalist rhetoric reflected the relative insignificance of republican virtue in Federalist political science.

Although Americans were not Spartan, they were blessed with an 'enterprizing spirit.' Their new federal government was needed to avoid a restriction of commerce that would 'cut off the life and source of industry; and pave the way for indolence, and a train of vices more destructive to community, than those arts of elegance and refinement (which it is said, and justly said) are the concomitants of commerce.'[27] This point was underscored in a Fourth of July oration delivered by Samuel Stillman in Boston in 1789. Stillman was a man of continental outlook: born in Philadelphia, educated in Charleston, he had become pastor of the First Baptist Church in Boston in 1764, and had been a delegate to the Constitutional ratification convention. On this first anniversary celebration of independence after the commencement of the new government, Stillman spoke on a theme suitable to the occasion: the benefits of independence from Britain These benefits, he thought, had become actual only with the actualization of the new government, for directly after the War,

> instead of adopting the methods of oeconomy, promoting agriculture and manufactures, and living as much as possible within ourselves; we rushed into the most extravagant importation of British goods. Many persons left their proper employments and set up for merchants, who were unacquainted with commerce.

And large debts, frequent bankruptcies and a destruction of 'mutual confidence,' had put a stop to business as a result of this extravagance. With the advent of the sobering and stabilizing influence of the new government, America could realize the potential of its deliverance from British restrictions on trade and manufactures.[28] David Humphreys indicated that he was of the same mind by claiming that the new regime was needed to make the most of Americans' ingenuity 'for making improvements.'[29]

Because Americans displayed this spirit of enterprise, Federalists were confident that they were amenable to both energetic government and a certain 'moral assistance,' which would encourage the virtues of 'industry, oeconomy and a true spirit of patriotism.' These alone could 'retrieve the distresses of our situation.'[30] For the 'prosperity and decline' of nations was connected not only with the 'systems of policy by which they are governed,' but also, and more directly, with 'the manners of moral conduct by which they are characterized.'[31] In the 1780s Federalists judged that a measure of moral improvement was in order. They felt that the fluctuation in the value of paper currency during and after the War had 'occasioned vague ideas of property, produced licentious appetites, and corrupted the morals of men,' producing 'private distress, bankruptcy, and breach of faith' throughout the country.[32] Americans needed 'industry in the proper occupations, and moderation in the various enjoyments of life.' They had had occasion to learn that 'from the prevalence of contrary habits, from a disrelish in business, inactivity in profitable and laudable pursuits, and a free indulgence in the varieties and pleasures of a dissipated life, arise the greatest dangers which a nation, especially in its infant state, has to fear.'[33]

Federalists had well-defined expectations of the American people and what Stephen Higginson (writing as 'Laco') referred to as 'those virtues proper to their situation, and necessary to their safety and happiness – such as temperance, frugality, prudence, and a love of their country.' These virtues had to be taught to the people 'both by precept and by example.'[34] By 1790, Higginson could detect much success in this project. He believed

> that a general alteration in the habits and feelings of the people has taken place for the better...Habits of industry and frugality are taking place of those of luxury and dissipation, more generally and with more celerity than I expected. it is a growing Idea, that the manners contracted during the War must be done away; and that every class of Citizens must expect only to thrive by the means comonly successful in a time of peace.[35]

On the same day that Samuel Stillman delivered his oration in Boston, Samuel Whitwell presented to the Massachusetts Society of Cincinnati his portrait of the pleasant prospects enjoyed by the new nation. The numerous benefits he expected from the triumph of Federalism were dependent on the rise of 'the sun of virtue' in America. A virtuous people would be inculcated with 'industry and frugality.' These virtues

> must be adopted as the means of our political salvation.
> Extravagance of all kind abolished – the distaff and the spindle must be assiduously employed. The barren wilds of America cultivated and made fertile and economy in every branch rigidly attended to – An introduction of foreign luxuries will degenerate us to slavery and the syren charms of pleasure and fancy will indelibly mark the escutcheons of our country with shame and dishonour.[36]

Of course, the prosperous grandeur and empire expected by Whitwell implied that domestic luxuries might be more permissible than their imported competitors. He appealed to temporary frugality, as a means to more solid affluence, independent of British control. Thus, in 1791, the June Election Day in New Hampshire gave Israel Evans the opportunity to celebrate how well things were going, and to contend that Americans' adherence to true liberty and republicanism – a course which the French were now emulating – allowed them to 'reap and enjoy the pleasant fruits of their honest industry.'[37] A month later, Evans' judgement of the benign currents of world politics was seconded by another New Hampshire orator, William King Atkinson, who rejoiced that the American Revolution had created a 'mighty shock' pervading 'the whole earth.' While he too exhorted Americans to be frugal and temperate in their use of foreign luxuries, Atkinson also extolled industry and praised the rapid advancement of American manufactures 'toward european perfection.'[38]

The Federalist expected much from the American people, but not as much as had been commonly expected by Revolutionary enthusiasts. He called upon the people to be honest and industrious, but he did not require them to regenerate themselves to prepare for a Christian Sparta. His rhetoric, although it chimed with the 'Protestant ethic,' did not resemble those Revolutionary Protestant jeremiads that Perry Miller pointed to as inspirations of the 'religious patriotism' of American resistance to Britain, so much as it did those less energizing appeals 'to the rising glory of America' characteristic of the 'genial Anglicanism' of the minority of Revolutionary clerics, whose persuasion relied on a 'piety hardly more than a species of Stoicism.'[39] The modesty of the moral vision articulated by the Federalist helps to explain his distance from the zeal of the reformer. His moderate call for moderation was generally less appealing than the rhetoric of the Revolutionary who preceded him and the Republican who soon superseded him.

Energetic government

Federalists adapted republicanism to American realities partly by exhorting Americans to live up to the ideal of honest industry and acquisition, and partly by redefining republican government to complement that social ideal. In their thoughts on both society and government, they betrayed their doubts about Revolutionary ideals by looking back on the Declaration of Independence and the war with Britain as a matter of harsh necessity rather than an opportunity for uplifting innovation. Stillman offered the opinion that the independence of America from Britain had been unforeseeable, and that the Declaration of Independence had been reluctantly assented to, 'as a matter of absolute necessity.'[40] Whitwell depicted the Revolution as a result of 'rashness in the parent, and necessity in the child.'[41] However, the rigors of a foreign war had held out to the nationalists of the early 1780s the possibility that support might be gained for their project of strengthening the central government and the national fiscal system, but when peace came in 1783, they had not yet succeeded in realizing this possibility.[42] The patriotism evoked by the War had encouraged attachment to national goals, but even in the War, Federalists saw the genesis of habits unsuitable for a united republic. By 1787, they had begun to discern an improvement in these habits, which they thought could both support and be heightened by an energetic national government. Federalists believed that the American people were not only more inclined than before to honest industry, but also now ready to admit the error of Revolutionary politics, the error of thinking that government was but a necessary evil and that the states needed little or nothing in the way of central government to replace British imperial rule. Their moral improvement was only moderate; therefore, the necessity of government could be better appreciated. Higginson was confident 'that many new circumstances have arisen; tending to increase the force and respectability of Government, and to give a strong impression of the necessity of its being supported.'[43] When Hamilton returned home from the Philadelphia Convention in July 1787, he reported back to George Washington that conversations he had had on his journey to New York had convinced him that

> we ought not to allow too much weight to objections drawn from the supposed repugnance of the people to an efficient constitution. I confess I am more and more inclined to believe that former habits of thinking are regaining their influence with more rapidity than is generally imaged.[44]

As 'Publius,' Hamilton wrote in a similar vein, 'I am much mistaken, if experience has not wrought a deep and solemn conviction in the public mind, that greater energy of government is essential to the welfare of the community.'[45] By Independence Day, 1789, David Humphreys could celebrate the recent success of Federalism as a refutation of the belief that mankind are 'averse to the coertions of government.' The Confederacy had 'no power of coercion,' but Americans learned by experience that 'the powers given by the members of the union to their federal head, were not sufficient to enable it to accomplish the purposes for which the body politic had been formed.' However, generally 'docile to duty,' no sooner had our countrymen felt the inconveniences arising from the feebleness of our former confederacy, than they seemed willing to invest a new Congress with a farther portion of their original rights, for the purpose of being more fully protected in the enjoyment of the remainder. Thus the dispositions [of] our Countrymen have been gradually matured to receive an energetic government.[46]

This willingness or anxiety of Federalists to believe that their persuasion was at one with an American consensus reveals some of the defects of that persuasion. For example, it is unlikely that Hamilton's conversations had brought him into contact with a very wide spectrum of opinion. He failed or refused to see any vitality in political opinions incompatible with the Federalist realism which was thought to be clearing the field. Nevertheless it probably remained true that 'the people' were 'less disposed in America than anywhere else to provide for the needs of government,'[47] Federalist hopes to the contrary notwithstanding. However, Federalists continued to hope that their political convictions would hold sway.

Central to those convictions was the opinion, contrary to Revolutionary rhetoric, that power and liberty could be mutually dependent. Whitwell suggested that the Articles of Confederation had been formed on principles 'adapted to the enthusiasm of the day, unforseeing the several incidents that would depend on a deficiency of power.' This episode taught that 'errours in government' could 'frequently arise from a want of a permanent, well grounded establishment.' Revolutionary enthusiasm had dictated an ineffective form of government, 'popular in a speculative mode, but dangerous in practice.' Federalist political theory took account of the fact that

> a relaxation in the reins of government is as productive of anarchy and confusion as the despotick law of an eastern monarch is of tyranny and oppression. It diminishes the dignity of any state, has a direct tendency to destroy subordination, and on slight pretences introduces factions and every commotion.[48]

Chief Justice John Jay included a summary of this theory in his first charge to grand juries:

> It cannot be too strongly impressed on us all, how greatly our individual prosperity depends on our national prosperity; and how greatly our national prosperity depends on a well organized, vigorous government, ruling by wise and equal laws, faithfully

executed – nor is such a government unfriendly to liberty – to that
liberty which is really estimable. On the contrary, nothing but a
strong government of laws, irresistably bearing down arbitrary
powers and licentiousness can defend it against those two formidable
enemies.[49]

Jay believed that a stable government was necessary 'to produce a
uniform adherence to what justice, dignity, and liberal policy may
require.'[50] American government needed 'that power of coercion without which no government can possibly attain the most salutary and
constitutional objects.'[51] This had been forgotten in the midst of the
opposition to British government:

> We have, probably, had too good an opinion of human nature in
> forming our confederation. Experience has taught us, that men will
> not adopt, and carry into execution, measures the best calculated for
> their own good, without the intervention of coercive power.[52]

Edward Gray's Independence Day oration in Boston in 1790 dwelt on
the same theme:

> Having severely suffered under a King and Parliament, whose
> constitutional powers were formidable, and having frequently
> experienced the fatal effects of those powers, when abused, we
> suspected that all rule naturally tended to oppression: That an
> authority in a government to check the licentiousness of man,
> involved in it a power to enslave him; that such must be its effect, and
> therefore that rulers, invested with that authority, were dangerous.

At this time, Americans did not sufficiently reflect

> that many powers were absolutely necessary to establish that
> freedom, so dear to us all; to procure our happiness as a people, and
> to support our dignity as a nation: And from a preposterous jealousy
> of our friends and fellow citizens, we would not arm them in our
> defence, lest they should turn against us. We forgot the honest
> lessons of history, which have taught, that a government without
> sufficient authority to protect those who live under it; which has not
> within itself the means of its own defence; which can exist only when
> faction slumbers; which cannot controul it, but is controuled by it;
> which pursues the happiness of the people, and yet is destitute of
> sufficient energy to enforce obedience, must inevitably fall.

Citing Montesquieu and 'Publius,' Gray remarked that, although 'it
seems agreed by political writers, that a people are without liberty, when
the legislative, executive and judicial powers are in one body of men,'

yet the examples of Greek history and recent American history demonstrated 'that a people are equally destitute of freedom, whose rulers do not possess those powers to a certain extent, and have not sufficient authority to execute them.' Gray joined in the Federalist denial of the inverse proportion supposed to exist between power and liberty; he reasoned that more power in government could mean more liberty, by preventing the degeneration to anarchy, which would of necessity be followed by tyranny, thereby exhibiting 'another instance of the degeneracy of man.'[53] Even if the old Confederal government escaped Federalist censure, the individual state governments were blamed. In New Hampshire in 1791, William King Atkinson produced a Fourth of July speech that failed to mention the Confederal government, but noticed instead the inadequacies of the state constitutions, which he claimed had been universally recognized. In contrast, the federal Constitution, avoiding the evils of monarchy, aristocracy and democracy, had 'energy and permanency.'[54] In Worcester, Edward Bangs delivered his remarks on the fortunate political homogeneity of America, which by no means restricted the need for government, as Thomas Paine and others would argue that it should do. Government was still needed for 'regulation,' as well as for defense against other countries, whether they were homogeneous or not. Bangs did not subscribe to the ideal of a peaceful world of self-regulating societies. The Independence Day ceremonies in Worcester included 'An Ode for the Day' (written by Dr. Oliver Fiske, to fit the tune 'God save the King'), which celebrated the 'rapid course' of freedom, now firing 'Gallia's shore.' But the poem itself was an ode to commerce and wealth as well, and the subsequent oration by Bangs repeated the Federalist formula, not Paine's plan, for the proper means to these goals. His theme: '*What cannot a wise choice of rulers, and a proper confidence in them, after choice, perform!*' He deprecated the political virtue of jealousy and over-caution in delegating power to governments; Americans had 'more room for *confidence*, and less occasion for jealousy, than any other people, ancient or modern.' He reasoned that because government 'in its own nature requires and always must and will have the necessary adequate powers of regulation and defence,' they would be assumed if they were not given. If they were granted in the first place, they would 'probably be exercised constitutionally.'[55]

The statement by John Quincy Adams in 1793, that 'federal' and 'confederal' were synonyms, and that the Constitution was more properly called 'national,'[56] is a reflection of early Federalist confidence. William Tudor of Massachusetts became so confident in the acceptance

of the Federalist theory of power and liberty that in 1790 he publicly
referred to the new government as a 'consolidated Republick,' prefer-
ring that term to 'Federal Republick' or (what was the same thing)
'confederated Republick' because these implied *imperium in imperio*, the
notorious solecism[57] – which, however, had been a useful absurdity in
Federalist rhetorical strategy in the struggle to ratify the Constitution.[58]
However, Federalists did not abandon the anti-monarchical bearing of
their republicanism. Indeed, some were bold enough to attempt to turn
American anti-monarchism against Antifederalists. 'Decius' (Dr. James
Montgomery), mildly supporting the nationalism and republicanism of
Washington, Jefferson and 'Publius,' claimed that Governor Patrick
Henry's administration in Virginia admitted 'the dregs of monarchy
both in measures and in men.'[59] Similar accusations were made by
Stephen Higginson's 'Laco', directed against the re-election of Governor
John Hancock of Massachusetts (who had been an Antifederalist until
a late hour). Higginson pointed to Hancock's wanton use of the 'prerogative' in his liberal distribution of offices to his friends, and contended
that Shays' Rebellion of 1786 had been caused by the people's sense of
this 'foulness' in the government.[60] The opposite use of this rebellion
by Federalist rhetoric, seeing it as an example of popular 'impatience
of government'[61] – too little government rather than too much – had
been more honest. Higginson, like most Federalist spokesmen, abhorred
the disorderly habits which had been fostered by state and confederal
governments whose 'foulness' consisted in their weakness and eagerness
to please, not in their overbearing, monarchical strength.

The importance of active, energetic government made it 'above all,
incumbent on us to appoint faithful watchmen on the walls of our
Jerusulem!'[62] If government was to be respected – and it was the 'duty'
of a 'free people...to support and encourage government'[63] –
Americans would have to use their freedom to elect to office 'the best
and wisest men.'[64] This seemed to be happening with pleasing regularity,
so that Robert Porter could report to the Pennsylvania Cincinnati Society
in 1791, 'The various departments of government are filled by men of
the first abilities and integrity.'[65]

Although the election of Federalists to administer the government was
a promising step, Federalists – unlike Republicans a decade later –
believed that 'much remains to be done.'[66] One of the most important
activities proper to this able government was the development of
America's economic potential. Whitwell eagerly looked forward to the
'prospects of future benefits' which would partner the new Constitution: 'Emigrations from remote as well [as] bordering countries will

immediately take place – Population increase – Commerce revive – Manufactures be augmented – Trade flourish – and the Arts and Sciences patronized.'[67] David Humphreys expected that 'national prosperity' would 'result from the administration of this government,' population would 'encrease beyond the power of calculation,' and the United States would become 'a commercial, a rich, and a powerful people.'[68] In 1790, delegates from the state Cincinnati Societies, meeting in Philadelphia, declared their sense of satisfaction with the state of America and its new government:

> we rejoice that our countrymen are rapidly recovering from the calamities occasioned by the late war, and that they are at last favored with a government which will probably secure to them the enjoyment of all the benefits they had a right to expect from the revolution. Already we perceive that agriculture, commerce, manufactures, private happiness and public prosperity, encrease in a wonderful manner, under the auspicious influence of this government.[69]

William Tudor congratulated the Cincinnati of Massachusetts on the success of the new 'consolidated Republick': 'Count the variety of her important and capital staples – See labour daily becoming more productive – Manufactures multiplying – the Mechanick arts improving.'[70] No longer restrained by British government, and encouraged by their own adequately powerful government, Americans could now

> entertain the whole peaceful circle of the industrious, enriching arts; and add to the virtuous number by new inventions...our ships may now explore the most distant coasts...Before our husbandmen the wilderness recedes, and fat herds, and smiling fields of corn appear, promising plenty, and inviting to partake the generous repast. These are the times in which a man should wish to live. Verily the lines are fallen to us in pleasant places; and we have a goodly heritage.[71]

With these pleasant lines Edward Bangs ended his oration in Worcester. William Linn, preaching a sermon to the Tammany Society of New York on the same day, began his remarks by quoting from Psalms xvi 6: 'The lines are fallen unto me in pleasant places; yea, I have a goodly heritage.' The political and religious freedom of America invited 'the oppressed from all quarters to repair hither,' where the fruit of labor did not go to support 'lazy priests and luxurious princes.' Linn extended the invitation:

> Forsake your hard task-masters. Refuse to dig an ungrateful soil which will not yield you bread. Haste you to the fertile plains of

America. Fill her new, and as yet, uninhabited territory. She opens
wide her arms to embrace millions, and waits to crown all the
industrious and virtuous with plenty and happiness.

The natural and political privileges of America called for 'faithful and
diligent improvement': 'Is our country pleasant and fertile? It is our
duty to contribute to the advancement of agriculture, manufactures and
commerce.'[72] Supporting the federal government was one way of
fulfilling that duty, for this government fostered economic development
and diversity. With independence from Britain made more secure
through union, Samuel Stillman saw that

> a new, extensive and animating scene opens to the view of the great
> body of American merchants; who, as to a spirit of enterprize are
> exceeded by no men on earth. They may extend their commerce to
> every part of the globe. By the revival and extension of commerce,
> shipbuilding will be encouraged, and the various classes of mechanics
> find employment. It is navigation that sets all the wheels in motion,
> and opens the way for the ingenious and industrious tradesmen to
> support themselves and families; and by encreasing the demand for
> the produce of our country, animates the farmer amidst the labor of
> the field.
>
> Without going three thousand miles for permission, we may
> establish manufactories in every part of the United States; work up
> our own materials, employ our own people, promote industry, the
> friend of virtue; lessen our annual importations, increase our
> exports; and rise thro' the blessing of God on our endeavors,
> superior to all those difficulties, with which for several years we have
> struggled.[73]

More positive steps in this direction could be taken by the new
government. By 1791, Thomas Crafts could offer a broad survey of its
achievements:

> In a period short of three years, we have seen our country raised
> from contempt, to the important rank she now holds among the
> nations of the earth. Our national faith is redeemed and established
> on a permanent foundation. The value of every species of property
> has been appreciated. The husbandman, no longer groaning
> beneath the weight of taxes, enjoys in peace the abundant fruit of his
> labours. *Commerce* also begins to rear her drooping head; new
> sources of wealth are daily opening to her view; her harbours are
> thronged with Ships, pouring into her lap, the rich exuberance of

every climate. *Manufactures* thrive, our publick *Seminaries of Learning* flourish; and the voice of gladness is heard throughout the land.'[74]

By the new government's 'wisdom and stability,' Robert Porter claimed,

Public and private credit has been restored, which has already become a mine of wealth to this country. Agriculture, commerce, and manufactures are regulated and shine with superior lustre. Every class and denomination of citizens feel the beneficent rays of the new constitution.

Porter mentioned the fact that L.Q. Cincinnatus, to whom the Cincinnati owed their name, had exemplified the agrarian virtue of the ancient republic of Rome; having saved his country, Cincinnatus had returned to the plow. But it was clear that Porter approved of the fact that the modern republic of America was equally concerned with the promotion of all classes of industry, and did not think agriculture was the only peacetime pursuit respectable enough for modern Cincinnati. In America the exertions of men were directed to making 'improvements in nature' by 'the hand of art'; the example chosen by Porter to illustrate this direction was the promotion of 'the improvement of roads and inland navigation. By this mean,' he added, 'our internal trade, manufactures, and population will rapidly increase.'[75] Federalists rarely mentioned the traditional association of agriculture and republican virtue without commenting as well on the interdependence of agriculture and other occupations. They seldom adopted 'the imaginary consequence too incident to the soil.'[76] As agriculture furnished a material foundation for commerce, 'so commerce gives life and spirit to agriculture.'[77] As Stillman had said, American farmers were 'animated' by commerce. The relationship of interdependence between farming and other business was psychological, not merely a matter of mutual convenience, for virtuous industry in agriculture arose from its being part of a complex economy. Apart from this industriousness in a pursuit where the 'progress of wealth' could be dependably 'regular and sure,'[78] the virtue associated with agriculture seemed to the Federalist to be nothing more substantial than a certain pastoral innocence, which, unlike a practiced virtue, could easily be lost, especially if farmers had to associate with non-farmers.[79]

When Stephen Higginson wrote about the 'general alteration in the habits and feelings of the people' in the late 1780s, he perceived the connection between this alteration and corresponding policies of the new government. He supposed that with the new, sober, industrious sentiments

impressed on the minds of the body of the people, and the
advantages they will derive soon from the System proposed by the
Secretary of the treasury, and from some general commercial
arrangements, which may soon be expected, the situation of
individuals will become more easy and eligible, and private happiness
be more generally enjoyed. from the same Causes, I expect, the
Government will be gradually increas'g in its energy and dignity, and
will daily extend its protection and blessings.[80]

Higginson and other Federalists believed that the new government had
enough independence and vigor to reinforce the honest industry of
Americans; this would increase their 'private happiness' and thereby
reinforce in turn their inclination to leave politics to their government.
The new confidence in government made it possible to secure policies
which would promote the people's cultivation of their own various
businesses.

The fundamental reason for encouraging a *variety* of businesses had
been explained by Madison's *Federalist*, Nos. 10 and 51, and Hamilton
set forth a corollary in his Report on Manufactures in 1791, where he
argued that the encouragement of manufactures would furnish 'greater
scope for the diversity of talents and dispositions, which discriminate
men from each other.'[81] Madison had been concerned to control factions,
but his method of doing this was to let them flourish and multiply, an
aim in which Hamilton concurred. The factious passions of men would
be more susceptible to governmental control if the interest groups
informed by those passions were 'various and interfering.'[82] In plain
terms, this required that the 'landed interest,' by far the largest, be
complemented with other kinds of business. In their public pronouncements, Hamilton and his assistant, Tench Coxe, seemed to concede some
of the special claims made on behalf of agriculture, but in their policies,
they, like other Federalists, treated it as one business – and a rather
overbearing one – among many equally eligible pursuits.

Coxe anticipated the directions of the new government's domestic
policies even before the government itself was formed. In May 1787 he
published an outline of the correct principles for the conduct of
American commerce, in a paper inscribed to the members of the Philadelphia Convention, read to the Society for Political Enquiries at Benjamin Franklin's house. Conceding that 'agriculture appears to be the
spring of our commerce and the parent of our manufactures,'[83] Coxe
nevertheless complained that Americans were too inactive in exploiting
the potential of America. 'The foundations of national wealth and

consequence' were there, but the 'enjoyment of these substantial bless-ings' was 'rendered precarious by domestic circumstances' – namely, the inability of the Confederal government to have any commercial policy at all.[84] Three months later, the Constitution having been produced by the Convention, Coxe's published statements were more confident, and somewhat less deferential to the claims of agriculture. It was possible to derive 'more profit to the individual and riches to the nation... from some manufactures... than from any species of cultivation whatever,' he asserted, and he proceeded 'to disencumber manufactures of the objections, that appear against them.'[85] He answered the charge that manufacturing had 'unfavourable effects on the health of the people' by pointing to the physical dangers involved in farming. He showed little concern for the moral effects of different pursuits, saving his suggestion that domestic manufacturing would 'lead us once more into the paths of virtue.' He had in mind 'frugality and industry,'[86] those Federalist cures for dependence on foreign manufactures, and the sum of popular virtue in Federalist psychology and political science. Like many other Federalists, Coxe had much higher expectations regarding the virtues which would animate the men who exercised 'the trusts and powers of the state.'[87] For these men had to have a vision of 'the general welfare of the nation,' and the ability to arrange that the multiple interests complement each other in order to secure the general good. Coxe indicated his idea of the general good when he proclaimed that the measures of a 'free government' ought to aim 'at the increase of the wealth of the people.' And a merely agricultural nation, he warned, could be neither 'opulent' nor 'powerful.'[88]

'It ought readily to be conceded,' wrote Hamilton in his Report on Manufactures, 'that the cultivation of the earth... as including a state most favorable to the freedom and independence of the human mind ...has intrinsically a strong claim to pre-eminence over every other kind of industry.' But he did not think that this question of the putative moral tendencies of agriculture needed to be answered in order to answer the question of the policy of promoting other kinds of industry. His case for an affirmative response to the latter question rested on 'fact and calculation.' First he argued that the alleged amoral, economic superiority of agricultural industry was false, that agriculture was not the most productive object of capital and labor, even in America with its abundance of land and scarcity of capital. Manufactures made 'the produce and revenue' of a society greater than they could possibly be without manufactures, by the division of labor and by the use of more machinery, more workers (women, children, immigrants) and more

3

diversified talents than were employed in a purely agricultural society: the 'busy nature of man' was better fulfilled in a mixed economy, where many avenues of success were open. Therefore such an economy was also more likely to produce the 'opulence' to which the 'political and natural advantages' of the United States 'authorize them to aspire.' Moreover, it was a 'moral certainty' that the trade of a mixed economy was 'more lucrative and prosperous' than a simply agricultural economy, because the fact that even the least agricultural nations grew some food meant that the demand for agricultural imports fluctuated, while an agricultural nation's demand for manufactured imports was constant. Hamilton added to these arguments, which he thought were sufficient to prove his case, the argument which made his case politically acceptable some twenty years later: 'independence and security,' he said, required every nation 'to possess within itself...the means of subsistence, habitation, clothing, and defence.'[89] Non-agricultural life became politically praiseworthy only as a necessity, not for the positive advantages postulated by Hamilton on the basis of the Federalist belief in their conformity with human nature. Accordingly, one hoped to avoid its pejorative tendencies by bringing to the life of the city the spirit of the country.[90]

In 1791 Hamilton had another argument to oppose. Was *laissez-faire* not the best as well as the simplest policy? If manufactures were so profitable, would they not grow on their own? No, urged Hamilton, for the strength of habit was such that 'the incitement and patronage of government' was required 'to produce the desirable changes.' And the time was now ripe, while disturbances in Europe occasioned an influx of money and potential workers, and while the present 'activity of speculation and enterprise' could 'be made subservient to useful purposes.' But would not this patronage give a 'monopoly of advantages to particular classes, at the expense of the rest of the community'? Here was a decisive political objection to Hamilton's program, and a test of how far he was willing to allow government to go in the regulation of society. In reply he could only point to 'the ultimate effect,' when goods produced by well-established and competitive domestic manufactures would be even cheaper than imported goods. This 'eventual and permanent economy,' as beneficial to farmers as to anyone else in the long run, required in the mean time something 'like monopoly.' Otherwise Americans would act on the 'common error of the early periods of every country,' the idea that agricultural and manufacturing interests were necessarily opposed to each other. Hamilton hoped that they would act instead on the 'truth' that 'every thing tending to establish substantial and permanent order in the affairs of a country, to increase the total mass of industry and opulence, is ultimately beneficial to every part of it.'[91] In 1792 Coxe suggested that the best interests 'of our landholders require the introduction of some kind of manufactory in almost every vicinity.' He reversed the usual formula for the interdependence of agriculture and manufactures, by citing an example in Great Britain, where the wool and liquor businesses showed the importance of manufactures to agriculture: 'They nourish and support it.' Closer to home, he cited chapter and verse on the progress of manufacturing in the South, and, by an analysis of the occupations of the families in several towns in the interior of Pennsylvania, he showed 'that manufactures are the best support of the interior landed interest.' In any case, Coxe said, the landed property of America 'has been constantly animated by the application of the monies of distant capitalists.'[92]

The promotion of manufactures in America did not require that the supply of land be reduced, but it did require that the supply of capital be increased. Hamilton noted that the velocity of money would be greater in a mixed economy, and that this alone would augment the money supply, as would banks – 'if administered with prudence,' he stipulated, probably thinking of the rapidly multiplying state banks, which he had called 'monsters.' But he placed most reliance on the funded national debt, which, like bank and private credit, could create 'an artificial increase of capital.'[93] Hamilton's intended policy of encouraging manufactures – a policy widely supported by Federalists – thus revealed some of the main purposes of the plans for funding the debt and establishing a national bank, plans which had been secured several months before the Report on Manufactures. It also added significance to his opposition to discrimination between original and subsequent holders of the debt. Discrimination would have created difficulty in the secure transfer of the certificates of debt. This could have dispelled the hope that these certificates might serve as money, and as capital.[94] Hamilton's proposals now specified that this capital was for the 'useful purpose' of creating a complex economy. This purpose gave coherence to the Hamiltonian program, and it related Federalist policies to Federalist political science and psychology.

The fate of the Federalist project was considered to be of immense significance: 'The attention of mankind is fixed on the event, and the happiness of numbers exceeding the powers of conception, depends on the issue.'[95] The American experiment in republicanism would determine the future of the entire world. America was a modern Israel, a people chosen to exemplify righteous liberty. Federalists did not fail to invoke this recurrent theme of American rhetoric by drawing parallels between the histories of the chosen peoples of the Bible and of modernity. According to John Cushing, 'God dealt with no people as with Israel: but in the history of the United States, particularly New-England, there is as great a similarity, perhaps, in the conduct of Providence to that of the Israelites, as is to be found in the history of any people.'[96] To the Reverend Dr. William Smith, in his sermon before the Pennsylvania Society of the Cincinnati, the United States appeared as a better fulfillment of the Old Testament prophecies than any nation in either the Old or New Testaments; Jews, Assyrians, Macedonians, Greeks, Romans – all had departed from the path of virtue and prosperity.[97] William Linn claimed that the natural and political privileges of America, like those of Israel, were granted by God.[98] In an election day sermon in Boston in 1791, Chandler Robbins propounded a variation on the theme of Israel and America. His text was from 2 Chronicles xii 12: 'And also in Judah things went well.' The United States, Robbins suggested, resembled Judah, rather than Israel. Like the United States, Judah had become a separate nation after a period of prosperity under a reign of kings, when it had been united with Israel. Arbitrary claims had been made by a prince, and the empire had been dismembered. Judah had no reason to regret the separation; God made it David's particular object of care, and soon 'things went well.'[99] Isaac Keith's sermon had used Deuteronomy xxviii as a text, from which he concluded:

> As long as religion and virtue have been generally honored and practiced among a people they have continued safe, flourishing and happy. When their morals have become generally vicious and dissolute, they have been soon involved in various calamities, and unless prevented by a timely reformation, have finally sunk into irretrievable ruin.
>
> In the Jewish history, in particular, the proofs of this are exhibited with the strongest and most convincing evidence.

Keith argued that the Jews were not chosen as the sole beneficiaries of prosperity. Rather, they were chosen as an example to the rest of mankind: 'In them God seems to have intended to give the world an illustrious example of the general method of his procedure with the various governments or societies of mankind in every age and country.' With an eye to recent American history, Keith noticed in his text 'a most gracious and encouraging promise made to the Israelites at the time when they had at length compleated their tedious march of forty years, varied with many astonishing scenes of divine mercy and judgement, through the wilderness, and were now on the point of entering into and taking possession of the long promised and long expected land of rest.'

The text held that the Jews' obedience to God and to His moral and political laws 'would prove the certain means of raising them to the highest stage of personal and national prosperity, of advancing them to an enviable pre-eminence in wealth, power and glory among the nations of the earth.' And Keith held that 'The hope set before them belongs equally to us.' By quoting with approval a portion of the preamble to the new federal Constitution, he made it clear why he thought 'the light of a brighter day has again broken forth upon us.'

The religious practice required by Keith was simply the acknowledgement of 'the superintending Providence of God in all our affairs, and especially in all the great events of a public nature and general concern which take place among us.' By 'providence,' Keith understood a certainty of the punishment of vice and the reward of virtue. Only in the closing words of his sermon did he remind his audience of their 'eternal interests.' He was preoccupied with the delineation of the kind of conduct in this world which would make certain not only a happy life hereafter, but also a prosperous life here and now. This conjunction of religion and worldliness, of nature and nature's God, could hardly have been shocking to Keith's audience, for it was not unusual in contemporary American thought. As the Reverend John Woodhull explained, with reference to Greece, Rome and especially Israel:

> The Judge of all the earth will do right; he will render to every individual and nation according to their works. And as nations exist only in this world, they must *here* receive *their* reward.

The punishment of national vice and the reward of national virtue were 'natural tendencies' because 'the frame of things' had been constructed by 'infinite wisdom and purity.'[100] This sanguine, utilitarian view of religion and virtue saw in this world far more guaranteed comfort than could be expected in a vale of tears, provided only that certain virtues were maintained. Thus it was perhaps less important 'to overcome the world, and all that is in the world.' This religious view of providence was not far distant from the secular version, wherein human history takes the place of divine providence: 'If we look into antient history, we find that nations were flourishing while they were industrious, temperate and frugal; but as soon as luxury was admitted, indolence and a train of evils soon followed her, sapp'd the foundations and the whole fabric tumbled into ruin.'[101] If Americans became 'corrupt and profligate,' 'national greatness and glory' would quickly depart, but Keith did not think this danger was imminent; indeed, he believed that Americans had just escaped a vicious episode – the threats of disunion and anarchy which followed the conclusion of the War: a 'criminal neglect of our own interests' – and were now recovered and therefore in line for 'better things.'[102] His sermon was more congratulatory than monitory, quite compatible with Whitwell's vision of

> that America which but a few years past was a lonely wilderness – rising to the zenith of her lustre – important in her councils, and impregnable in her strength – respected and courted by distant nations, like the antient mistress of the world, displaying her grandeur throughout the Universe.[103]

Samuel Stillman was equally confident. He thought that Americans could now 'reasonably anticipate America's golden age, when science, arts, industry, religion, freedom, and public happiness, shall exalt her to the most distinguished eminence among the nations of the world.' But he showed little concern for the promotion of the arts; in fact he said that historians, poets and painters were already as plentiful as heroes in the New World. As for religion, Stillman, like Keith, made God's 'unalterable purpose' less mysterious than he himself felt obliged to claim that it was. On the other hand, he held that American independence was unforeseeable and thus 'altogether providential.' But he also claimed that it was inevitable because of the absurdity involved in the government of a continent by a distant island. Mystery and apparent absurdity are not incompatible. For Stillman, providence was subject to knowable laws; wisdom and virtue have caused the rise of nations, he said, and 'by ignorance and vice they have been ruined. The same causes will invariably produce the same effects.'[104]

Federalists thus presented their project in terms of the appealing idea of America as the promised land of a chosen people. In the early years of the French Revolution, they could imagine that the righteous American example was being followed abroad. They adopted Thomas Paine's denunciation of English politics and his praise for the French Revolution.[105] But they continued to think of their Constitution in terms of their political science which was if anything more attuned to British practices than to the doctrines developed by Paine. They paid homage to Paine, but maintained a consistent loyalty to both Revolutionary and Federalist realism. Likewise, their rational deism and confident utilitarianism militated against a fuller development of the Old Testament element of political religion in America. A less enlightened, less disillusioned and more apprehensive view of the promise of American life was presented by Republicans, who were able to make the forty years in the wilderness tally more closely with American history by making the Revolution of 1800.

PART II
THE ORIGINS OF PARTY POLITICS

4

The Federalist practice of politics and the origins of the Republican party, 1789–92

A false beginning

John Adams, who believed that American politics was returning to the natural order of things, did not leave it to nature to discover its ways of returning to the American political scene. He offered himself as its instrument in 1789, when he and an Antifederalist Virginian Senator, Richard Henry Lee, led the new Senate's advocacy of honorific titles for the highest offices in the federal government. Adams is reported to have remarked that titles were 'all nonsense to the philosopher; but so is all government, whatever.'[1] The remark sounds like him, and it is not flippant, it merely expresses Adams' understanding of the irrational way of politics. The episode of the titles proposal and the reaction to it was the false start of American party politics. Historians sometimes give it more significance than it deserves, for they anticipate that monarchism was to appear as one of the issues between Federalists and Republicans.[2] It is misleading to trace the origins of party politics directly to the controversy over titles, although it is interesting that it should appear so much of a piece with those origins.

Madison's commentary on American politics in his letters to Jefferson, who was in Paris, furnish a fair appraisal of the atmosphere surrounding the first session of Congress, in which the titles debate began and ended. His letters of December 1788 (delivered to Jefferson by Madison's nationalist ally, Gouverneur Morris) show his gratitude at the outcome of the Congressional elections, which were providing 'both a certainty of [the government's] peaceable commencement in March next, and a flattering prospect that it will be administered by men who will give it a fair trial'; 'if prudence should be the character of the First Congress,' the elections would lead 'to measures which will conciliate the well-meaning of all parties, and put our affairs into an auspicious train.'[3] George Washington, the President of the new Republic, echoed this

65

satisfaction with the continued national rejection of Antifederalism.[4] In April, Fisher Ames, a Federalist from Massachusetts complacently reflected on the number of 'sober, solid, old-charter folks' in the House of Representatives, who were however so 'republican' in character that 'the *antis* will laugh at their own fears. They will see that the aristocracy may be kept down some years longer.'[5] Adams' support for titles reflected his desire to prevent the anarchy of state-centered politics, a desire which he shared with all Federalists,[6] but other Federalists rejected his proposed means to this end.

For the most part the confidence of these more orthodox Federalists was unshaken during the first session of Congress. But in May 1789, Madison was obliged to inform Jefferson that the Congressional calm had been disturbed by the titles proposition. On the twenty-third – after the brief controversy had ended by the House of Representatives flatly refusing even to agree to the title 'Honorable' for Senators – Madison sent this summary of the dispute to Jefferson (the italicized words originally in cipher):

> My last inclosed copies of the President's inaugural Speech and the answer of the House of Representatives. I now add the answer of the Senate. It will not have escaped you that the former was addressed with a truly republican simplicity to G.W., Presid^t of the U.S. The latter follows the example, with the omission of the personal name, but without any other than the Constitutional title. The proceeding on this point was in the House of Rep^s, spontaneous. The imitation by the Senate was *extorted*. The question *became a serious one between the two Houses, J. Adams espoused the cause of titles* with great *earnestness,* His *friend, R. H. Lee, altho elected as a Republican enemy* to an *aristocratic Constitution,* was *a most zealous second.* The *projected title was, His Highness the Presid^t of the U.S. and protector of their liberties.* Had the *project succeeded, it would have* subjected the *Presid^t to a serious dilemma,* and given *a deep wound to our infant Government.*

On the twenty-seventh Madison could report sanguinely that the spirit characterizing Congress 'is already extinguishing the honest fears which considered the [new federal] system as dangerous to republicanism.'[7] The episode had ended; its only substantial result was the presentation to John Adams of the title 'His Rotundity.' On the same day that Madison reported the failure of the titles proposal to Jefferson, Fisher Ames turned in a similar report to his old friend George Minot:

> The business of titles sleeps. It is a very foolish thing to risk much to secure; and I wish Mr. Adams had been less undisguised...He has

been long absent, and at first he had not so clear an idea of the temper of the people as others who had not half his knowledge in other matters.[8]

Ames noted that Adams was still 'greatly respected'; nevertheless he confirmed Madison's judgement of the unfortunate nature of the titles proposal. By the beginning of June, a 'delightful accommodation,' 'much harmony, politeness and good humour' could be said to prevail in both Houses of Congress.[9]

Adams' indiscretion even elicited a lamentation at 'the depravity or weakness of human nature, in tracing the incentive and the end of action to the gilded ear, or ceremonial ribband,' from the orator at the Independence Day meeting of the Society of Cincinnati in Philadelphia.[10] And in Boston a versifying pamphleteer contrasted Adams with Washington, who was 'untainted' by royal ambitions, and pointed out that a king would not long remain limited, for he would have creatures, who would have creatures, and so on.[11] But it was not yet argued that these creatures might precede a king, and for the moment Madison was as anxious as anyone to bury this episode. He never made Adams' mistake of thinking that public monarchism could be a viable part of American national republicanism. And at this time Madison was particularly concerned to cultivate American loyalty to orthodox Federalist republicanism; open monarchism would play into the hands of Antifederalists by verifying their predictions. Madison's detailed letters to Jefferson from 1787 to 1789 show how anxious he was to maintain the Federalist loyalty of his older but more volatile friend, who had seen only from a distance the sobering scenes of the final years of the Confederacy, and who had played little part in the Federalist redefinition of republicanism. In 1791, Jefferson would be tutoring Madison, and they would find it profitable to revive the specter of monarchism that haunted the minds of John Adams and a few others. Only then would they connect monarchism with certain national policies instigated by Hamilton. And by then monarchism was being not considered but strenuously denied by friends of the administration, and Adams had retreated to the quasi-anonymity of his 'Discourses on Davila' to demonstrate with clean logic the truths that would ever fail to be politically logical. Adams' political longevity, such as it was, depended on his abandonment of serious attempts to put his theories into practice, and on his consequent pragmatism, which enabled him to attach the loyalty of moderates.[12] After all, he always defined republicanism as the rule of law, even if he did propose unacceptably realistic devices to establish the rule of law. Adams' political theorizing subsided not (as has been suggested) after his defeat and retirement in 1800 but after this defeat of 1789: not because his political thought was closely tied to his political activity, but because his actions could not follow his thoughts.

Political disunity

It is less accurate to trace the origins of party politics to the confident reaction to the overt advocacy of monarchism, than to the later and more fretful accusation of covert monarchism. The publication of this accusation, which marks the origins of the Republican party, was preceded by – but not identical with – the collapse of Federalist unity. Politicians who had supported orthodox Federalism continued to agree – with various degrees of wholeheartedness – on many of the 'realistic' tenets of Federalism, but they found themselves at odds on the reduction of Federalist principles to practice. They differed both over the way in which policies should be decided and over the substance of the policies themselves. Both procedural and substantive differences took roots in radically different notions of the nature of man and government in the New World. The fuller articulation of these notions and further development of Federalist realism encouraged the fainthearted to abandon Federalism and to create the Republican party.

Procedure. Even those politicians who would remain loyal to Federalism found reason for disappointment in the Federalist practice of politics. In 1790 there were heated disputes in Congress. They seemed like the kind of disputes that Federalist political science had anticipated; they were mainly economic issues, which the system was supposed to be capable of managing as long as they remained independent from ideological issues. Yet there was also a disappointing decline in the dignity of this management. John Steele, a Federalist from North Carolina, who arrived in New York to take his seat in Congress in April, was greeted by disconcerting evidence of a lack of sympathy between Northern and Southern Congressmen; in June he reported that there was 'little prospect of doing anything in this session that will terminate for the good of the whole.'[13] But a great deal was accomplished in this session, though not by the methods anticipated by Steele and other Federalists. The most prominent issues dividing Congressmen were the permanent residence of the national capital, and the federal assumption of the states' war debts. In 1790 these two issues were deemed negotiable by Jefferson,[14] but they were fiercely fought over by Congressmen.

A not unsympathetic French diplomat prefaced his report of the political squabbling and deals made on the residence and assumption issues with some reflections on the character of American republicanism:

The hypothesis upheld by one of the noblest geniuses of this century that virtue is the principle of a republic would do much honor to humanity if it could pass without alteration through the crucible of experience. For eleven years I have examined carefully one of the freest people on earth and I have found here so little virtue in the political sense of this word that I am very far from subscribing to the opinion of this philosopher who knew republics only through books or through isolated and too rapid observations. The intrigues, the cabals, the underhanded and insidious dealings of a factious and turbulent spirit are even much more frequent in this republic than in the most absolute monarchy where they are concentrated in the palace without infecting the mass of the nation. Here the intrigues begin in the smallest parochial assemblies whence they pass to those of the district, from there to the state legislatures and from the latter to Congress where they act through accelerated movement with more energy. But as it is impossible to deceive an entire nation about its true interests, it generally happens that the private egoism concentrated in that of the nation leads to an honorable end by means which are hardly so and by men who desire the good only because it is personally useful to them.[15]

Fisher Ames, who had referred to the debate on residence as a 'despicable grog-shop contest, whether the taverns of New York or Philadelphia shall get the custom of Congress,' reported the residence–assumption deal with shame for his colleagues and pleasure at his ability to keep clear of it:

the world ought to despise our public conduct, when it hears intrigue openly avowed, and sees that great measures are made to depend, not upon reasons, but upon bargains for little ones.[16]

Log-rolling of the sort that stirred up such shuddering as this was typical of a much lower tone of conduct than was anticipated by the Federalist understanding of politics. Far from approaching the dangerous heights of principled, uncompromising politics, American legislators were in danger of disappointing even the Federalist expectation of disinterested statesmanship presiding over a multiplicity of compromisable interests. Even the ideals of Federalism, estimated as lower

than those of Revolutionary republicanism, seemed to be too high. The
representatives of the people seemed to display little more virtue than
the people. How had this come about?

What Madison called 'the spirit of this City,' which he related to New
York City's 'Anglicanism,' had abetted commercial policies that scotched
his proposal in 1789 for commercial discrimination against Great Britain.
In this proposal, Madison's ideals were wholeheartedly nationalist, for
he was leading a crusade to retaliate against British restriction of American commercial expansion. Furthermore, Madison's proposal could be
construed as a corollary of the Federalist project; as 'Publius,' he had
claimed (and Hamilton agreed) that a great variety of interests –
including 'a manufacturing interest, a mercantile interest, a moneyed
interest, with many lesser interests' – was essential to 'civilized nations,'
and he now saw that he was asking farmers and planters to subsidize
the growth of the relatively feeble commercial and and manufacturing
interests.[17] Not surprisingly, Virginia's U.S. Senators (who had been
Antifederalists) joined in the Senate's rejection of this proposal. Ironi-
cally Fisher Ames' opposition to commercial discrimination was also
justified on nationalist grounds: he thought it a 'little and mean' measure, smugly dissociated himself from the New England Representatives
who had voted in favor of it, and proudly proclaimed, 'I wish I may
never sacrifice national principles to local interests.' A few weeks later
Ames saw that his position was in fact aligned with Eastern commercial
interests, who now feared that they would suffer from a trade war with
Britain.[18] Willy-nilly, Ames had reflected the local interests of his
constituents. Madison too soon began playing in spite of himself the role
of the representative as agent, faithfully following his constituents'
interpretation of their interests, when in 1790 he proposed the discrimination between original and subsequent holders of the certificates
of national debt, and the assumption of state debts as they had stood
in 1783 rather than as they stood in 1790. Both of these expensive
propositions, which Madison had based on the principle of national
equity, were popular in Virginia, where they were thought to be
profitable to Virginians. (Henry Lee and James Monroe advised Madison of the Virginian opposition to Hamilton's policy of undiscriminated
funding and assumption.)[19] Both proposals were defeated – the first,
partly because of its great expense, the second, by the South's acceptance
of the capital residence and a system of compensatory grants in its
stead.[20] New York City – the established center of financial speculation
in America[21] – was an appropriate scene for the wheeling and dealing
of the first federal Congress. Difference of principle lay behind the

political divisions, but the principles were not party principles and they were not publicized as such. They help to explain the divisions among some of the leading politicians, but they do not explain the support that these men received or failed to receive from other politicians and from the people responsible for electing them.[22] Federalists had known that the people would display short-sighted selfishness, but they had hoped – and their political science had depended upon it – that politicians would be able to maintain some distance and independence from popular passions. But even in their attempts to do so, politicians became more and more closely identified with those passions. Federalists deplored this procedural development; Republicans would be more receptive to it.

Substance. Foreign policy was one of the most important areas of substantive disagreement among federal politicians. Party was to be created and first publicized with emphasis on domestic issues, and both Republicans and Federalists would have occasion in the course of their conflict to wish that this emphasis had continued. The vagaries of public reaction to foreign affairs helped to delay the triumph of the Republican party in spite of its natural superiority. However, the first substantive divisions of principle among the politicians in the new government concerned policies toward Britain and France. The nationalism that had been hitherto the companion of Federalist realism diverged into a proud, defiant, idealistic Republican foreign policy, and a Federalist foreign policy of shockingly consistent 'realism.' The foreign policy debates that took place within the government from 1789 to 1792 did not produce political parties. However, they provide a fine prologue to the play of partisanship, not because of the fact that they themselves enter in the second act, but because they reveal the basic doctrines at issue between Federalists and Republicans.

Supporters of the foreign policy that was to become identified with the Republican party started from the assumption shared by most Federalists in the 1780s, that a stronger national government would enable America to adopt a more vigorous posture toward British domination of commercial navigation. What earthly use was the Revolution if it was not to mean that American commerce would be freed from colonial shackles? But the British government had decided that to continue to rule the waves meant to continue to bar the former colonists from unrestricted trade with the remaining imperial possessions, particularly the West Indies, a nursery of British seamen which the United States with its geographical advantage would soon spoil if let into it. So

Americans were to have the trouble of independence without some of its most tangible fruits, if British policy was successful. Between 1783 and 1789, when the United States had little power to pursue any foreign policy, everyone continued to insist on the Revolutionary ideals of free trade, which held up the possibility of an end to war and power politics in relations between nations. British power and policy was keenly resented. In 1789 with the means now apparently in hand to promote these ideals, James Madison and Thomas Jefferson determined to make the new government serve this, its proper end, and they steadfastly tried to initiate commercial retaliation against Britain in order to compel it to behave with respect for principles of international justice. The Constitutional ban on export duties, which had been insisted on by the South, deprived them of one of their potentially most effective weapons,[23] but tariff and tonnage duties could be used with some effect. The threat of retaliation by these means did at least help bring the British to negotiate.[24]

Federalists once more turned away from Revolutionary ideals, toward a harder line. By 1789, a revived Anglo-American commerce was proving profitable to Americans in spite of British restrictions, and there was little substance in the vision of a flourishing Franco-American trade that was supposed to be the alternative to the British connection. The only other option was a Spartan self-sufficiency, and Federalists knew that Americans had lost whatever taste they had ever had for that. Besides, Hamilton's scheme for the finance of American manufactures – a long-term way of procuring real independence – depended partly on British capital and even more on a reliable revenue from commercial duties, which was bound to be interrupted by the commercial warfare that Republicans favored. The cultivation of the American spirit of enterprise required the United States to avoid antagonizing Britain rather than prematurely to challenge it in commercial competition.

The foundation of Federalist foreign policy was the same as that of Federalist domestic policy. Neither individual nations nor individuals within nations could be expected to act on very elevated principles. Nations had as great a need for some kind of artificial government as individuals had. The possibility of a world government not having been laid open, nations had to make do with imperial systems. The federal government stood in the same relationship to the international system as individual Americans to that government. Thus, it was not wholly inconsistent for Hamilton to use before 1789 an argument that he would reject after 1789: to say that the new government would be in a position to defy British power was a good way to induce respect for the power of this government; when acting as that government itself, however, Hamilton had to acknowledge a higher sovereign in the necessities of international relations. The anarchy of free trade, which Republicans continued to advocate, seemed utopian, since it relied on men and nations being other than they are. Republicans enlarged – and, after 1800, acted – upon the principles of this utopia, where 'legislative interference,'[25] whether by a national government or by an international empire, was considered always a necessary evil that could be reformed away. However, they first challenged the Federalists on domestic ground.

There were many throughout the country in 1789 and 1790 who did not silently acquiesce in the domestic measures of the new government. Determined opposition was heard, especially in Virginia, New York and Pennsylvania. Charges of Anglophilia were hurled at the funding and assumption systems. But these charges were made by Antifederalists, and they found little representation in the counsels of the national government, which was controlled by Federalists.[26] Madison did not yet repeat the apprehensions that a Philadelphia physician, Benjamin Rush, expressed to him: 'the "public blessing" of a debt contracted to foreigners and a few American speculators...will lay the foundations of an aristocracy in our country,' said Rush, who believed that when the 'country people' were informed of this vile scheme, it would affect the elections of Representatives in several states in 1790 and 1791. Rush declared himself 'only a spectator of public measures,' however, and did not yet act on this 'matter of opinion only.'[27] In New York in 1790 there appeared a brief pamphlet called *Considerations on the Nature of a Funded Debt*, the first of a proposed series which was not continued; its author was Robert R. Livingston, who would soon emerge as one of New York's Republican leaders.[28] The excise on whisky roused appropriately spirited resentment in western Pennsylvania. But a Pittsburgh politician, Hugh Henry Brackenridge, who would claim in 1794 that he had opposed the Hamiltonian program from the very beginning, had first tried to maintain his wealthy Federalist connections; even in his *National Gazette* articles in February 1792, he expressed the need for strong federal power to secure the frontier, as vigorously as he warned of the dangers of the frontier's opposition to the excise.[29] There was strong opposition to funding and assumption in New Hampshire and in Virginia; the Virginia legislature, by a vote of 75 to 52, sent to Congress a formal protest against the injustice and unconstitutionality of the assumption system, in December 1790. The Virginians also judged it to be opposed to 'republican policy,' for they had discerned a striking resemblance between this system and that which was introduced into England at the Revolution – a system which has perpetuated upon that nation an enormous debt, and has, moreover, insinuated into the hands of the Executive an unbounded influence, which, pervading every branch of the Government, bears down all opposition, and daily threatens the destruction of every thing that appertains to English liberty. The same causes produce the same effects.[30]

But the protest occasioned no stir in Congress; the move was of so little avail that one of the most powerful Virginia Federalists, John Marshall, judged that the fight against Antifederalism was over, and withdrew from state politics.[31] It was not until charges similar to these were entertained and elaborated by men who had supported Federalism that Antifederalists were mobilized into an effective national force, as a wing of Republicanism.

This deference to Antifederalism did not occur in 1790. Madison's leadership of an opposition to Hamilton's funding policies appealed to equity, not to anti-monarchical republicanism. The proposal for discrimination in funding had previously been made by a Federalist colleague, Pelatiah Webster;[32] and 'Decius' had pointed out that Antifederalists were far from absent in the ranks of the 'political stock-jobbers' who made a killing by buying up government securities before news affecting their price was broadcast.[33] Hamilton's Report on Public Credit had anticipated the kind of opposition made by Madison;[34] it did not anticipate, and did not yet receive, considerable opposition on the grounds of its monarchical tendencies. In 1790 'exaggerated republicans' could be treated with simple circumspection by President Washington.[35] At the end of the year, Washington was compelled to find diversion in the minute supervision of the redecoration of his carriage, political questions being so little engaging. Jefferson could report to a French correspondent,

> Our second experiment is going on happily; and so far we have no reason to wish for changes except by adding those principles which several of the states thought were necessary as a further security for their liberties.

Benjamin Franklin Bache's *General Advertiser* – not an administration organ – looked forward to the commencement of 'a new, happy series of years' in the new decade. Elections to the second Congress brought many changes of personnel, but few of political persuasion, contrary to Rush's prediction.[36] Partisan elections require political party, which did not yet exist, though political disunity can be seen to have cried out for it.

Political party

In January 1791 Hamilton's proposal for a national bank raised some opposition in Congress on the grounds of the intrinsic evils of banking, but Edmund Randolph, Jefferson, even Madison on the floor of the House, appealed mainly to 'the cool dictates of reason' and raised the question of strict versus loose construction in Constitutional interpretation.[37] This appeal showed how far some nationalists were willing to veer towards Antifederalism when they disliked national policy. But it was not a very effective appeal, divorced as it was from the true reasons for the opposition – especially when Hamilton could paraphrase Madison's *Federalist* writings to support loose constructionism. Nor was it the kind of appeal that was to define Republicanism, which did not reject nationalism as such, but was opposed to the Hamiltonian nationalism characteristic of the Federalist project. The year 1791 saw much preparation for some kind of concerted action by men who doubted the wisdom or benefits of the policies being unfolded in Hamilton's overpowering Reports. In January R. H. Lee was answering James Monroe's inquiries about the excise and the bank. In February, Jefferson began to write letters to political leaders throughout the nation, to sound out the opposition raised by the measures of the government.[38] (The bank bill had quickly passed, and was signed by Washington on February 25.) On February 28, Jefferson offered Philip Freneau a job in Philadelphia that would leave him time to publish a newspaper. He (inadvertently, it seems) raised a sensation in the spring when his letter praising Paine's *Rights of Man* was published as a preface to that extremely Anglophobic republican work. In May, he began his famous botanizing excursion with Madison.[39] He returned to Philadelphia in June to find a controversy raging between 'Publicola,' a series of essays by John Quincy Adams replying to Jefferson's endorsement of Paine, and a 'host' of republican volunteers in response.[40]

These events convinced Oliver Wolcott, Jr., that the convening of the new Congress in October 1791 would reveal an opposition party appealing to the principles discussed in the press. 'Mr. A. H. and Mr. J. seem much disposed to quarrel on...whether Tom Paine or Edmund Burke' is the greater fool, he wrote to his father.[41] But the debates of Congress were not disturbed on the scale that he predicted. At the end of October, Ames could report that the first arrangements for the Bank of the United States had 'passed over smoothly. Though mutual jealousies were felt, yet all parties saw and yielded to the necessity of harmonizing.' But he also saw that 'faction glows within like a coal-pit.'[42] The glow was visible in the allusions to corruption and anti-republicanism made in Congress in November by Representatives Giles and Page of Virginia.[43] That it did not yet flare up into anything as fiery as the Giles Resolutions of January 1793 indicates that the Republican protagonists were keeping their eyes on the political objectives to be won by republican partisanship. They did not want to start a total war, they only desired a quickly won and quickly forgotten campaign. Before 1792, they had even hoped that reapportionment following the census of 1790 might alleviate the necessity of larger-scale partisanship. It was not their unfamiliarity with political partisanship, but their very experience with it in the disputes of 1776 and 1787 that made them think of it as an extraordinary and temporary expedient. At first, they thought that one republican partisan election would be sufficient to secure their objective, and 1792 was to be the one. They looked not to the floor of Congress, but to the elections of the next Congress. For not only had Congress failed to provide the disinterested, statesmanlike adjustment of interests that was anticipated by Federalism; in its less dignified role as a kind of broker, it had not properly felt the weight of certain interests, because of executive interference or 'corruption.'

In December 1791, Jefferson was writing to a fellow Virginian about the natural monarchical tendencies of the national government.[44] In that same month, Hamilton presented to Congress his Report on Manufactures, which made clear the kind of society his funding, assumption and bank had been designed to promote. However, though Freneau's *National Gazette* had begun publication in October, the powerful pens of Republican publicists were restrained until February 1792, when the campaign of 1792, the first and by intention the last of its kind, was unleashed. Only then did contemporary observers begin to talk about two parties in Congress, and 'right' and 'wrong' voting by Congressmen. At the same moment, party opposition appeared for the first time in New Jersey, and in New England, the Federalist fastness which Republicans already recognized as the greatest test of their siege tactics.[45]

The changing character of newspaper publications in the national capital indicates first the absence and then the sudden presence of republican partisanship in the first years of the new government. In early 1789, there was no particularly Federalist newspaper in New York; *The Federalist* had first appeared in the *Daily Gazette*, a commercial sheet. John Fenno set up his *Gazette of the United States* in the spring, and in spite of the continual adulation of 'His Excellency' George Washington in the *Gazette's* articles (which were copied by editors throughout the country), Jefferson found it a congenial place to publish – with Washington's approval – translations of articles from a French newspaper, in order to correct the bias of the British sources of published news from abroad. Indeed, the only anti-administration newspapers of 1789 and 1790 were the Antifederalist newspapers of 1788, and they criticized the administration indiscriminately. For example, Aaron Burr's friend Thomas Greenleaf, in his *New York Journal*, attacked Madison and Jefferson as well as Hamilton and others.

In the spring of 1791, Fenno had followed the government to Philadelphia, and his style mellowed, in the absence of a rival like Greenleaf. The adulation of Washington dwindled. There even appeared in the *Gazette* a few anti-Bank articles. In October, Freneau's *National Gazette* commenced publication, as a rival national newspaper. (Articles in both *Gazettes* were reprinted by newspapers North and South.) But until the end of February 1792, Freneau, possibly on the advice of his patrons, published a politically circumspect journal.

The calm of editorial opinion was not broken until the concerted spring offensive on administration policy in *National Gazette* articles by 'Brutus,' who assailed Hamilton's funding system; 'Sidney,' who assaulted his excise; and 'A Farmer' (George Logan), who leveled the important charge that, in spite of the failure of the titles proposal two years before, the principles of aristocracy were still prevalent. This offensive began during the last week of February. On February 27, Freneau himself charged that the funding system was responsible for the 'thirst for rank and distinction' afflicting too many Americans. 'Foreigners have observed, in *this* country, that the inhabitants...are only republican in name,' he proclaimed. 'Brutus' was the most notorious of the anonymous writers. On March 26 he warned that, steered by the funding system, 'Our political bark seems to be gently sliding down that stream leading from freedom to slavery.' At this time the House of Representatives were considering measures following up the assumption of state debts, and Hamilton's system suffered new accusations of being an imitation of British policies that were inappropriate to the young republic; on March 31 Madison adverted to the Virginia Resolutions of 1790, which he and the rest of the House had ignored since their being quietly tabled fourteen months previously.[46] On April 5th 'Brutus' advised, 'Let the Secretary of the Treasury and his adherents beware...let them remember, that altho' the republican jealousy of the people may sleep for a time, that it is not extinct.' It seems likely by the timing of this offensive that it had as its objective the autumn and winter elections of Representatives and the Vice-President (Washington's re-election to the Presidency being granted). On May 31, Freneau divined that the Congressional elections would bring a 'new era' in which 'republicanism flourishes and is again in fashion.'

Fenno, even though advised by Hamilton, was taken by surprise. He opposed Freneau's Republican army with the charges of Antifederalism and electioneering. The first charge was answered by 'Brutus' on September 1, with these words: 'It does not appear to me to be a question of federalism or antifederalism – but it is the Treasury of the United States against the people.' To the second, Freneau replied on June 21, admitting that a 'faction' existed, but insisting that it comprised 'a very respectable number of the anti-aristocratical and anti-monarchical people of the United States, whom we shall be proud to serve at all times.'

The Republican propaganda campaign, coupled with the questioning of Treasury policy in the House of Representatives, spurred Hamilton to accuse his accusers. In May he wrote to Colonel Edward Carrington in Virginia a lengthy indictment of Madison's opposition to him, suggesting that Madison was acting under the influence of Jefferson, who was 'a man of profound ambition and violent passions,' aiming to be elected President.[47] A month later Hamilton advised Adams that Clinton would be a competitor for the office of Vice-President at the next election, and remarked, 'If you have seen some of the last numbers of the National Gazette, you will have perceived that the plot thickens & that something very like a serious design to subvert the Government discloses itself.'[48] The accusations of systematic opposition and collusion between Jefferson and Madison made in the letter to Carrington were amplified and published a few months later by Congressman William Loughton Smith of South Carolina. Smith accused Jefferson of having tried to 'depress his rival,' the good Secretary of the Treasury, by 'endeavoring to persuade his fellow citizens that they were miserable, and that the Secretary of the Treasury was the author of their misery.'[49] And Hamilton reported to Adams:

> I have a letter from a well-informed friend in Virginia who says: 'All the persons I converse with are prosperous and happy, and yet most of them, including the friends of the government, appear to be much alarmed at a supposed system of policy tending to subvert the republican government of the country.' Were men ever more ingenious to torment themselves with phantoms?[50]

Hamilton and his friends may have prophesied more than they guessed the actual ambitions and collusion of the leading Republicans, but they pointed to a fact worth considering when they indicated the connection between the Republicans' cause and a state of doubt regarding economic accomplishments and purposes. Prosperity had brought as much anxiety as it had the much-desired 'tranquility.'

In October and November, John Adams became the chief target of both the *National Gazette* and the *New York Journal*. This tack had been preceded by a decision[51] by leaders of the interstate 'faction' – which, considering its respectability, preferred to call itself 'the republican interest' – to try replacing Adams with Governor George Clinton of New York. (Clinton's candidacy for the Vice-Presidency had been opposed by Madison in 1788, because of Clinton's Antifederalist leanings.)[52] In December it became clear that Adams had retained his office; the official voting in January gave him 77 electoral votes to Clinton's 50 (including all the second votes of New York, Virginia, North Carolina and Georgia), Jefferson's 4, and Burr's 1. From then until Inauguration Day in March 1793, Freneau turned on Washington himself. He expressed scorn at the splendid celebration of the President's birthday in February. In March he appealed to Washington to abandon courtly splendor in his second term of office.

It has been asked whether Freneau's preoccupation with Washington in these four months was a mark of 'the bitterness of frustrated Republicans,' or, alternatively, 'a calculated plea to the best instincts of the President to renounce Federalism, as designed by Hamilton, in the years of office before him.'[53] The second alternative would seem to be more accurate. The Republicans had failed to remove Adams. But Clinton was not loved by all Republicans, and his election would have been more a symbol than a means of policy changes. The national Republican leaders were more concerned with the results which their efforts to publicize Congressional party divisions would have on the nation's election of Representatives. They were satisfied with these results, especially in New York and Pennsylvania, where the publicization of Congressional parties in terms of republicanism *versus* monarchism and aristocracism had been extensive.[54] North Carolina, which had been a marginally Federalist state, failed to elect a Federalist majority in its Congressional elections (which took place early in 1793).[55] Fisher Ames predicted that the next session of Congress would 'be the pitched battle of parties.'[56] Jefferson even believed that, while there was no reason 'to expect many instances of conversion' in the outgoing Congress,

some will probably have been effected by the expression of the public sentiment in the late election. For, as far as we have heard, the event has been generally in favor of republican, and against the aristocratical candidates. In this State [Pennsylvania] the election has been triumphantly carried by the republicans; their antagonists having got but 2 out of 11 members, and the vote of this State can generally turn the balance. Freneau's paper is getting into Massachusetts, under the patronage of Hancock and Samuel Adams, and Mr. Ames, the colossus of the monocrats and paper men, will either be left out or hard run. The people of that State are republican; but hitherto they have heard nothing but the hymns and lauds chanted by Fenno.[57]

Jefferson dared to hope that a single year could encompass the beginning and the end of American party rivalry. He thought the republican genius of the American people – even those who lived in Massachusetts – would make partisanship unnecessary after 1792; 'this government,' he believed, 'will, from the commencement of the next session of Congress, retire and subside into the true principles of the Constitution,' supported by those who felt themselves 'republicans and federalists too.'[58]

This piece of optimism was to prove ill-founded. But it was the same optimism that carried Jefferson through the unanticipated remainder of the partisanship of the 1790s to the victory of 1800 and beyond. He was always certain that this victory would come, that republicanism would be saved. And he would describe the party victory of 1800 in words remarkably similar to those he used to describe what he thought was the final party victory in December 1792 and January 1793. The year 1800, like 1792, saw a victory of 'republicans and federalists too.' Moreover, although the eight years following the false final victory of 1792 introduced many new issues, they were all argued in the terms established in the campaign of 1792 – terms of republicanism and gov-ernment 'frugality' *versus* monarchism and that monarchical device, extravagant government.[59] The entry of foreign policy disputes and their domestic repercussions lent their urgency to the partisan warfare, but the partisan warfare was already there to receive it, and foreign policy was often argued in terms of republican policy. Besides, foreign and domestic policy conflicts were based on the same doctrinal disputes about the nature of man and government. The partisan elaboration of these disputes continued throughout the decade culminating in the Revolution of 1800. The abiding issue that embodied these disputes was executive ('monarchical') corruption of the legislature, and a subsequent corruption of the people by governmental promotion of speculation and other unhealthy activities. These activities were compatible with the 'selfish passions' that the Federalist science of politics relied on, though not perhaps with the honest industry which Federalists wanted so much to see and talked so much to encourage in Americans. But they were not at all consistent with the popular and representative virtues demanded by Jeffersonian Republicanism. Jefferson expressed the orthodox version of the party division in these terms in January 1793:

> The tide which after our former relaxed government, took a violent course towards the opposite extreme, and seemed ready to hang everything round with the tassels and baubles of monarchy, is now getting [back] as we hope to a just mean, a government of laws addressed to the reason of the people and not to their weaknesses.[60]

Or, as Madison had expressed it in an unsigned article in the *National Gazette* nine months before: the 'real friends to the Union' are not those who

> avow or betray principles of monarchy and aristocracy, in opposition to the republican principles of the Union, and to the republican spirit of the people; or who espouse a system of measures more accommodated to the depraved examples of those hereditary forms, than to the true genius of our own.[61]

Not Adams' political monarchism, but Hamilton's economic 'monarchism,' had produced the beginnings of American party politics. The Republicans' confusion of the two kinds of monarchism assisted their cause, but if Adams had disappeared, Hamilton's measures would have been just as unacceptable to the 'republican interest.' Hamilton could and did defend his policies in terms of the republicanism of 'Publius.' And it cannot be denied that Madison had deserted the position of 'Publius' by 1792, to join Jefferson's demurrer to the unconcealed realism of Federalist republicanism.

The roots of Republican persuasion: a provisional view

What brought the men who became the leading Republicans to tap the force and even some of the logic of Antifederalism? Both Madison and Jefferson were more conscious than Hamilton of the dangers of reaction to measures that appeared to pay too much attention to certain northeastern interests. Or if they were not more conscious of these dangers, they were less inclined than Hamilton to use coercion to meet them. The whole fabric of Jeffersonian Republicanism could be seen as a statesmanlike effort to defuse this reactionary Antifederalism by co-opting it. As early as 1790, Edmund Pendleton had warned Madison that the proposal to assume the states' debts had raised 'a suspicion of a Government by a Junto,' a suspicion which Pendleton feared would help the cause of the unconverted Antifederalist minority.[62] In one of his letters of 1791, sounding out the reaction of the country to the new government, Jefferson remarked,

> there are certainly persons in all the departments who are driving too fast. Governments being founded on opinion, the opinion of the public, even when it is wrong, ought to be respected to a certain degree.[63]

Or was their reaction to Federalism merely a rationalization of the recognition that Federalist policy was working against their constituents' interests? Was it, in other words, a mobilization rather than a defusing of the interested opposition to Federalist policies? This alternative is made the more probable one – but also more complex – by our recognition of the passionate sincerity of the Republicans. There is no evidence that Jefferson, for example, was consciously acting the part of the statesman realistically deferring to 'wrong' public opinion; there are few chinks in his armor of righteousness.[64]

However that may be, the motives of the politician are admittedly difficult to draw from the place where Hamilton, for one, claimed they must remain: the depository of his own breast.[65] Perhaps it is best to think of politicians' calculations as something akin to the instinctive prudence which is also possessed by non-human animals.[66] However, the character of the Republican party may be judged by the circumstances surrounding its origins and growth as well as by the professions and other activities of its leaders. However obscure the motives of these men may remain, the political and social context of the persuasions they roused helps explain their success.

In January 1792 Fisher Ames had noticed that the 'mad bank schemes of New York,' which 'justly scared and disgusted' sober people, were providing 'an handle to attack the government.'[67] And the political party offensive coincided with the stock market panic brought on by the bullish activities of William Duer. Joseph Davis describes the scene as one of

> violent over-speculation and over-extension of credit; failures of a few entailing failures of many and severe losses to more; a shock to business confidence affecting mercantile activities themselves entirely unconnected with speculation; a tumble of prices

not only of securities, but also of real estate and commodities; thoroughgoing confusion, uncertainty of mind on the part of the abler business men, and excitement and irritation on the part of the crowd; a temporary stoppage of building, improvements, and even of more essential economic activities, – a temporary derangement of the whole economic machinery. Exaggerated though the picture may be which is revealed by letters and newspaper articles written in the midst of the excitement, the main facts stand out clear, and the exaggeration itself reveals further the mental atmosphere which prevailed.[68]

The encouragement of these speculative schemes was not part of Federalist policy – although Duer's erstwhile position as a Treasury official lent a certain cogency to those who argued that it was. Hamilton's system, intended to establish firm national loyalties throughout the nation, was also intended to stop speculation in government paper, be it the depressive sort which preceded the Federalist movement or the manic sort which Duer promoted; once the price of paper was stable, it would be money usable as capital for productive enterprise, especially for undertaking manufactures. Confronted with the charge that 'Paper speculation...nourishes in our citizens vice and idleness, instead of industry and morality,' Hamilton admitted that 'this proposition, within certain limits, is true.' But he insisted that 'the effect upon our citizens at large is different. It promotes among them industry, by furnishing a larger field of employment.'[69] The proper Federalist attitude was assumed by Joseph Blake, Jr., in his Independence Day oration in Boston in 1792. Blake commended the American 'commercial spirit,' anticipated the growth of 'the darkest forest' into a 'crouded town,' and praised Hamilton's direction of the country's finance, which was opening 'all the springs of wealth.' But he also approved of the 'lessons' given by the recent bursting of the bubble of speculation. He did not, however, make this episode an excuse for censuring the federal government; on the contrary, Blake condemned 'the whispers of jealousy' in the air, and urged the continuance of 'a generous confidence in government as most productive of publick peace': 'We elect with caution, but once elected we dare think our rulers honest.'[70]

The speculative temperament evident in the panic of 1792 played a part in the other fluctuations in 'the most sensitive economic activities' in the 1790s; none of these fluctuations was wholly rational, since a gradual, solid economic growth was taking place throughout this period.[71] The growth was a part of the Federalist program, but the temperament was alien to Federalist intentions. This temperament was nevertheless widely displayed by Americans in the Federalist era. Davis reports, 'One of the impressive facts of the day...was the way in which all sorts and conditions of men and women became devotees of the stock market.'[72] Federalists had been unrealistic in their vision of sober, industrious Americans untempted by the prospect of a quick killing. The realistic beliefs of Federalism proved in practice to be too idealistic in regard to society just as they had done in regard to government. Just as representatives had found themselves dealing with affairs in a manner inappropriate to the passionate disinterestedness expected of them, so their constituents showed themselves unaddicted to the virtues allotted to them: honest industry, patient cultivation of presumptively equal opportunities and deference to the wisdom of leaders of their choice. From the Federalist standpoint, 'the people' had failed as miserably as their representatives in fulfilling even the lowered expectations of Federalism. Perhaps the very publicity Federalists gave to the notion of a fearful state of nature helped to sap the civilized confidence that they had hoped for, thus making way for the Republicans. At any rate, a less censorious interpretation of the political and social origins of American party politics should be visible from the viewpoint of Republican idealism.

PART III
THE REPUBLICAN PERSUASION

5

The idealism of the Republican challenge

The transition from the political disunity of 1790 to the party politics of 1792 was marked by the Republican party's becoming an effective instrument of effective rhetoric. This is one of the first jobs of modern political parties, and it reveals something of the nature of modern parties to see why the Republican party was better able than the Federalists to do this job. Federalism was less successful in creating 'enduring bonds of nationality,' which required 'the cementing force of an ideal sprung from human hearts and minds.'[1] Republicans fashioned such an ideal from the Revolutionary traditions of America. Even Alexander Hamilton had been able to use Revolutionary rhetoric in Revolutionary circumstances; he appealed to the farmers of New York: 'How would you like to pay four shillings a year, out of every pound your farms are worth, to be squandered...upon ministerial tools and court sycophants?'[2] But Republicans were more equal than Federalists to the task of reviving this rhetoric and making it a part of the regime rather than a merely revolutionary device. Republicans were also able to speak as authentic agents of progress, rather than merely to lapse into the reactionary postures associated with the Revolutionary appeals to pristine liberty. Both of these capacities can be attributed to the character of their principles. They are partly attributable as well to their situation in opposition, but there had been a shorter-lived alternative to Federalism: the Antifederalists. Many former Antifederalists found their way into the Republican party; however, the party was led by friends of union. In exploring the principles of Republican partisanship, it helps to see the differences as well as the similarities between Antifederalism and Republicanism.

Antifederalism and Republicanism

It has been noticed that 'the most prevalent Antifederalist belief' was
the idea of the small republic.[3] In their letter to Governor Clinton
explaining their reasons for quitting the Constitutional Convention, the
New York delegates, Robert Yates and John Lansing, recorded their
allegiance to this idea: 'we entertained an opinion...that however wise
and sympathetic the principles of the general government might be, the
extremities of the United States could not be kept in due submission
to its laws, at the distance of many hundred miles from the seat of
government.'[4] In the guise of 'Cato,' in the *New York Journal* in October
1787, Clinton himself elaborated the idea in these terms:

> whoever seriously considers the immense territory comprised within
> the limits of the United States together with the variety of its climates,
> productions, and commerce, the difference of extent, and number of
> inhabitants in all; the dissimilitude of interests, morals, and politics in
> almost every one, will receive it as an intuitive truth, that a
> consolidated republican form of government therein, can never *form
> a perfect union, establish justice, ensure domestic tranquillity, promote the
> general welfare, and secure the blessings of liberty to you and your posterity.*

Clinton was consistent enough to add, probably with an eye to the
factious politics of his own state:

> The extent of many of the states of the Union, is at this time almost
> too great for the superintendence of a republican form of
> government, and must one day or other revolve into more vigorous
> ones, or by separation be reduced into smaller and more useful, as
> well as moderate ones. You have already observed the feeble efforts
> of Massachusetts against that insurrection; and is not the province of
> Maine at this moment on the eve of separation from her? The reason
> of these things is, that for the security of the *property* of the
> community – in which expressive terms Mr. Locke makes life, liberty,
> and estate to consist – the wheels of a republic are necessarily slow in
> their operation. Hence, in large free republics, the evil sometimes is
> not only begun, but almost completed, before they are in a situation
> to turn the current into a contrary progression.[5]

It may be doubted that Clinton had in mind to try to change New York
into a monarchy or into a plurality of republics, although it is worth
remembering that his was a relatively energetic executive office, which
he used vigorously, and which served as one of the models for the

Presidency.[6] In any case, the belief he expressed in the necessity of small size and moral homogeneity for the operation of republican government was a genuine article of faith for Antifederalists, not only in New York, but throughout the country.[7] It was recognized as such by Federalists, and James Madison developed the Federalist counter-argument: precisely a large and heterogeneous society was necessary for modern republics. Clinton's 'intuitive truth' was controverted by Madison in the Philadelphia Convention and in *The Federalist*; Federalists were grateful for Madison's demonstration that property and republicanism were not less but more secure with a larger sphere of government.

The reason that Federalists could make this claim and Antifederalists remain unconvinced lay in their different anticipations of the character of political representatives in an enlarged republic. Federalists insisted that more elevated characters would be elected as representatives in an enlarged republic – men 'whose enlightened views and virtuous sentiments render them superior to local prejudice, and to schemes of injustice.'[8] Antifedcralists disagreed. They clung to the small republic theory perhaps less because of their speculative belief in the impotence of a republican government over a large territory, than because of their real fear that local interests and views – Antifederalists' interests and views – would not be taken into account by a few representatives in a distant legislature. Yates and Lansing opined

> that if the general legislature was composed of so numerous a body of men, as to represent the interests of all the inhabitants of the United States, in the usual and true idea of representation, the expense of supporting it would become intolerably burdensome and that if a few only were vested with a power of legislation, the interests of a great majority of the inhabitants of the United States, must necessarily be unknown; or if known, even to the first stages of the operation of the new government, unattended to.[9]

Clinton again restated their opinion:

> Is it...reasonable to believe, that inhabitants of Georgia, or New Hampshire, will have the same obligation towards you as your own, and preside over your lives, liberties, and property, with the same care and attachment? Intuitive reason answers in the negative.[10]

Antifederalists were united in the expression of this localism, as they shared a connection with local interests.

Local connections, when they did not have to do with sectional fears and rivalries, primarily meant state connections. However, as Clinton's logical consistency indicates, more restricted localities were possible, and perhaps necessary for republican liberty. The greatest restriction would make each individual autonomous, and at the bottom of Antifederalist localism was a tendency to trust people rather than government, be it ever so small a territory governed.[11] Thus, objecting to the Federalist notion of representation by the best men of a large republic, R. H. Lee (as 'The Federal Farmer') could affirm that 'of far more importance than brilliant talents' was 'a sameness, as to residence and interests, between the representative and his constituents.'[12] The Pennsylvania Antifederalist dissentients wanted representatives to be 'sufficiently numerous to possess the same interests, feelings, opinions and views which the people themselves would possess, were they all assembled.' Faith in an unqualified re-presentation of popular views implied faith in the wisdom and public-spiritedness of 'the people,' a faith unshared by Federalists. Antifederalists had a corresponding lack of faith in governors, even in republican governors, who were therefore to be kept on a short rein, and allowed nothing like the freedom of action left to them by Federalists. Another reason offered by the Pennsylvanians for a numerous representation was 'to prevent bribery and undue influence'; and they required that representatives be 'so responsible to the people, by frequent and fair elections, as to prevent their neglecting or sacrificing the views and interests of their constituents to their own pursuits.'[13] Again Yates and Lansing objected to a large republic perhaps less on account of the impotence of such a government than because of their anticipation of

> the insuperable difficulty of controlling or counteracting the views of a set of men (however unconstitutional and oppressive their acts might be) possessed of all the powers of government; and who from their remoteness from their constituents and necessary permanency of office, could not be supposed to be uniformly actuated by an attention to their welfare and happiness.[14]

Antifederalists required little convincing that the new government would be sufficiently 'energetic'; their faith in the small republic had more to do with their reluctance to join Federalism in expecting more political virtue in rulers than in ruled.

The difference over the proper size of a republic coincided with the obvious division of opponents of the proposed Constitution and its defenders – though it was admitted by some of the former that a few of the states themselves were too large to qualify for the small republic *cachet*. So to a lesser extent did the division between those with faith in people and those with faith in governors, for Antifederalists claimed that the states were closer to the people than to the central government, and in any case, unlike Federalists, they were not claiming to have discovered a new solution to the problem of power and liberty. The arguments fitted the purposes of the two sides. Whether the choice of arguments was controlled by the purposes, or the purposes by the beliefs in the arguments, is hard to say. What can be stated with some confidence is the curious fate of the arguments, and their entanglement with other purposes.

Jefferson's use of the large republic argument *against* Federalists epitomizes the Republican debts to both Federalist and Antifederalist logic. In retirement in 1795, to a foreign correspondent he expressed what could be taken as a rather orthodox Federalist version of the large republic doctrine:

> I suspect that the doctrine, that small States alone are fitted to be republics, will be exploded by experience, with some other brilliant fallacies accredited by Montesquieu and other political writers. Perhaps it will be found, that to obtain a just republic (and it is to secure our just rights that we resort to government at all) it must be so extensive as that local egoisms may never reach its greater part; that on every particular question, a majority may be found in its councils free from particular interests, and giving, therefore, an uniform prevalence to the principles of justice.[15]

This is compatible with *The Federalist's* argument on the 'coalition of a majority' in 'the extended republic of the United States,' by which unjust popular pressures were to be removed from national representatives so that their public-spiritedness could prevail.[16] Jefferson probably had 'Publius' before him while composing his letter. However, he was faced with a situation in which he judged that a kind of 'local egoism' had managed to gain control of the government, so he was actually adapting rather than adopting 'Publius.' In the same period, Jefferson was complaining about the lack of cohesion displayed by 'the agricultural interest,' dispersed as it was 'over a great extent of country' and therefore unable to dispel the appearance of strength and numbers enjoyed by 'the anti-republican party.'[17] (His 'agricultural interest' was not, it seems, merely one of those 'particular interests' which were to be kept out of the nation's councils.) And six years later, at his inauguration as President in 1801, at the zenith of his political career, Jefferson was propounding a reinterpretation of the large republic doctrine incorporating Antifederalist assumptions about the different characters of people and representatives. The victory of the Republicans, he now alleged,

> furnishes a new proof of the falsehood of Montesquieu's doctrine, that a republic can be preserved only in a small territory. The reverse is the truth. Had our territory been even a third only of what it is, we were gone. But while frenzy and delusion like an epidemic, gained certain parts, the residue remained sound and untouched, and held on till their brethren could recover from the temporary delusion.[18]

The 'extent' of the republic had saved it: 'While some parts were laboring under the paroxysm of delusion, others retained their senses and time was thus given to the affected parts to recover their health.'[19] Jefferson thus reinterpreted the Federalist case for a large republic to fit the case for the Republican party. He was 'peculiarly pleased' when party rhetoric contained 'not a sentence from which it could be conjectured whether it came from north, south, east or west.'[20] In the original Federalist view, the large size of the country was directed to the diversification and the consequent weakening of the influence of the people and groups outside government, so representatives would have some independence. Jefferson came to depend on this same large size for opposite ends. It was now seen as a means of strengthening the eventual influence on government of people outside government: if the republic had been smaller, the noxious policies and personnel of its government might have beaten the popular challenge of the Republicans. In a paragraph from Hamilton's draft of Washington's 'Farewell Address' (included in Washington's final manuscript, but omitted in the published speech), Hamilton implicitly acknowledged the force of Jefferson's observations on partisanship in a large republic. In republics 'of large extent,' Hamilton wrote, in response to Republican indictments of Federalist policy, the 'powers and opportunities of resistance of a numerous and wide extended nation defy the successful efforts of the ordinary military force or of any assemblies which wealth and patronage may call to their aid' to effect a partisan victory. 'In such republics it is perhaps safer to assert that the conflic[t]s of popular faction offer the only avenues to tyranny and usurpation.'[21] Jefferson's formulation of the same phenomenon was very similar, but he approved the popular influence that Hamilton feared. Hamilton's fear was in keeping with the original Federalist outlook; Jefferson's approval was a modification, based on a different assessment of human nature.

Jefferson and other Republicans could claim with some justice to be good Federalists, for they were loyal to the idea of the enlarged republic.

Nevertheless they deferred to Antifederalism by accepting Antifederalist (and un-Federalist) ideas about the amount of trust that one could
place in peoples or societies. Both Antifederalists and Republicans were
men of great faith in the virtue of republican peoples. The only time
when Antifederalists set this faith aside was when Southerners, fearing
Northern commercial domination, echoed Federalist apprehensions of
the tyranny of popular majorities.[22] On the other hand, unlike both
Federalists and Republicans, they generally stuck to the political despair
handed down by opposition theorists for decades. No political solution
of Federalist proportions presented itself to their eyes. They 'lacked ... a
theory of leadership.'[23] But Republicans developed a theory of governments consistent with the spirit of trust in peoples. Their political
solution rivaled that of the Federalists' in confidence.

Thomas Paine and Joel Barlow

Federalist distrust of 'the people' was associated with a realistic psychology. The dissent from this psychology took many forms. Sometimes
there was expressed an explicit disagreement with the maxim of Hume,
repeated by Hamilton, that in political science 'every man must be
supposed a knave.'[24] In 1791 Robert Coram of Delaware published a
collection of 'Political Inquiries,' addressed to the reform of American
education. His educational reforms were based on the hypothesis that
mankind's alleged proneness to vice was 'chimerical'; in civilized nations,
vice was the effect of bad government. This was proved by the fact that
the aborigines in America were both happier and less vicious than the
subjects of any government in the 'Eastern world.' Government on the
harsh, European model, ostensibly designed to check vice, was ridiculous: 'They first frame an hypothesis, by which they prove men to be
wolves, and then treat them as if they really were such.' Yet it was
asserted at the same time than men owed everything to education.
Coram agreed with the second half of the contradiction; he thought that
civilized men were miserable because of their grossly imperfect
education, which left them worse off than the brutes, for many a
civilized man 'has no where to lay his head.' It was unfair to praise the
blessings of government above the state of nature, as Locke and
Blackstone did, while ignoring some of the concomitants of government
hitherto: 'poverty, vices innumerable, and diseases unknown in the state
of nature.' There was no satisfactory reason to believe, though it was
'generally held,' that government originated from the 'wants and vices
of mankind.' The abundance of uncultivated land disproved the first

cause, and the fact that 'the savages of North-America, are infinitely more virtuous than the inhabitants of the most polished nations of Europe,' threw doubts on the second.[25]

Coram's work was a plea for 'incorporating education with government.'[26] He had in mind not the idea of a national university (an idea cherished, but never realized, by a few leading Federalists and Republicans), but the improvement of the wretched state of country schools throughout the United States. His close relation of morals or education to politics was rather classical; it formed only a residual part of American political science. Federalist political science was explicitly based on the hypothesis that Coram rejected. So, in a more qualified way, was Republican political science. 'Common Sense,' the famous Revolutionary tract written by that Republican oracle, Thomas Paine, was reprinted in Philadelphia and Albany in the same year in which Coram's 'Inquiries' appeared; Paine had written, in contrast to Coram: 'Society is produced by our wants and government by our wickedness.' Government was 'rendered necessary by the inability of moral virtue to govern the world.'[27] What distinguished Republicanism from Federalism was not a forgetfulness of human knavery, even though Paine can be said to have been a little blind to 'the dark side of human nature.'[28] It is nonetheless true that Republicanism hoped to overcome vice where Federalism would rest satisfied with harnessing it. Overshadowing the political realism of Paine and American Republicanism was the confidence that the knavery of men could be reduced, if not altogether eliminated, by proper political arrangements. The pursuit of realistic ends – not moral virtue, merely life, liberty and property – was qualified and enhanced by the choice of idealistic means, which rose superior to Federalist expectations of 'virtuous materialism' in society and fame-seeking patriotism in government. Paine's experience of American politics in 'the critical period' did not make him 'more realistic.'[29] He continued to discern in the writings of Jean-Jacques Rousseau and the Abbé Raynal 'a loveliness of sentiment in favour of Liberty, that excites respect, and elevates the human faculties'; but, he complained, they failed to describe 'the means of possessing it.'[30] This he proposed to do.

What did clearly distinguish between Republican and Federalist political understandings is indicated in Paine's un-Federalist views on the ability of society to fend for itself, without the class of public-spirited men above if not beyond society in the Federalist scheme. He whole-heartedly concurred with Coram's contrast of happy Indians and miserable Europeans (a contrast made innumerable times by Jefferson as well).[31] But, in opposition to Coram, he emphasized not the perfection of education under the fostering hand of government, but the removal of the influence of government wherever possible, for 'government, even in its best state, is but a necessary evil.' And, in opposition to Federalism, he emphasized how very little government was necessary in a modern, civilized nation. The British constitution 'was noble for the dark and slavish times in which it was erected,' but not suitable for modern, enlightened times.[32] Modern idealists accept much of the realistic assessment of the nature of government, but stress that government based on realistic principles, however well-perfected by devices like the general will, does not answer the higher human needs. Modern idealists like Rousseau conclude from this that the best individuals must seek their perfection outside the mainstream of political society. Perhaps something of this modern tension between humanity and politics can be glimpsed in the ambivalence that leading politicians displayed toward their calling; Jefferson in particular was forever withdrawing from the stormy seas of politics. But as a politician, Jefferson resembled the other kind of modern idealist, who, like Paine, concludes from the disproportion between humanity and actual political societies that society must become less government-oriented – less political and therefore more human. They develop the idea of representative, non-ruling government somewhat further than their predecessors, by suggesting that a state can be reached in which government hardly need impinge upon man at all.

The assumptions underlying Paine's un-Federalist tone were made clear in 'Common Sense,' where, in spite of his denigration of the political relevance of moral virtue, he certainly did not abandon reliance on a kind of republican virtue, a kind which was not simply the passionate patriotism connected with republicanism by early modern political philosophers. The three parts of the British constitution, Paine suggested (he did not yet deny, as he would in 1791, that Britain had a constitution), were 'the base remains of two ancient tyrannies, compounded with some new Republican materials,' which consisted in 'the persons of the Commons, on whose virtue depends the Freedom of England.' The first two parts – King and Lords – were hereditary, and 'independent of the people'; the Commons was the only forum where society could be properly reflected – where all society's natural interests, and none of the artificial, independent interests of government itself, could be represented. Paine suggested a Continental Congress of 'at least 390' members for the purpose of sufficient representation.[33] His support for an extensive republic rested on the assumption that a representative system would convene local knowledge: 'It admits not of a separation between

knowledge and power.' A true republic would have no 'political super-
stition in its government.'[34] Not a city ruled by philosopher kings, but
a national, representative republic was the solution to the political
problem. Antifederalists shared Paine's view of comprehensive interest
representation; like George Mason of Virginia, they found themselves
in the odd position of praising the House of Commons over the House
of Representatives on this account:

> The people of Britain have a representation in parliament of 550
> members, who intimately mingle with all classes of the people,
> feeling and knowing their circumstances. In the proposed American
> government – in a country perhaps ten times more extensive, we are
> to have a representation of 65, who from the nature of the
> government, cannot possibly be mingled with the different classes of
> the people, nor have a fellow-feeling for them. They must form an
> aristocracy, and will not regard the interest of the people. Experience
> tells us, that men pay most regard to those whose rank and situation
> are similar to their own.[35]

Federalists, while agreeing that hereditary powers, with a will 'independent of the society,'[36] had no place in a republican government, nevertheless rejected the idea of a one-to-one correspondence between
society and political representation. According to 'Publius,'

> The idea of an actual representation of all classes of the people, by
> persons of each class, is altogether visionary. Unless it were expressly
> provided in the constitution, that each different occupation should
> send one or more members, the thing would never take place in
> practice.

For however more or less numerous the representation should be, it
would 'consist almost entirely of proprietors of land, of merchants, and
of members of the learned professions.' This was not only inevitable,
it was good. For such men would 'truly represent all those different
interests and views,' because they would be those virtuous (public-spirited)
and talented souls required for true interest representation, in whom
Americans of all interests could confide.[37]

Not confidence but jealousy was the attitude toward government
assumed by Antifederalists and, at least provisionally, by Republicans.
Their alternative to the social regulation that Federalism placed in the
hands of justly proud governors, was the self-regulation of society.
Paine's Revolutionary 'Common Sense' again established the theme:
society 'promotes our happiness *positively* by uniting our affections,'

whereas government could only promote happiness '*negatively* by re-
straining our vices.' That is why even at its best, government was only
a necessary evil, while society was always 'a blessing.'[38] Belief in the
self-sufficiency of society was the basis of the insistence on the strict
correlative representation of society in whatever government was
deemed necessary. And the more society was left free to promote men's
affections, the less government was necessary to restrain their vices. The
independence and scope granted to governors by Federalism was
inadmissible, both because the Federalist notion of governors motivated
by the virtuous passion for fame was too optimistic, and because the
Federalist concern with the regulation of society was too pessimistic: it
neglected the positively virtuous tendencies of society itself.

This alternative republicanism was elaborated by Paine in his *Rights
of Man*, the first part of which, 'being an answer to Mr. Burke's Attack
on the French Revolution,' was first published in London in 1791, and
reprinted in several American editions the same year; the second part
was published on both sides of the Atlantic in 1792. The British reaction
to the French Revolution, and the response to this reaction, had more
impact on American politics than the Revolution itself. When the *Rights
of Man* appeared, Paine was still respectable in American society; *The
Age of Reason* had not yet brought him into the disfavor that Gouverneur
Morris would implicitly predict by his wry comment that Paine 'amuses
himself with publishing a pamphlet against Jesus Christ.'[39] Americans
were generally in agreement with Joseph Priestley on the dispute between Burke and Paine. Before the publication of the *Rights of Man*,
Priestley had anticipated Paine's and the general American sentiment:
'That an avowed friend of the American revolution should be an enemy
to that of the French, which arose from the same general principles, and
in a great measure sprung from it, is to me unaccountable.'[40] In 1794,
Priestley – now living in Pennsylvania – anticipated Paine's decline in
popularity when he wrote *An Answer to Mr. Paine's Age of Reason*, urging
that revealed religion, when divested of its 'shocking corruptions,' was
more free from difficulties than natural religion. Priestley was even more
congenial than Paine to the moral idealism (and its low-church
overtones) which characterized the American alternative to Federalism.

Whereas Priestley signaled and signalized the moral aspect of un-
Federalist republicanism, Paine was nevertheless more authoritative on
its political aspect. Priestley – whose friend Thomas Cooper was ostra-
cized for his political conservatism in Pennsylvania, as Priestley had been
for his political and religious liberalism in Birmingham – was more
friendly than Paine to Lockean whigs and the Revolution of 1688, which

had established not a republic but a limited monarchy.[41] Paine emphasized that 'the rights of man were but imperfectly understood at the Revolution.' The 'Glorious Revolution,' he asserted, 'has been exalted beyond its value'; it 'is already on the wane, eclipsed by the enlarging orb of reason, and the luminous revolutions of America and France.' And 'Publicola,' who disagreed with Paine's assertion, was widely contradicted.[42] Paine judged that America was exhibiting the best practical proof of the theory of the *Rights of Man,* and Americans were inclined to agree.[43] Americans of the Republican persuasion agreed with more justice, for Paine's version of representative or republican government had more in common with the political science of Republicanism than that of Federalism.

Driven by 'the passion of humanity,' Paine propagated the idea that man, though not naturally political (Federalists were correct in assuming this), was naturally social. Man was by nature 'a creature of society,' a 'social being.' 'As Nature created him for social life, she fitted him for the station she intended.' As in 'Common Sense,' Paine noted that one thing that impelled man into society was his 'natural wants': 'No man is capable, without the aid of society, of supplying his own wants.' For the realization of these realistic ends, Paine had great faith in the ideal of a multiplicity of interests in a modern commercial society, apart from government:

> Great part of that order which reigns among mankind is not the effect of government. It has its origins in the principles of society and the natural constitution of man. It existed prior to government, and would exist if the formality of government was abolished. The mutual dependence and reciprocal interest which man has upon man, and all the parts of a civilized community upon each other, create that great chain of connexion which holds it together. The landholder, the farmer, the manufacturer, the tradesman, and every occupation, prospers by the aid which each receives from the other, and from the whole. Common interest regulates their concerns, and forms their law; and the laws which common usage ordains, have a greater influence than the laws of government. In fine, society performs for itself almost everything which is ascribed to government.

Society functioned autonomously, spontaneously generating the peaceful prosperity of diverse interests, without the assistance of any energetic government of the sort advocated by Federalism. This autonomous functioning was due not alone to a natural harmony of the human wants which lay behind the various interests, but to another faculty implanted in man by nature: 'a system of social affections, which, though not necessary to his existence, are essential to his happiness.' Natural social affections acted as a kind of republican virtue, uniting men by benevolence, a more dignified motive than their reciprocal interests. Given these two natural characteristics – reciprocal wants and social instincts – government was

> no further necessary than to supply the few cases to which society and civilization are not conveniently competent; and instances are not wanting to show, that everything which government can usefully add thereto, has been performed by the common consent of society, without government.

Paine illustrated this assertion by the appealing example of the temporary absence of established government in the American states for more than two years following the commencement of the War of Independence. The resourcefulness of Americans in this instance showed that the abolition of formal government merely brought out the 'natural aptness' of man and society, spurred on by reciprocal benefits and the 'Natural instinct' of sociality. The use of government and coercion in international affairs was very dubious as well. Commerce provided 'a pacific system, operating to cordialize mankind, by rendering nations, as well as individuals, useful to each other.'[44]

In 'Common Sense,' Paine had postulated that government was 'the badge of lost innocence': 'were the impulses of conscience clear, uniform, and irresistibly obeyed, man would need no other law-giver.'[45] He did not say that these subjunctives could be made indicative, but in the *Rights of Man* he did say, 'The more perfect civilization is, the less occasion has it for government, because the more does it regulate itself.' if civilization were perfected, perhaps innocence might be retrieved. Paine saw 'a Regeneration of man,' and 'a renovation of the natural order of things,' in political developments in America and France. The step in the perfection of civilization most evidently in the offing, from Paine's point of view, was the transformation of the old to the new systems of government. There was 'a morning of reason rising upon man on the subject of government.' By midday, government might appear even less necessary than it did in this morning light; it might become, as it ought, 'a thing more in name and idea than in fact,' 'no more than some common centre in which all the points of society unite.' After all, it was the unnecessary impositions by governments which very often disturbed 'the natural propensity to society,' and the sanguinary punishments of inhumane governments 'which corrupt mankind.'

(Jefferson had observed from Paris Shays' Rebellion in Massachusetts in 1786, and written about 'incroachments on the rights of the people' which produce such outbreaks.)[46] Given his divine origins, man, 'were he not corrupted by governments, is naturally the friend of man, and...human nature is not of itself vicious'; but 'upstart governments' had been 'presumptuously working to *un-make* man.'[47]

However, in this morning of progress the mists of government – government of a particular kind – were still required. 'That *civil government* is necessary, all civilized nations will agree; but civil government is republican government.' And republican government was a kind of interim caretaker, which would be far better than old, non-republican government, but would also fall 'far short of that excellence which a few years may afford,' after 'the condition of the present moment' has been improved. Like deism between revealed religion and secularism, republican governments had to begin as a halfway house between old governments and perfect governments. The task of republican government was now mainly 'to undo what was wrong' in the preceding governments, to undo the corruption of 'the natural dignity of man.' They could begin in their own beginnings, which – in contrast to the understandable obscurity of 'the origins of all the present old governments' – could be honorable and memorable, like 'the origin of the present government of America and France.' Their positive duties thereafter consisted in removing the effects of the abusive former governments. This was the rationale of the £4 million *per annum* Paine allowed for the relief and education of the poor in his proposed budget for Britain in the second part of the *Rights of Man*. Paine anticipated Jefferson's vision of 'the sum of good government' as

> a wise and frugal government, which shall restrain men from injuring one another, which shall leave them otherwise free to regulate their own pursuits of industry and improvement, and shall not take from the mouth of labor the bread it has earned.[48]

'Government,' said Paine,

> is nothing more than a natural association; and the object of this association is the good of all, as well individually as collectively. Every man wishes to pursue his occupation, and to enjoy the fruits of his labours, and the produce of his property in peace and safety, with the least possible expense. When these things are accomplished, all the objects for which government ought to be established are answered.

There was no reason for the true principles of government 'to throw a Nation into confusion by inflaming ambition.' Rather, they would 'call forth wisdom and abilities, and...exercise them for the public good, and not for the emolument or aggrandizement of particular descriptions of men or families.'[49] Republican government required cold, dutiful civil servants, knowing the simple things that were good for society, not Federalism's ambitious politicians, knowing more their desire to serve famously, and encouraged to aggrandize themselves in aggrandizing the country.

Following in the wake of Thomas Paine was an American in Europe, Joel Barlow. His *Advice to the Privileged Orders in the Several States of Europe*, like the *Rights of Man*, was published on both sides of the Atlantic, in two parts, each of them first appearing in the years after the respective parts of Paine's work first appeared. In the midst of the first party campaign in America, Jefferson wrote to Barlow:

> Be assured that your endeavors to bring the trans-Atlantic world onto the road of reason, are not without their effect here. Some here are disposed to move retrograde, and to take their stand in the rear of Europe, now advancing to the high ground of natural right.[50]

Like Paine, Barlow raised man's sociality over his politicality. The experience of the American Revolution, he repeated, 'when the people in some States were for a long time without the least shadow of law or government...[and] acted by committees and representation,' showed that under 'a settled belief in the equality of rights...*there is no danger from Anarchy.*' The old regimes, feudal systems aided by the church and the military system, had debased human nature. It was 'generally understood' that the administration of justice was

> merely to *restrain* the vices of man. But there is another object prior to this; an office more sacred, and equally indispensable, is to *prevent* their vices – to correct them in their origin, or eradicate them totally from the adolescent mind.

This object was made simpler by the fact that

> Men are gregarious in their nature; they form together in society, not merely from necessity, to avoid the evils of solitude, but from inclination and mutual attachment. They find a positive pleasure in yielding assistance to each other, in communicating their thoughts and improving their faculties. This disposition in man is the source of morals; they have their foundation in nature, and receive their nourishment from society.

The true object of the social compact is to improve our moral faculties, as well as to supply our physical wants; and where it fails in the first of these, it certainly will fail in the last. But where the moral purpose is attained, there can be no fear but that the physical one will be the inseparable consequence.

The only sure foundation for society and government was in 'establishing the moral relations of men on the moral sense of men,' and not in nurturing men's 'selfishness.' The inordinate attachment to property was one of the bad effects of 'unnatural and degrading systems of government,' which had given rise to 'erroneous' opinions of 'the human heart,' by making wealth rather than moral character the distinguishing mark among men. It was exhibited among Americans, to a limited extent, only because they imported European customs and manners with European merchandise; Americans had not formed a 'national character.' Fortunately, the old oppressions had not been so great there, and the moral features of man not so distorted. It was wrong for Americans to be guided by European ideas of public expenses and public debts. The funding system, as an engine of politics, had taken the place of religious enthusiasm in the promotion of wars. This was perhaps an improvement, since the spirit of commerce taught men that they had no natural enemies in one another; but it could be improved upon in free republics, where national credit – not often necessary in a peaceful republic – could rest on the nation's reputation for performing its duties.[51]

Thomas Jefferson

The 'moral sense' school of moral philosophy, to which Paine and Barlow alluded, had its origins in an opposition, on Thomas Hobbes' own materialist grounds, to the latter's morose view of human nature. It insisted that while Hobbes correctly dismissed the Aristotelian idea of man as a political animal, he missed the natural moral sense in man, and therefore failed to see that man is a social animal. Shaftesbury was one of the founders of this school.[52] The conclusion of his thought on this subject was accurately assessed by Leibniz:

The Iroquois and the Hurons, uncivilized [*sauvages*] neighbours of New France and of New England, have upset the too-universal political maxims of Aristotle and Hobbes. They have shown, by their surprising conduct, that entire peoples can be without magistrates and without quarrels, and that as a result men are neither taken far enough by their natural goodness nor forced by their wickedness to provide themselves with a government and to renounce their liberty. But the roughness of these savages shows that it is not so much necessity as the inclination to advance to a better [condition], and to arrive at felicity through mutual assistance, which is the foundation of societies and of states.[53]

A number of authorities – most prominently, Adam Smith and David Hume – associated themselves with this school of thought without going so far as to believe that the natural moral sense and sociality of man could be utilized directly by political society. The most famous American adherent to this school – though he is not so famous for this – was Thomas Jefferson, who, along with Paine and Barlow, suggested that the tension between politics and natural human sociality could be greatly reduced if not completely released.

Jefferson believed that the evidence of natural right 'is not left to the feeble and sophistical investigations of reason, but is impressed on the sense of every man.'[54] His confidence in the natural moral sense allowed him to amalgamate the teachings of his two great moral authorities: the philanthropy of Jesus and the materialism of Epicurus. Jefferson believed that the moral sense belonged to man in his pre-political state. The war of everyone against everyone had been mistaken for the natural rather than the abusive state of man. Natural men, as the example of the American Indians showed,[55] were not totally selfish brutes in a continual state of war. Jefferson did not share the anxiety of Hobbesian political science to escape from the alleged horrors of the state of nature; indeed, his observations of European civilization impelled him to write to Madison, 'It is a problem, not clear in my mind, that the 1st condition ['without government, as among our Indians'] is not the best.' For man, though not naturally political, was naturally social. The purpose of civilization and politicization was to cultivate his natural sociality, by subduing – not, as 'Publius' suggested, utilizing – those 'selfish passions' that interfered with the operation of the socializing moral sense. The desirable traits of natural man were not to be civilized away.[56]

In Jefferson's mind, republicanism always owed its eligibility to its connection with morality. He indicated this connection in his public papers, and elaborated it in his 'private' correspondence (his letters were given to finding their way into publicity; both in 1791 and in 1797, Jefferson was put before the public by the publication of private remarks, his comments on Paine's *Rights of Man* and his famous letter to Philip Mazzei). For Jefferson, as for Paine and Barlow, republican virtue was more than passionate patriotism. It was closer to what John Adams had contrasted with this simple love of country: 'universal benevolence.'[57] Jefferson commended the morality of Jesus for improving on classical morality by inculcating 'universal philanthropy.' Jefferson rejected classical morality not only because it was political and particular instead of social and universal, but also because it depended on the 'feeble and sophistical investigations of reason.' The moral sense was a non-rational faculty of the soul, by which 'every human mind feels pleasure in doing good to another.' This hedonistic belief allowed more idealistic aspirations than those usually associated with hedonism, by grafting other-regardingness onto self-regardingness. Jefferson thought that political society could have a more dignified foundation than the Hobbesian contract based on fear, and justice a higher foundation than self-preservation.[58]

Jefferson's concern with moral virtue often took the form of his vision of agrarian virtue, so eloquently expressed in his *Notes on Virginia*. But Jefferson did not restrict virtue to farmers. Whereas Federalists (and later, Tocqueville) emphasized the businesslike character of American farmers, Jefferson asserted that American businessmen displayed something like agrarian virtue in their independence and moderate pursuit of wealth. He claimed that 'as yet our manufacturers are as much at their ease, as independent, and moral as our agricultural inhabitants.' In his view, the existence of vacant lands in America, the potential for farming, made the actual practice of farming unnecessary. The abundance of land was a means to prevent economic inequalities on the European scale, for 'whenever it shall be attempted to reduce' any Americans 'to the minimum of subsistence, they will quit their trades and go to labouring the earth.'[59] As long as this abundance of land existed, there was no need for the fears and hopes of excessive acquisitiveness to be tolerated – much less to be fostered – in any class of Americans. While Hamilton spoke of British possessions on 'our left' and Spanish ones on 'our right,' Jefferson's 'empire of liberty' looked to the West[60] – not for the sake of pure agrarianism, nor for the sake of unencumbered capitalism (although this was the practical effect), but for the preservation of the morality of the various occupations of the American people. Jefferson regretted that the American people would 'forget themselves, but in the sole faculty of making money, and... never think of uniting, to effect a due respect for their rights.'[61] Federalist political science counted on their doing precisely that: to spend their energy in divisive but peaceful economic pursuits. Jefferson's Republican party was in part an attempt to avoid this forgetfulness, to unite the people, and to revive the spirit of '76.

What about the political representatives of the people? Jefferson's thoughts on the limited 'sum of good government' have been quoted above. Jefferson shared Paine's disapproval of imposing governments. Furthermore he believed that 'Every government degenerates when trusted to the rulers of the people alone.' He wanted to see unadornedly governing *aristoi* and mildly governed people living in peaceful coexistence rather than in the adversary relationship he saw in the old regimes. Comparing the Virginian and ancient Roman constitutions, he did not contrast a democratic Virginia with an aristocratic Rome. The important difference was this: Rome's had been a 'heavy-handed unfeeling aristocracy,' its people 'ferocious and rendered desperate by poverty and wretchedness'; Virginia's people, on the other hand, were 'mild...patient...united...and affectionate to their leaders.' Jefferson's idealistic partisanship was directed against the tumultuous partisanship that Machiavelli had realistically suggested was healthy in imperial republics.[62] The realistic Machiavelli was the first modern advocate of party government, but this advocacy was aided by its amalgamation with modern idealism, which made partisanship itself more respectable. The conspiratorial, Machiavellian devices that flourish more or less openly in party government today would not have become so well established and acceptable without the impetus afforded by this mixture.

Jefferson held that a 'leader may offer but not impose himself, nor be imposed,' on the people.[63] Unlike John Adams, he hoped and believed that an uncorrupted people would willingly and knowingly defer to the leadership of the *aristoi*; thus the *aristoi* could lead the people without fearing them, and therefore would neither oppress them in order to protect their leadership, nor feel the need to impress them with signs of their superiority. There was no call for European-style inequalities, because a moderate attachment to wealth and a security in the tenure thereof would allow man's better nature to prevail, and the useless complications of government designed to humble the people could therefore be abandoned. Both people and governors could be better than many Federalists imagined. Federalism also contemplated popular confidence in governments, but it was much less concerned than Jefferson with governmental deference to the people, for in the Federalist outlook popular virtue was little more than this confidence itself. In Republican eyes, popular virtue was sufficiently substantial – as long as an imposing government did not corrupt society – to make the virtue of governors equivalent to their faithfulness to popular wishes. The confidence in governments allowed by Republicans was provisional; it was only the reverse side of the jealousy of governments independent

from peoples. It was more than Antifederalism allowed – some Antifederalists had wanted to make political careers impossible[64] – but more
qualified than the political careerism anticipated by Federalism.

Although Jefferson's initial reactions to the Constitution were usable
by Antifederalists,[65] he did favor the ratification of the Federalist's plan
of government. From Paris in 1789, he judged that the Republic faced
little danger from the quarter of American monarchism:

> I know that there are some among us who would now establish a
> monarchy. But they are inconsiderable in number and weight of
> character. The rising race are all republicans. We were educated in
> royalism: no wonder if some of us retain that idolatry still. Our
> young populace are educated in republicanism. An apostasy from
> that to royalism is unprecedented and impossible.[66]

To his friend the Marquis de Lafayette he wrote from New York in April
1790, expressing his delight that 'The opposition to our new constitution
has almost totally disappeared,' and that 'habits of authority and obedience' were being generally established under the influence of
Washington.[67] But his expectations and ideals were rather different from
those of the Federalist science of politics, and the differences soon
manifested themselves in his perception of and disagreements with
Federalist policies. His eventual success in joining and directing opposition to those policies would seem to indicate that his dual personality
– his 'sanguine ideology' overlaying a 'sense of expediency'[68] – was at
home in America. The aegis of Washington covered a variety of ideals,
some more idealistic (if no more utopian) than others.

In June 1790 Jefferson protested to George Mason (who had been an
Antifederalist) that his duties as Secretary of State prevented him from
mingling in the questions of capital residence and debt assumption, and
that he did 'not pretend to be very competent to their decision.' In
general, he said, 'I think it is necessary to give as well as take in a
government like ours.'[69] Eight months later, Jefferson had begun to
entertain – even to court – Antifederalists' objections to the proceedings
of the new government, and he again wrote to Mason, assuring him of
the continued esteem of his fellow Virginian (but recent opponent)
James Madison, and asked:

> What is said in our country of the fiscal arrangements now going on?
> I really fear their effect when I consider the present temper of the
> Southern states. Whether these measures be right or wrong
> abstractedly, more attention should be paid to the general opinion.
> However, all will pass; the excise will pass, the bank will pass. The

only corrective of what is amiss in our present government will be the augmentation of numbers in the lower house, so as to get a more agricultural representation, which may put that interest above that of the stock-jobbers.[70]

Fisher Ames and other Federalists had become disillusioned about the new government's conduct – and especially the conduct of the House of Representatives, which was expected to be the legislatively supreme part of the new government – in 1790, when representatives began to act as mere bickering and dickering agents of their constituents. Jefferson seemed satisfied that this was their proper role, and happy to provide Paine's 'common centre' for social forces to meet and resolve themselves in a friendly manner at his own dinner table, where the residence-assumption deal was discussed. He did not become disappointed with the new government until 1791, and then not because he thought (like Ames) that representatives were acting too much like agents, but because he had discovered (or so he thought) that they were not acting like agents at all. Sufficient numbers of them had been corrupted to prevent the free play of social forces in their 'common centre' temporarily situated in Philadelphia. The policies coming out of the government were therefore not accurately representative policies, and therefore not strictly republican policies, either in form or in substance. They were policies of a corrupt government which were in turn corrupting society, by fostering manners more appropriate to the old regimes than to the modern republic. From the Republican point of view, as Mason had written to Jefferson in a letter that had evoked Jefferson's pointed questions, the funding system was a 'Circumstance, tho' it's [*sic*] Consequences have been little attended to, or thought of, which is continually sapping and contaminating the Republicanism of the United States, and if not timely altered, will corrupt the rising Generation.'[71] Thus, in July 1791 – after the Paine–'Publicola' controversy had erupted[72] – Jefferson wrote to Edmund Pendleton, 'I am afraid it is the intention to nourish the spirit of gambling by throwing in from time to time new aliment.' At the same time Jefferson made it clear that he opposed 'the delirium of speculation' not on agrarian grounds, but for reasons similar to Hamilton's: he thought it withdrew capital from the 'useful pursuits' of 'commerce, …manufactures … buildings, etc.'[73]

He also mentioned to Pendleton his hope that the French Revolution would continue its success, in order to 'ensure the progress of liberty in Europe and its preservation here.' He thought the failure of the

French Revolution 'would have been a powerful argument with those who wish to introduce a king, lords, and commons here, a sect which is all head and no body.'[74] This does not mean that he had not yet connected American monarchism with Federalist policies, for as early as March he had urged a friend to come join 'the republican scale' in Congress, to help weight down 'future heresies preached now, to be practised hereafter,'[75] when the anti-republican manners would be matched by non-republican forms of government.

Jefferson elaborated his position on a republican Federalist policy in conversations and correspondence with President Washington. At the end of February 1792, when the campaign of 1792 had just begun, Washington called in his Secretary of State to ask him not to retire, and urged the current discontent with the measures of his administration as a reason for staying on. Jefferson took the conversational opportunity to express his opinion that 'there was only a single source of these discontents' – namely, the Treasury system, which was encouraging immoral speculation and had introduced 'its poison into the government itself' by making 'particular members of the legislature' into instruments of the Treasury. By this means, and by extravagant Constitutional constructions, permitting 'congress to take everything under their management which *they* should deem for the *public welfare*,' the system had been fixed. Jefferson expressed his hope that Hamilton's proposition for 'bounties for the encouragement of particular manufactures' would be rejected, not because manufactures were immoral, but because of its assumption of this unlimited nature of Congressional power. Defeat of this measure would prove 'that things were returning into their true channel,' and he expected that changes in the representation which would shortly take place would 'remove a great deal of the discontent.'[76]

A week later, Jefferson judged that 'Treasury influence was tottering' in the House of Representatives, but in April he still expressed fear that the indefatigable contrivances of 'the chickens of the treasury' would yet succeed in establishing their doctrine 'that a public debt is a public blessing...a perpetual one is a perpetual blessing.'[77] In May it was his turn to urge Washington not to retire. Jefferson used this opportunity, as he had used the opposite occasion, to present the Republican objections to the fiscal system and monarchism. He wrote the objections in 'the form, real or imaginary, under which they have been presented' – a hypothetical posture gradually abandoned in the body of his letter. He repeated the charge that an artificial enlargement of the debt, giving rise to barren speculation, had been secured by the corruption of a portion of the legislature, which turned the balance between the honest voters. Jefferson and the Republicans simply could not accept the possibility that an uncorrupted representation might produce corrupting policies. The ultimate object seemed to them to be a monarchy on the British model; indeed, Jefferson claimed that the former monarchists added to the 'corrupt squadron' made a majority of both houses of Congress, against a minority of Republicans and a few unacknowledged Antifederalists. He warned:

> The only hope of safety hangs now on the numerous representation which is to come forward the ensuing year. Some of the new members will be, probably, either in principle or interest, with the present majority; but it is expected that the great mass will form an accession to the republican party.

If this happened, all Federalist measures would not be undone, but much would be reformed; if this did not happen, Jefferson trembled at the evils involved in 'a continuance of the same practices.' He even suggested to Washington that a division of Southern from Northern states might follow if Washington were to retire.[78]

Jefferson anticipated a conversation with Washington to follow his receipt of this controversial letter, and in preparation he asked Madison for a list of names, so that 'if the P. asks me for a list of particulars, I may enumerate names to him, without naming my authority, and show him that I had not been speaking merely at random.' In the meantime, he expressed to Lafayette the substance of his partisan passion:

> A sect has shown itself among us, who declare they espoused our Constitution not as a good and sufficient thing in itself, but only as a step to an English constitution, the only thing good and sufficient in itself, in their eye. It is happy for us that these are preachers without followers, and that our people are firm and constant in their republican purity...too many of our Legislature have become stock-jobbers and king-jobbers. However, the voice of the people is beginning to make itself heard, and will probably cleanse their seats at the ensuing elections.

True to Republican convictions, viciousness had appeared not in the people but in energetic governors.[79]

In July Jefferson had the expected conversation with Washington. It was disappointing; so was a similar one in October, which followed a similar letter (now clearly in Jefferson's name) in September. In these confrontations, Washington began to deny Jefferson's complaints, and to suggest that opposition to his administration was perhaps limited to

Freneau and a few others.[80] Jefferson had failed to secure Washington's
membership of the Republican party; perhaps this failure helps to
explain the Republicans' finally turning their propaganda against Washington himself in December. Washington's endorsement of the Constitution had been 'an argument that Antifederalists could never
surmount,'[81] so this failure must have been keenly felt. Nevertheless,
Jefferson faced the future with confidence, since the elections of the
third Congress proved satisfactory. He placed much of the credit for
this result with the campaign led by Freneau's newspaper; privately, he
defended it from Washington's criticism:

> His paper has saved our Constitution, which was galloping fast into
> monarchy, and has been checked by no means so powerfully as by
> that paper. It is well and universally known, that it has been that
> paper which has checked the career of the monocrats.[82]

James Madison

One of Freneau's most powerful contributors during this campaign had
been Congressman James Madison. Federalist regret at the loss of
Madison's allegiance went as far as wishing that he had originally
opposed the Constitution, so that he would now have less influence on
public opinion.[83] Madison's unsigned essays in the *National Gazette*
(seventeen of them appeared, from November 1791 to December 1792)
showed that his change of allegiance extended to principles as well as
to parties.

As 'Publius,' he had stressed the benefits of an enlarged sphere of
government that lay in the ease of preventing therein the formation of
majority interests or combinations of interests. Now he spoke up against
government consolidation, and in favor of social consolidation. He now
feared, as he had then hoped, that any further consolidation of the
government, tending to the abolition of the state governments, would
prevent the voice of the people from carrying as far as the national
government. It would become impossible to act together, and 'the
inefficacy of partial expressions of the public mind' would be succeeded
at length by 'a universal silence and insensibility.' This would leave the
government 'to that *self directed course* which, it must be owned, is the
natural propensity of every government.' How far this is from his belief
of only three years before, that American governments tended to a
'relaxation' of power.[84] Now he urged that 'a consolidation should
prevail' in the 'interests and affections' of 'all parts of the Union.' Having

been disappointed in the results of legislation that tried to preside over a multitude of interests, he now sought to promote a 'uniformity' of 'interests and sentiments' as the necessary social basis of national legislation. Another reason he offered for social consolidation hinted at the incipient party opposition:

> the less the supposed difference of interests, and the greater the concord and confidence throughout the great body of the people, the more readily must they sympathize with each other, the more seasonably can they interpose a common manifestation of their sentiments, the more certainly will they take the alarm at usurpation or oppression, and the more effectually will they *consolidate* the defence of the public liberty.

Madison also showed this opposition's prospects for alliance with Antifederalists, when he called upon Antifederalists ('those who are most jealously attached to the separate authority reserved to the states') 'to watch every encroachment, which might lead to a gradual consolidation.' Those more inclined to think of America as one nation, on the other hand, should not now promote further government consolidation and social diversification, but should 'employ their utmost zeal, by eradicating local prejudices and mistaken rivalships, to consolidate the affairs of the states into one harmonious interest.' In a word, it should be

> the patriotic study of all, to maintain the various authorities established by our constitutional system: and to erect over the whole, one paramount Empire of reason, benevolence, and brotherly affection.[85]

Thus Madison now employed his singular powers of persuasion to promote not a diversity of social groups in order to control them, but a diversity of governments in order to control them. He pointed his slogan 'Divide et impera' in the opposite direction.[86] He subscribed to the hope, discounted by 'Publius,' that a just majority coalition could be erected on the basis of a single 'harmonious interest' rather than on the basis of a diversity of interests. This single interest – the 'republican interest' – unlike the multiple, self-seeking, economic interests, could be reasonable, benevolent and fraternal.

In an essay published two weeks later, Madison developed the idea of 'a general intercourse of sentiments' in the free formation of true public opinion. He stressed the disadvantage of extensive territory. In a large country, public opinion was more respectable when it was known, but the larger the country the more difficult it was to ascertain public opinion, and the easier it was to presume and to counterfeit it. Whereas this state of affairs was 'favorable to the authority of government,' it could be 'unfavorable to liberty': 'the more extensive a country, the more insignificant is each individual in his own eyes.' Gone was the harmony between power and liberty seen in the large republic by 'Publius.' To counteract the illiberal tendencies of extensive territory, it was necessary to facilitate 'a general intercourse of sentiments' by such means as 'good roads, domestic commerce, a free press, and particularly a *circulation of newspapers through the entire body of the people, and Representatives going from, and returning among every part of them.'*[87] Gone was the distance between representative and represented, which 'Publius' had thought was healthy.

Another two weeks brought the publication of Madison's essay on 'Government,' the argument of which anticipated Paine's contrast of the wisdom of republics and the ignorance of hereditary governments.[88] One of the dangers in monarchies was that a prince, however well-intentioned, is not always able to learn all he ought to know about the country in order to govern it. A representative republic, on the other hand, could choose the wisdom which was available to hereditary governments only by chance. A representative republic could be both large and knowledgeable. This advantage of large republics was familiar to all good Federalists. However, it now appeared that the only reason against small republics was that they could not attain 'the force of monarchy'; Madison mentioned nothing about the evil of undiversified social interests. Moreover, he added a different, distinctly un-Federalist advantage of representative republican government for a large territory: whereas monarchs and aristocrats were more deterred by 'the fear of combinations among the people' in a small than in a large country, that reason for small size did not exist in a republic, *provided* that

> every good citizen will be at once a centinel over the rights of the people; over the authorities of the federal government: and over both the rights and the authorities of the intermediate governments.[89]

Madison now argued that combinations of the people were important positive forces in republics large and small. The small republic was no longer the only kind of republic that had governors who required constant watching by jealous guardians of popular liberty.

From January 19 to February 6, 1792, five more of Madison's essays appeared in quick succession, further developing Republican theories, and further betraying some departures from Federalist republicanism.

An essay on 'Parties,' though not partisan like the later 'Candid State of Parties,' nevertheless qualified the statements on parties made by Madison in the 1780s. This essay still treated parties as factions or economic interests: 'A difference of interest, real or supposed, is the most natural and fruitful source of them.' And they were still contrasted with the 'artificial parties' of '*kings* and *nobles*, and *plebeians*.' But the policy Madison now drew from the acknowledgement that such parties were 'unavoidable' consisted not only in 'making one party a check on the other, so far as the existence of parties cannot be prevented nor their views accommodated,' but also in fostering an even distribution of wealth, and 'abstaining from measures which operate differently on different interests.'[90] 'Publius' had sought to multiply rather than to prevent factions, and had not been so concerned to correct directly the unequal distribution of property underlying them; Madison now questioned the naturalness of parties produced by policies which favored 'an inequality of property.' Moreover, while Federalist political science was interested in encouraging economic enterprise of all kinds, it did not exclude absolutely the use of what Hamilton admitted was something 'like monopoly' in order to do this. Madison himself had acted consistently with this policy in 1789.

An essay on 'British Government' followed, detracting from its 'boasted equilibrium' and suggesting that so far as it did exist it was 'maintained less by the distribution of its powers, than by the force of public opinion' in support of limited monarchy. On the subject of 'Universal Peace,' Madison expressed the belief that societies ought to restrain themselves by making each generation bear the burden of its own wars. Then 'avarice would be sure to calculate the expenses of ambition; in the equipoise of these passions, reason would be free to decide for the public good'[91] – the reason of society, not of government.

Writing about the 'Government of the United States,' Madison stated more explicitly the altered direction of 'Divide et impera': 'If a security against power lies in the division of it into parts mutually controuling each other, the security must increase with the increase of the parts into which the whole can be conveniently formed.' As 'Publius,' Madison had mentioned the necessity of such precautions auxiliary to the 'dependence on the people,' which was, 'no doubt, the primary control on the government.' But he had rejected Jefferson's suggestion (made in the *Notes on Virginia*) that conflicts between the separate powers of government be decided by popular referenda, because, he thought, 'The passions...not the *reason*, of the public, would sit in judgment.' Furthermore, he had doubted that there was *any* satisfactory solution to the problem of encroachments by one department on another; 'the legislative authority necessarily predominates' in republican government. One could not place much reliance on the separation of powers. This brought him back to the social diversification he had previously expounded, as the safe background to representation (this explains the repetition of an argument made forty papers earlier).[92] Only with this diverse background did 'Publius' have any real faith in 'the primary control.' In the *National Gazette* essay, Madison reversed field, and stressed the 'auxiliary precautions' and 'the primary control' without its prophylactic diversification. The 'internal checks of power,' by the separation of powers, were important, but were

> neither the sole nor the chief palladium of constitutional liberty. The people, who are the authors of this blessing, must also be its guardians. Their eyes must be ever ready to mark, their voice to pronounce, and their aim to repel or repair aggressions on the authority of their constitutions; the highest authority next to their own, because the immediate work of their own, and the most sacred part of their property, as recognizing and recording the title to every other.[93]

The constitutionalism of 'Publius' had donned a democratic robe.

Thus far Madison's essays had been theoretical, although hardly academic, since criticism of federal policies could easily be inferred from them. After an interval of a fortnight, there appeared his essay with the theoretical title 'Spirit of Governments.' This was published on February 20, and it set the stage for the 1792 political campaign, which began about this time, by posing the possibility of sharp criticism of administration policies. Presenting his own distillation of the spirits of governments, in answer to Montesquieu, Madison distinguished three types of government. The first operated on the European model, by permanent military force; they were governments which burdened and submitted the people to their burdens. The second category operated on the British model, by corrupt influence, 'substituting the motive of private interest in place of public duty,' with bounties, bribes and interested propagandists 'supplying the terror of the sword.' Such 'impostor' governments were happily not found on this side of the Atlantic, Madison said, but he added:

> It will be both happy and honorable for the United States, if they never descend to mimic the costly pageantry of this form, nor betray themselves into the venal spirit of its administration.

The possibility of such a betrayal was to loom large in the propaganda of the Republican party for the next eight years. The third type of government defined by Madison derived its energy from the will of society, and operated by society's judgement of the reasonableness of its measures. This was republican government, the kind that philosophy had sought and humanity had fought for from the most remote ages. This was the theory of the American model. Madison concluded his essay by asking that the glory of the United States

> be compleated by every improvement on the theory which experience may teach; and her happiness be perpetuated by a system of administration corresponding with the purity of the theory.[94]

'Experience': it had already altered Madison's outlook, as indeed he had indicated it might when he had delivered his judgement on the relationship between power and liberty in American government three years before:

> It is a melancholy reflection that liberty should be equally exposed to danger whether the Government have too much or too little power; and that the line which divides these extremes should be so inaccurately defined by experience.[95]

Madison's experience had taught him that the new government suffered from no lack of energy, and he was thrown back on to the virtue of the people much more quickly and urgently than he had imagined possible.

Three more of Madison's essays were published by Freneau in March. With regard to a 'Republican Distribution of Citizens,' implicit exception was taken to Hamilton's and Coxe's forgetfulness of the morally unhealthy effects of manufacturing and mechanical industry:

> Whatever is least favorable to vigor of body, to the faculties of the mind, or to the virtues or utilities of life, instead of being forced or fostered by public authority, ought to be seen with regret as long as occupations more friendly to human happiness, lie vacant.

Husbandmen and sailors, Madison suggested, were the two extremes in the hierarchy of virtuous occupations. (Republican foreign policy again worked against Republican domestic ideals.) The least desirable occupations were those dependent on 'Fashion.' Opting for a generous definition of 'Property,' Madison perceived injustice in governments

> where arbitrary restrictions, exemptions, and monopolies, deny to part of its citizens that free use of their faculties, and free choice of

their occupations, which not only constitute their property in the general sense of the word; but are the means of acquiring property strictly so called...

and in governments 'under which unequal taxes oppress one species of property and reward another species.'[96]

In April a paper on 'The Union' defended the Republican party from the charge of Antifederalism. The 'real friends to the Union,' Madison claimed, were those who,

considering a public debt as injurious to the interests of the people, and baneful to the virtue of the government, are enemies to every contrivance for *unnecessarily* increasing its amount, or protracting its duration, or extending its influence.

Unnecessary enlargement of the debt increased 'the causes of corruption in the government, and the pretexts for new taxes under its authority.' Furthermore, true supporters of the Union were not those who tried to pervert its government into 'one of unlimited discretion,' nor those who espoused monarchy and aristocracy or 'a system of measures more accommodated to the depraved examples of those hereditary forms, than to the true genius of our own.'[97] There is considerable agreement between these formulations of Madison's, and Jefferson's remarks in his record of correspondence and conversations with Washington from February through October.

Toward the end of September, while the leaders of the 'republican interest' were discussing tactics for the Vice-Presidential election campaign, Madison's second new statement on political parties appeared in the *National Gazette*. In the previous paper, published nine months before, parties had still been equated with interest groups. Now, in 'A Candid State of Parties,' Madison distinguished these lesser parties, 'not within the present review,' from the 'general' political parties of three different periods of American national history. These emphatically political parties were different in kind from the lesser, local ones, which were the 'factions' of 'Publius,' closely tied to economic interests. Up to 1789 there was the small British Loyalist party, opposed to the rest of the population. Madison now found it fruitful to emphasize this conflict – which Federalists like Edward Gray had attributed to non-partisan necessity – as an example of respectable partisanship which could be imitated by Republicans. From 1787 to 1788, he went on to say, there had been the division between those in favor of and those opposed to the Constitution. Madison was careful to add that there had been friends to union and good government in both of these parties of the second period, but he also felt it necessary to say that there were some either openly or secretly friendly to monarchy in the party that favored the Constitution. This second period ended with 'the regular and effectual establishment of the federal government.' Out of the administration of this government had arisen a third division. This division comprised parties which were not only as general as the previous four, but also, Madison asserted, 'natural to most political societies' and therefore likely to endure for some time. These were the 'anti republican party, as it may be called,' and the 'republican party, as it may be termed.'[98] The Republican party founded by Jefferson and Madison did not have to go as far as the Patriots of '76, partly because they were more persuasive than the Federalists of '89, but Madison found it useful to be able to appeal to these apparent precedents for his political innovation.

This essay departed significantly from Madison's previous reflections on parties. As 'Publius,' he had discounted the necessity of the future existence of a respectable, general political party in America, and he had relegated theoretical political differences to the realm of the 'accidental.' The most natural and persistent differences were economic. He had not found it necessary to speak of natural *political* parties, though he was quite aware of the difference between factions, often economic and always selfish, and parties based on 'zeal for different opinions concerning...government,' which could be respectable; majority parties – Revolutionary Patriots before, and Republicans now – were not necessarily majority factions, with an orientation 'adverse to the rights of other citizens.'[99] He did not foresee the necessity for further *political* partisanship on a national scale. Now that this necessity had arrived, he changed his mind about the naturalness or inevitability – though not about the scope and possible respectability – of political parties.

The natural political parties Madison now delineated were defined in terms of their attitude toward republicanism, a different kind of republicanism from that which had animated the party of 'Publius.' The natural republican party supported the kind of republic described in the essay on the 'Spirit of Governments.' Republicans,

> believing in the doctrine that mankind are capable of governing themselves, and hating hereditary power as an insult to the reason and an outrage to the rights of man, are naturally offended at every public measure that does not appeal to the understanding and to the general interest of the community.

The other division supported the second or perhaps even the first spirit of government. It consisted

of those who, from particular interest, from natural temper, or from
the habits of life, are more partial to the opulent than to the other
classes of society; and having debauched themselves into a
persuasion that mankind are incapable of governing themselves, it
follows with them, of course, that government can be carried on only
by the pageantry of rank, the influence of money and emoluments,
and the terror of military force. Men of those sentiments must
naturally wish to point the measures of government less to the
interest of the many than of a few, and less to the reason of the many
than to their weaknesses; hoping perhaps in proportion to the ardor
of their zeal, that by giving such a turn to the administration, the
government itself may by degrees be narrowed into fewer hands, and
approximated to an hereditary form.[100]

Madison suggested that the numbers of the republican party would have
some difficulty in overcoming the strategem of the anti-republican party,
but that it would not be surprising if they should establish their
ascendance, considering that their

superiority of numbers is so great, their sentiments are so decided,
and the practice of making a common cause, where there is a
common sentiment and common interest, in spight of circumstantial
and artificial distinctions, is so well understood.[101]

He did not now look forward, as 'Publius' had, to an overwhelming
political consensus in America. Only an 'ascendance' was possible, for
both parties were natural. More than thirty years later, Madison would
maintain this altered view of political parties. Explaining 'the Republican
Ascendancy,' he would insist that there had been 'a deep distinction
between the two parties or rather, between the mass of the Nation, and
the part of it which for a time got possession of the Gov^t,' and that this
distinction had its origin in 'the confidence of the former, in the
capacity of mankind for self Gov^t and in a distrust of it by the other
or by its leaders.'[102] He would emphasize what 'Publius' had neglected:
that parties 'seem to have a permanent foundation in the variance of
political opinions in free States,' as well as in the variety 'of occupations
and interests in all civilized States.'[103]

Madison's last *National Gazette* article was published in December.
Under the title 'Who Are the Best Keepers of the People's Liberties?'
was a dialogue between a 'Republican' and an 'Anti-republican,' the
pithiness of which is due to the fact that it is in many ways a dialogue
between Madison's former Federalism and his new Republicanism.

'Republican' quickly answers the title question: 'The people themselves.' 'Anti-republican' objects:

> The people are stupid, suspicious, licentious. They cannot safely trust themselves. When they have established government they should think of nothing but obedience, leaving the care of their liberties to their wiser rulers.

In an overstated fashion, this is indeed the voice of Federalism, and even of 'Publius.' 'Republican' responds by suggesting that the ignorance and servility of the people have been imposed on them, for 'all men are born free.' Was the correct inference therefore

> that because the people *may* betray themselves, they ought to give themselves up, blindfold, to those who have an interest in betraying them? Rather conclude that the people ought to be enlightened, to be awakened, to be united, that after establishing a government they should watch over it, as well as obey it.

'Publius' had been willing to depend only on a divided people, and even then had presumed that less jealousy was warranted.

'Anti-republican' replies: 'It is not the government that is disposed to fly off from the people; but the people that are ever ready to fly off from the government.' To the people, then, 'never pronounce but two words – *Submission* and *Confidence*.' But 'Republican' refuses to see a 'centrifugal tendency' in the people, and calls it 'a perversion of the natural order of things' to place power at the center and reduce liberty to a 'satellite' in the 'social system.' In a rejoinder remarkably like Madison's reflections of 1788 on power and liberty, 'Anti-republican' says,

> The science of the stars can never instruct you in the mysteries of government. Wonderful as it may seem, the more you increase the attractive force of power, the more you enlarge the sphere of liberty.

Madison's own similar thought – like those of William Hillhouse, Edward Gray, Samuel Whitwell and John Jay – had been consistent with Federalist republicanism, but he now made 'Anti-republican' connect this formula with hereditary governments, and this revealing dialogue therefore ended with mutual recriminations of atheism and anarchy on one side, and blasphemy of popular rights and idolatry of tyranny on the other.[104]

Pennsylvanians and New Englanders

Jefferson and Madison were no doubt the 'great collaborators' of the Republican party; Paine might have joined them, and in a very useful capacity, too, had Jefferson's proposal of 1791 that Paine become Postmaster General been acceptable to Washington.[105] As it was, there were many others who contributed both to party rhetoric and to party organization in the Middle and Northern states.

Another writer in Freneau's *Gazette* was 'A Farmer,' George Logan, a physician and farmer residing in Pennsylvania, formerly a young friend of Benjamin Franklin in Europe. He became a Republican member of the Pennsylvania legislature in 1795, and unofficial emissary to Talleyrand in 1798 (the 'Logan Law' thus bears his name). Six of his *Letters Addressed to the Yeomanry of the United States* were printed in pamphlet form in 1791. His argument in these letters was couched in purely agrarian terms, but his opinions coincided in their policy conclusions with the Republican rhetoric of 1792. His point of departure was, in fact, an implicit disagreement with Madison's 'Anti-republican' interlocutor: he asserted the existence of a parallel between mathematics and politics. In both fields, the one thing needful was correct first principles. Logan's first principles in politics were clearly more Republican than Federalist. He demanded that the discovery of the origin of government be made not by 'recourse to the vague opinions of the scholiasts, or to the contradictory accounts of civilians,' but by a 'careful investigation into the nature of man.'[106] He believed that such an investigation would demonstrate the Creator's intention that man live in society: 'His sensations, his faculties, his wants in childhood and in old age, render this state necessary.' The 'Great Being' who had created man had also established both a reciprocity of human wants and a dependence of every man's happiness on 'his benevolence and services to others.' Thus, the 'horrid system' of Machiavelli, Hobbes and Spinoza (and of Federalists like William Hillhouse and Josiah Bridge, one might add) had been based on the erroneous belief

> that the natural state of man is that of a savage animal, perpetually at war with his fellow creatures; that it is force alone which renders him submissive to government; and that self-interest constantly engages him to take the advantage of his neighbors by force or by stratagem.

This belief supported an unjust and unnecessary system of oppression by governments.

Given his social nature, man in society was not abandoned to 'the arbitrary and capricious decrees of man.' Along with the rest of creation, man

> has laws ordained by God for his government: these laws are simple and evident; they have their foundation in the reciprocal duties men owe to each other, and their rights arising from such duties.

It was not necessary for government either to make men good, or to remind them of their duties.

Logan held more firmly than many Republicans to the school of physiocracy and *laissez-faire* economics. Physiocracy primarily meant government with a due regard to the social nature of man, and Republicanism certainly included that aspiration. But orthodox physiocrats also believed, as Logan believed, that the nature of civil society was intimately connected with the 'divine science' of agriculture. Logan discounted the need for any government in hunting and pastoral societies, and discovered its origin in the necessity of supporting 'each individual in the right of soil, and the advantages and profits arising from his labor,' after the growth of population had made society become agricultural. He never tired of repeating the physiocratic consequence: agriculture was the only source of wealth, and the only just revenue was an unhidden, direct tax on property, leaving commerce unfettered, manufactures unsubsidized, 'chimerical wants' unstimulated and foolish wars unfinanced. Logan deplored the annihilation of the 'independent yeomanry of England,' who, in their lethargy, had been duped into the belief that their support of the commercial and manufacturing classes promoted their own interest:

> The farmer, after paying one-tenth of the produce of his labor to support the clergy, two or three more tenths to the government, and a very heavy tax for the support of a numerous poor, rendered so large by manufacturing towns: after this weight of taxes, the free sale of the remainder of his produce is restricted to satisfy the avarice of merchants and manufacturers.

Like Barlow, Logan thought 'the unjust principles of fiscality' were the modern equivalent of the tyrannical religious opinions of former ages. Unfortunately, the false fiscal principles of Britain had infatuated too many Americans. Congress was establishing a system of finance similar to Britain's. The fundamental maxim of the British government seemed to be 'to divide the interest of the people.' Thus it was 'constantly engaged in making laws to regulate its agriculture, its commerce, and its manufactures,' and the new American government was following this

5

example. (Rightly so, according to Federalist political science.) Left to themselves, farmers and merchants would never have become enemies, for they would be 'obliged to submit to the common law of competition.' Society should be 'regulated by Liberty,' not by government. Government was as little needed to restrain vices as it was to encourage virtues.

Although government ought to have 'energy' and 'great power,' energetic government in the Federalist style was uncalled for. What was needed was rather an energetic vigilance of 'every act of government,' for, even if legislators were disinterested, they might be ignorant of 'the dependence of civil society on the physical order of cultivation,' their legislation therefore 'arbitrary, mutable, and contradictory.' Because the science of legislation had been rendered as obscure as Christianity by its 'pretended teachers,' it was no wonder that lawyers were particularly 'ignorant of the fundamental principles of government.' Logan called for an end to the 'indignant silence or lethargy' of American citizens, which he thought was being construed as approbation of the unjust measures of their new government, promulgated in 'thick clouds of political ignorance' by a 'dangerous aristocracy' of 'half-informed Lawyers and mercenary Merchants': 'Come forward – tell your servants in Congress that it is you who must feel the effects of their Machiavellian politics.' He had confidence that 'experience, reflection and truth' would one day overcome the tyrant, opinion. But, he admonished,

> When a people are inattentive to the fundamental principles of their original compact, or to the conduct of those men interested with the supreme power of the state, they must expect that the prosperity and happiness of the community will be continually sacrificed to the ambition and avarice of a few.[107]

Enlightenment had to come to society before justice would come to government.

Logan was too unequivocal about farmers being the only 'real citizens' to have an extensive following, though it must be remembered that in the 1790s most Americans were farmers or planters. But his volleys at 'the phantom of public credit'[108] and Federalist policy in general were welcomed by some of the men who had rather less of 'the imaginary consequence too incident to the soil.' And in 1792 he was welcomed into the ranks of the writers in the *National Gazette*, which (along with several other newspapers) printed his *Five Letters Addressed to the Yeomanry of the United States*. The second letter of this second collection was the one that referred to the prevalence of aristocratic principles in America in spite of the defeat of the titles proposition more than two years before.

It also joined an attack on the New Jersey Society for Useful Manufactures. This attack formed part of the party campaign of 1792, and it displayed the dual character of the appeal of this campaign, addressed as it was both to certain interests and to Republican dogma and anxiety. The society was perceived as inimical to the interests of small manufactures, and by January 1792 its incorporation was accused of being a violation of the principle of equal opportunity. However, these charges did not much affect public confidence in or support for the society. But when Hamilton actively engaged in financial support of the society in the summer, August and September brought a storm of protests at the use of such monopolies as 'political engines.'[109] The suggestion of political corruption was more effective than the suggestion of political and economic inequity.

The same year that Logan's first *Letters* were published, Thomas Lang of Philadelphia printed a fifty-page pamphlet on *Commerce and Luxury*, the argument of which was somewhat more typical of Republicanism as a national and socially comprehensive movement, with a less strictly agrarian orientation than Logan's. This work was unsigned, and in the publisher's preface, Lang claimed that it was being reprinted from the original London edition, on the advice of 'several enlightened patriots,' who, although they 'set a proper value on the conveniences and ornaments of civilized life,' were nevertheless concerned at 'the base alloy of imposition and gaming' that was being mixed into the nation's commerce.[110] The author acknowledged that he was writing in 'the trading age,' and, although he too believed that agriculture was the source of all real riches, he gave commerce its due. He did not count himself among those 'friends to barbarism, lovers of paradoxes, who, for our comfort, would persuade us, that we are undone by ease, and rendered miserable by the arts and sciences,' which were often, if not always, the fruit of commercial riches. Progressive developments of the human mind were interdependent:

> A neglect of the mechanic arts would be an omen far from favourable to the fine arts and sciences...The suavity of manners, too, which commerce inspires, the tranquillity it occasions, and the facility of instruction which it procures, incline men to peaceful occupations, and to the culture of the mind.

However, he alleged, there were 'bounds prescribed by nature' to commerce, beyond which lay merely superfluous luxury. Thus,

> If a moderate trade preserves a people in the vigour of manhood, too vast a trade hastens on it's old age. Cupidity, stimulated by the

fortunes made in trade, seizes the minds of all. Interest, the only idol of a trading nation, banishes virtue and talents.

As proof of this contention, he noticed the histories of ancient Persia, Tyre, Carthage and Marseille, where 'the mass of the nation' had been possessed by 'the spirit and ardour of trade,' and 'enlightened knowledge, virtue, and talents' had absented themselves. And 'was not the poor, the frugal Sparta, the rival of Athens in politeness and knowledge, and her superior in virtue and merit?' In modern Europe, there was only one exceptional instance: Britain, whose constitutional 'singularity' had hitherto mitigated 'the bad effects of a vast commerce,' and would not do so much longer. Furthermore, moderate commerce was the only assurance of population; the only immoderately trading countries where depopulation had not occurred had avoided it only by an 'inundation of foreigners.' Depopulation was advanced as well by the pointless wars which were made possible by the vast quantities of money accumulated by rampant trade. Besides, it was possible for 'a poor and brave people' to 'prove to effeminated nations that victory depends on men, and not on gold.' A large quantity of money could add nothing to the real wealth of a country; public debts and paper credit were therefore mischievous, tending to stimulate 'imaginary wants,' 'fantastical superfluities' feeding the 'little passions' of man. Federalism, we have seen, accepted and encouraged such passions in American people, calling for frugality mainly as a means to independent affluence. And nothing in the Federalist science of politics precluded the proliferation of dependence effects. Madison Avenue is not a perversion of the 'Madisonian system.'

The author believed that the degeneracy of luxury was a cause and an effect of a 'too great inequality of fortunes,' introduced by the 'superabundance' of money. Thus, it was more likely to take place in monarchies than in republics. 'Luxury prepares the chains of despotism,' but republics could be and should strive to be the polities where real wants were satisfied, but luxury was discouraged, and merchants were cautioned to be

> superior to their professions, to guard against the spirit of that profession, which, kept within due bounds, is a copious spring; but exceeding those bounds, becomes a torrent, and sweeps away virtue and talents.[111]

Republicanism supported and was supported by the same desire, the wish that the 'spirit of capitalism' might be avoided even by those engaged in capitalist activities. Republican capitalists were capitalists 'superior to their professions.'

Something of this paradoxical mode is apparent in the outlook of the author of another pamphlet published anonymously in Philadelphia. It was written in 1790 by Benjamin Rush, like Logan, a Philadelphia physician.[112] In the form of a letter to a London Quaker, Rush offered *Information to Europeans Who Are Disposed to Migrate to the United States.* This pamphlet was a handbook on how to succeed in the New World, and its advice was agreeable to the Federalist vision of an industrious and enterprising America. Men of independent fortunes were advised not to come. So were literary men with no professional pursuits: 'Our authors and scholars,' he warned, 'are generally men of business, and make their literary pursuits subservient to their interests.' Unlike certain other Federalists, Rush felt no need to apologize for the weaknesses of the fine arts in America, for the present was 'the age of reason and action in America. To our posterity we must bequeath the cultivation of the fine arts and the pleasures of taste and sentiment'; American conversation generally ran to 'the best means of acquiring and improving an estate.' Unlike certain other Republicans, Rush had few doubts as to the wisdom of promoting immigration. The descriptions of people who could 'better their condition by coming to America' included farmers, but not gentlemen farmers; mechanics, and manufacturers, for mechanical occupations were respectable in America, and post-Imperial 'experience and reflexion have taught us that our country abounds with resources for manufactures of all kinds,' so that 'a few European adventurers' with sufficient 'capitals...would soon find an immense profit in their speculations'; laborers, who, like mechanics and indentured servants, could expect to rise or to see their sons rise to 'more respectable occupations'; members of the professional classes; and schoolmasters. Thus, the United States was 'a hot-bed for industry and genius in almost every human pursuit'; in contrast to the overcrowded conditions of all occupations in the old world, industry, frugality and prudence would assure business success in America. This situation was being improved by the new government, whose influence 'in invigorating industry, and reviving credit,' was already intense. 'Order and tranquility' was proving to be 'the natural consequence of a well-balanced republic.'[113]

What, then, were Rush's objections to Federalist fiscal policies? Like many others, he voiced concern at the inequitable nature of Hamilton's undiscriminated funding system. Yet this meant much more to Rush than injustice. It meant anti-republicanism. Thinking in the terms of a physician, Rush believed that a republic was the proper form of government for 'the health and vigor of youth and manhood,' whereas monarchy and aristocracy were suitable for the corruption of 'old age.' And Rush's notion of a healthy republican government comprehended Christian morality as well as free enterprise: 'The precepts of the Gospel and the maxims of republics in many instances agree with each other.' The depth of his criticism of Federalist policies, in spite of their concurrence with many of his own expressions, can be explained only with reference to the tension between the moral republic and the capitalist republic. The 'domestic virtues' of Rush's republican people were more substantial than Federalist industry and prudence, for they were more self-sufficient than these qualities were in the science of Federalism. Rush attributed the vigor and stability of the Federalists' government not to its quasi-monarchical and -aristocratic features, nor to its energetic regulatory stance, but to its simplicity, its symmetrical balance, and its equality of representation. An independent king or senate was 'an abcess in the body politic which must sooner or later destroy the healthiest state.' Another century might bring the necessity of 'absolute monarchy' in the United States, because of the gradual ageing and 'corruption of our people.' But there was no reason to hasten this natural decay by political means.[114]

It comes as no surprise, then, to find Rush praising the reason of Paine's *Rights of Man* and its congruence with the revelation of Christianity. He wrote: 'It is the Spirit of the Gospel (though unacknowledged) which is now rooting monarchy out of the world.' (Along with slavery, capital punishment, public debt, war and ecclesiastical aristocracy.)

> It is possible we may not live to witness the approaching regeneration of the world, but the more active we are in bringing it about, the more fitted we shall be for that world where justice and benevolence eternally prevail.[115]

Justice *and benevolence*: that is the leaven that raised Rush's republicanism to Republicanism.

There is little evidence of Dr. Rush having been 'active' in politics after 1790. Yellow-fever epidemics caused him to spend most of his energy fighting that other scourge of mankind, disease.[116] However, there survives an interesting letter from Rush to Aaron Burr, written at the height of the 1792 campaign, showing Rush's intimacy with 'the republican interest.' After recommending the carrier of the letter, John Beckley (Clerk of the House of Representatives and Republican organizer), Rush called on Burr's support:

The republican *ferment* continues to work in our State, and the time I
think is approaching very fast when we shall universally reprobate
the maxim of sacrificing public justice and national gratitude to the
interested ideas of stockjobbers and brokers whether in or out of the
legislature of the United States.

Your friends every where look to you to take an active part in
removing the monarchical rubbish of our government. It is time to
speak out – or we are undone. The Association in Boston augurs well.
Do feed it by a letter to Mr. S. Adams.[117]

Mr. Samuel Adams, who became Lieutenant Governor of Massachusetts
in 1789, and Governor (on Hancock's death) in 1793, was well prepared
for links with the Republicans. He had shared Hancock's Antifederalism,
and was converted to Federalism only under pressure from Boston
shipbuilders and merchants.[118] After the federal government commenced, he was still wary of its potential. He expressed fear that

> more power might be assumed by the Government than the People
> ever intended they should possess. Few men are contented with less
> power than they have a right to exercise, the Ambition of the human
> Heart grasps at more. This is evinced by the experience of all ages.[119]

James Sullivan, Attorney General of Massachusetts, was one of Adams'
Republican colleagues. He was to be the unsuccessful Republican candidate for Governor in 1797, and a successful candidate for that office in
1807. Sullivan had been a Federalist, but he had supported John
Hancock for the first Vice-President of the United States (Hancock
himself had been converted to Federalism by the promise of more of
such support,[120] which was not forthcoming). And in 1791 his unfanatical
Observations upon the Government of the United States of America[121] included
the remark that, while 'imperium in imperio' must be avoided, the
United States could not be governed as a single large republic, for the
ratio of representation was too large. Rejecting the alternative which he
heard proposed by some, of the replacement of the House of Representatives by a king, lords and commons, Sullivan held that a division of
the large republic would be less destructive of civil liberty. He also
suggested (in Jeffersonian fashion) that if, on the other hand, the Union
could be regarded as an assemblage of republics, the possible conflicts
between local and central authorities could be settled by 'the people,'
by delegating conventions to establish the proper boundaries between
the two jurisdictions.

A more revealing testimony of political faith was published by Sullivan,
as 'A Citizen of Massachusetts,' in 1792. Although he did not repeat his

reference to the anti-republican alternative mooted in some quarters, he did indict the 'very deep' game being played by Hamilton for its inconsistency with 'a free and equal government.' What most concerned him was Federalist bank policy, which was encouraging a corrupting extension of the 'factitious' wants of man. The propensity of men to seek wealth, this wealthy 'Citizen of Massachusetts' admitted, had 'a manifest tendency to the advancement of the public interest,' for it produced 'the prosperity of the community.' Commerce was 'intended to give great and beneficial advantages to mankind'; he expected it would eventually 'form a chain of confidence and friendship throughout the world' – an 'important and glorious event.' However, acquisitiveness could go too far. It would be counter-productive if 'the public mind' became 'so corrupted, as to embrace wealth, in preference to virtue' – by which Sullivan understood not only industry but also 'integrity ...learning, and ability'. This corruption, in Sullivan's view, occurred only when man was encouraged to start a 'war with his own nature, and with his natural necessities,' by being incited to 'the deadly and corrosive passion of envy.' Emulation (like commerce, in the mind of the author of the pamphlet *Of Commerce and Luxury*) was one thing, envy (like luxury) another. Sullivan did not envisage anything like an equality of property:

> The divine Author of the human race, has seen fit to place us under various, and very different situations. Some men appear, as if they were formed for successful enterprise; and others, as if disappointment was given them, as the fruit of every undertaking. This is, no doubt, wisely ordered by HIM whose plans are incomprehensible to us, and whose measures are all founded in the most perfect wisdom.

But he insisted on an equality of opportunity, and he insisted that this principle was not being taken seriously by Federalists, who were making it possible for individuals or particular groups to obtain 'an accidental opportunity, or a superior privilege, for the acquirement of property.' When these few men

> accumulate fortunes, and live in unequalled splendor, it corrupts the taste of the other part of the community, and draws their attention from their ordinary means of business. It produces a spirit of envy, and renders those unhappy, who had been quite contented with their situation.

It was on these grounds that Sullivan objected to the Bank of the United

States (three-quarters of the stock of which was composed of the funded national securities). This measure stimulated demands for banks all over the country, schemes 'to accumulate wealth by peculiar and exclusive advantages.' All this tended 'greatly to the disquiet and unhappiness of civil society.' Sullivan conceded: 'Since the taste of the public [in Massachusetts] is raised insatiably for a bank, it may be necessary to have one.' But this concession had a republican stipulation: the bank 'ought to be upon such a plan as will allow a great number of the people to participate of its advantages, and to be for the good and benefit of all the citizens in the state.' This stipulation was made not for the sake of equity itself, but for the sake of the republican purity of enterprise, which would be corroded by base envy if inequitable aggrandizement were permitted. The concessive bank, like Paine's government, was to be set to undo, not to perpetuate, the mischievous policies of its predecessors.[122]

Society and politics in the Republican persuasion

There is little doubt that many Federalists failed to practice the principle of equality of opportunity that Federalism preached. The Hamiltonian system, which drew much fire on this score, was actually meant to advance this principle; for all its appeal to particular interest groups it represented a progressive development of the impersonal character of economic affairs which is a hallmark of successful commercial capitalism.[123] However, as John C. Miller points out, the gradual defection from Federalism of a part of the business community originated in a disgust with the narrow policies pursued by Federalist banks and their cohorts in Federalist-dominated state legislatures: 'It represented an effort on the part of enterprising and ambitious men who saw no future for themselves either within the Federalist party or the Federalist business community.'[124] Alfred Young shows how the panic of 1792 was coupled with a 'bank war' in New York, where a movement for a new bank was led by those 'disappointed in the direction of the existing banks, foremost among whom were the Livingstons.'[125] Benjamin Labaree's study of Newburyport suggests that the leaders of the Republican party, with some exceptions, were still 'working their way up from the quarterdeck to the countinghouse,' whereas Federalist leaders 'had "arrived" first.'[126] Lisle Rose claims that the core of Republican leaders in Virginia were all upwardly-mobile middle class (lower gentry), whereas the Federalist leadership included many of the great planters as well.[127] Richard Purcell discusses the situation in Connecticut after the Revolution of 1800 in comparable terms:

Republican politicians, with exceptions, were men of little standing in
the community. They were described, and not without some tinge of
justice, as lawyers of uncertain practice and dubious morality; as
holders of federal patronage; as 'mushroom candidates' and
self-seeking demagogues who were deluding the ignorant vote. They
were not of the elect, old ruling families, but new men rising up from
the people under improving opportunities.[128]

David Fischer's summary of the sociological patterns of partisan allegiance throughout the country in the election of 1800 confirms and adds
detail to this picture. Jeffersonian Republicanism flourished where the
'entrenched elites' were challenged by 'new men' riding the waves of
socio-economic dynamism.[129] In principle, Federalists promoted the
equality of opportunity, which encouraged men to spend their energy
in economic pursuits, which could be managed to yield peace and
prosperity. In practice, Federalists were slow or at any rate indirect in
their expansion of equal opportunities, and they were supported by
established and exclusive interests, reluctant to be challenged by newcomers exercising their rights to equal opportunity. The Republican
party rested on the support of these newcomers.

In effect, Republicans were pushing the principle of equality of
opportunity to include not only the able among their sons – as all good
Federalists permitted – but also themselves. But Republican spokesmen
were not content to rest their case on an appeal, even an impatient
appeal, to the Federalists' own professed ideals. The cool, dry liberalism
implicit in such a stance is absent even in the restrained prose of James
Sullivan, who insisted that Americans were not naturally envious, and
would have been 'quite contented with their situation' if unfair competition had not produced outlandish inequalities and 'a spirit of envy.'
Federalists would come to believe (mainly because of Republican activities) that the American people were even worse than they had supposed;
from their viewpoint, Republicans insisted that the people were or could
be even better. They never doubted that dismaying spectacles like the
financial panic of 1792 were a product not of the natural inclinations
of American society, but of the impositions on society of a government
bent on bad policies by the corrupting bias of Treasury influence, on
the English model. It did Federalists no good to point out, as 'Publicola'
did in his critique of Paine, that 'The principal and most dangerous
abuses in the English Government arise less from the defects inherent
in the Constitution, than from the state of society; the universal venality
and corruption which pervade all classes of men in that kingdom, and

which a change of government could not reform.'[130] For Republicans knew that government and not society was the primary source of the corrupt manners of society.

The Republican party displays not the paradox of agrarianist Jeffersonians yielding in practice to capitalistic interests,[131] but the more complex paradox of capitalists of all occupations denying the spirit of their occupations. The Republican party advanced the desire for ungoverned enterprise, not directly, but by an appeal to popular virtue. It appears that many Republicans wanted what the Federalists were offering, but they wanted it faster, and they did not want to admit that they wanted it at all. They did not march to victory under the banners of equal opportunity, for the Republican party was in principle opposed to the emancipation of men's acquisitiveness promoted by the Federalist project. They saw it as an imposition on rather than an emancipation of human nature, for human nature was not as low as Federalists assumed.

6

Principles and rhetoric in the critical elections of 1793–1800

The political principles and rhetorical characteristics evident in the election campaigns of 1792 can be seen in the rest of the partisan conflicts which led to the Revolution of 1800. In these conflicts, some aspects of Republicanism and Federalism became less clear at times; at others more was revealed of their nature than before. However, the party principles remained the same throughout; therefore, their changing relationships to party rhetoric, party Congressional and electoral strategies and public opinion can be traced through the course of events. Two things in particular delayed the Republican revolution until 1800. One was George Washington's Presidency, which shielded Federalist weak spots. The other was foreign policy. Although party principles were associated with the foreign policies of Federalists and Republicans, critical elections do not as a rule take place in the United States on issues on foreign affairs, and the first critical elections were not exceptional in this respect. Historians have noticed that the repercussions of the wars of the French Revolution and the debate over Jay's Treaty helped to spread the party dispute in America from Congress to the country. But this enlargement of the parties had already begun, and if problems in foreign policy had not come up, partisan appeals would still have continued. Perhaps they would not have continued so long as they did, because the Republican appeal could have been more immediately effective, and the Federalist defeat much sooner. The Republican ascendancy at the beginning of the nineteenth century coincided with a calm period in the stormy international relations of the times. Both before and after 1800, the Federalists were strongest when wars threatened and issues of foreign policy were agitated. The most effective Republican arguments were concerned with domestic affairs, but circumstances did not allow them to restrict the party conflict to that ground, even if they had always desired to do so, until the turn of the century. Republicans found themselves unable to wield the majority they enjoyed in the House of Representatives from 1793 to 1797 to enforce Republican policies. But the Federalists' return to unquestioned supremacy in the federal government in 1798 merely displayed their highly questionable political (as opposed to administrative) competence, and helped to ensure the Republican victories of 1800.

1793–4

The third Congress, in which the Republicans placed so much hope, would not meet until December 1793, as provided in the Constitution, which did not anticipate party politics. In the meantime, the first lame duck session of Congress met, and the Republicans inaugurated the policy of limping through such sessions. The ailing but energetic Fisher Ames complained: 'The session of Congress has not been very efficient. The acknowledged object of the opposition is to prevent any important business being done.' Conversely, Jefferson was wary that his cabinet colleagues were working to shorten 'the session of the *next Congress*.'[1] Throughout 1793, the Republicans in Philadelphia attempted to safeguard their electoral victory of 1792.

The failure of the Giles Resolutions, in the last session of the second Congress, justified Republican doubts as to the possibility of effecting any reforms until the newly elected Congress was convened. Congressman William Branch Giles of Virginia, in a series of resolutions offered to the House from December 26, 1792, to the beginning of March 1793 (when the session ended), obtained from Hamilton certain Treasury records, on the basis of which he proposed a formal censure of the Secretary's conduct of official business. Republicans, including Madison, now objected to the Treasury Secretary's use of the discretion which Madison had spoken so well to establish four years before. The failure of the censure motions, by a substantial majority, was a Federalist victory which was thought by some to be 'as glorious as it was unexpected.'[2] But Jefferson, for one, had expected this failure; considering the composition of the House, he noted that he was not sanguine about the fate of the resolutions.[3] In fact, and perhaps in intention, the resolutions figured more saliently in the Virginia Congressional election campaign, which (unlike those in most states) they preceded, than in the reform of Federalist policies.[4]

The Republican policy of temporary inactivity did not extend to partisan propaganda, which was needed not only for the last of the elections to the third Congress but also in order to maintain the intended purpose and Republican morale of this next Congress. The campaign of 1792 began in earnest in Virginia only in March 1793, with the publication in Richmond of a pamphlet produced by John Taylor of Caroline. After the rejection of the Giles Resolutions by the House, Taylor reviewed recent federal politics in a Republican light. Taylor had been chosen to fill the U.S. Senate seat left vacant in 1792 by the illness of R. H. Lee. Like Lee, he had been an Antifederalist, though he had not participated in the proceedings of the Virginia ratifying convention. And his review started with the expression of an Antifederalist opinion shared by Republicans. He complained of the 'thin' representation, in a ratio of 30,000 to 1, in the House of Representatives, which, he claimed, tended to make the ties between the members of the House and their constituents more apparent than real in many cases. Because of this defect, and because of the weakening of the separation of the powers of the central government by their joint conflicts with the states, Taylor suggested that the legislative branch of the federal government, though meant to be the guardian against invasions of liberty by the other branches, paradoxically required more popular vigilance than these other branches. This tendency to irresponsibility in the legislature should have been remedied, but had in fact been aggravated, by federal policies. The Senate met secretly; and taxes on newspapers discouraged the meliorative effects of the press. Even more damaging was the accumulation of an immense debt, under the control of the Secretary of the Treasury, and a bank based thereon. A class of public creditors had been created who had little concern for the interests of 'the land-holder, the merchant, and the artist,' upon whose labor they lived. Taylor did not argue on agrarian grounds. He simply pointed out that the interests of the public creditors consisted only in a 'rigid collection' of high taxes, so they would support any government who found the means to supply this end. Perhaps they should not 'be branded with reproach or infamy'; but they certainly should be perceived as 'an interest, which without due restraint, may endanger the general welfare.' They resembled 'a ministerial corps, leagued together upon principles to a certain degree hostile to the rest of the community.' An 'impartial review' of recent legislation showed that this noxious system had been practiced effectively; therefore, the public could no longer count on the independence of the national legislature. A 'powerful faction,' formed 'upon principles dangerous to the rights and interests of the com-munity,' had entered both the executive and the legislative branches of the new government. It already embraced 'a very extensive circle of society,' and it could be expected to acquire 'additional strength, in proportion as the public debt shall be accumulated';

> its progress in undermining the great pillars of the government, by the establishment of an institution, in express violation of its powers and capable, as an engine of corruption, of sapping the foundation of public virtue, and polluting all its measures, has been already great.

The Bank of the United States should be declared null and void, as a violation of the Constitution; or, at least, 'its present impure connection with the government' should be repudiated. A 'thorough reform' of the Treasury Department would restore its subordination to the Presidency, against which it had revolted. In spite of his annoyance at the irresponsibility displayed by Congress of late, Taylor had high praise for those who had 'maintained the conflict' against the corruption of the 'fiscal corps,' and he subscribed to the Republican hope that the next national legislature would provide the necessary remedies, measures which would restore the Constitution 'to its pristine health' and bring America back to 'a dignified simplicity and genuine republicanism.'[5]

At the end of Taylor's first U.S. Senate session, in March 1793, were proposed two Constitutional amendments, which conformed to the Republican party's policy designs. In the section listing Congressional powers (Article I, Section 8), the power of taxation to 'provide for the common defence and general welfare of the United States' was to be qualified by the phrase, 'in the cases hereinafter particularly enumerated.' Furthermore, the elastic 'necessary and proper' clause in the last paragraph of this section was to be qualified by the prohibition, 'but no power to grant any charter of incorporation, or any commercial or other monopoly, shall be hereby implied.' A second amendment would add to the section limiting Congressional powers (Article I, Section 9) another prohibition:

> no member of Congress shall be eligible to any office of profit under the authority of the United States, nor shall any person entrusted with the management of money of the United States, or concerned in the direction or management of any bank or other moneyed corporation, within the United States, be capable of a seat in either House of Congress.[6]

These proposals were laid on the table of the Senate. They appear never to have seen light of day outside the Senate chamber. Neglected by their contemporaries almost as much as by historians, these proposed amendments nevertheless illustrate the well-formed direction of Republican domestic policy in the beginning, before the public debate on foreign policy complicated party issues and loyalties.

The crystallization of partisan differences on American foreign policy was quickened in the spring of 1793, when news of Louis XVI's decapitation reached America, and the likelihood of Britain's entry into the European conflicts increased.[7] As late as 1792, Federalist opinion had publicly favored the French Revolution.[8] But the coming of the first French Republic and its war with Britain, in early 1793, divided public opinion to some extent along pre-existing party lines, for many Federalists now found it more difficult to agree with Thomas Paine that 'the cause of France is the cause of all mankind.'[9] They drew distinctions between the suitability of republican government in America and its inappropriate application to France,[10] and, unlike Jefferson, who had also first favored a limited monarchy in France, they did not accept the advent of the Republic as a progressive step. On the other hand there were those who said that Britain, whose Revolution of 1688 'had bound the nation with a zone of mingled woof – a public debt – a standing army – a numerous navy – with various other auxiliaries of despotism' was doomed in any case.[11] They agreed with Joel Barlow that 'kings can do no good,' and showed little pity for the French King, believing that 'It was scarcely in human nature that he should not be guilty.'[12]

The changes in international relations presented a problem to Washington's administration. After consultation with his cabinet, Washington issued a proclamation of neutrality (the omission of the word 'neutrality,' which Jefferson argued could fetch a high price, proved to be pointless) on April 22, 1793. Federalists rushed into print in support of this action. Rufus King published a short essay pointing to the 'golden harvest' made available by American neutrality.[13] As 'Marcellus,' in one of the essays that would soon earn him a diplomatic appointment to The Hague,[14] John Quincy Adams argued that the United States was under no obligation to continue its alliance with France, who had declared war on Britain and was therefore not fighting a defensive war, which would have made the treaty of 1778 operative; in the first place, he said, such an alliance would be against the natural law of self-preservation.[15] As 'Pacificus,' Hamilton repeated these arguments, and added his opinion about the irrelevance of gratitude and generosity, as opposed to justice and faith, in international relations.[16] In his private cabinet opinion against the suspendability of the French treaty, Jefferson had admitted Adams' and Hamilton's point about the supremacy of the principle of self-preservation, but he disagreed that things had reached that pass, and therefore maintained his belief that the 'moral duties' (apparently more demanding that Hamilton's 'justice and faith') naturally existing between states, like those between individuals, could safely be allowed room to operate.[17] One of the most controversial opinions of 'Pacificus' (widely recognized as Hamilton) was his justification of executive independence in matters of foreign policy. Though Congress had the power to declare war, and the Senate shared the executive functions of appointment and treaty-making, the executive branch, with its general grant of 'executive power' by the Constitution, had the power and the responsibility of conducting peace;[18] the neutrality proclamation was an exercise of this function. It was Hamilton's expansion of 'the executive power' that stirred Jefferson to urge Madison to pen a public reply to 'Pacificus,' which would appear in August and September.

Meanwhile the new issues thrown on to the American public scene began to be expressed as parts of the divergent republican persuasions. On the Federalist side, the Reverend Dr Samuel Parker spoke sadly of the 'dark veil' now overspreading 'the fair countenance of freedom' in France. Parker thought, in any case, that it was America's interest to stay out of European quarrels, and to enjoy God's blessing of peace. Indeed, that men might 'live quiet and peaceable lives, in all godliness and honesty,' was the 'design of civil society and government'; in other words, the purpose of civil society was 'to secure the rights and properties of its members, and to promote their welfare and happiness.' This end was dictated by the origins of government. Parker was willing to admit the notion that the 'social affections of our nature, and the desire of many conveniences, not to be obtained without the concurrence of others, probably first induced men to associate together.' But he declared that civil society and government had a different origin, which could not be overcome or replaced by socialization:

> the depravity of our nature since the apostacy, and the great
> prevalence of lusts and corruptions, have obliged mankind to enter
> into closer connections and combinations, for mutual protection and
> assistance...in this way Government comes from God, and is his
> ordinance.

The duties of honesty and 'equity' appeared to be more conformable to the nature of man than the duty of benevolence, which Parker also enjoined.[19]

The virtue of benevolence was more important in the Republican persuasion. And more congenial to that persuasion was a sermon closely following the one by Parker in Boston, by a Unitarian minister, Aaron

Bancroft (father of America's first progressive historian, George Bancroft) to the Massachusetts Freemasons in Worcester. 'The Parent of Man,' preached Bancroft, 'has fitted him for all the purposes of his existence. Social affections and benevolent principles, are an essential part of the human constitution.' Love was often 'stifled,' and benevolence 'corrupted by selfish and dissocial passions.' But social organizations like the Masons could help 'to check the undue influence of every dissocial passion.' The perfections wrought by such 'voluntary associations' could reproduce 'the golden age,' in which 'the common bounties of heaven would be sufficient to supply the wants of all mankind.'[20]

Many Americans warmly sympathized with the second modern republic, and equated neutrality with 'desertion.' The 'impartiality' enjoined by Washington's proclamation might suit

> the disposition of those who drew from the funds; but of none else. The fact is, the American mind is indignant, and needs to be but roused a little to go to war with England, and assist France. Let all who think with me, SPEAK.[21]

And speak they did, in the summer of 1793. The Independence Day proceedings that year were in many places a celebration of Franco-American fraternity. In Boston, where even John Quincy Adams judged it prudent to discuss in his oration the fall of European feudalism, some fiery toasts were proposed:

> The Gallo-Columbian fraternity of Freeman! – May the Union of *France* and *America* be as durable as the Ocean which divides them! (3 *cheers and* 15 *guns.*)

> The Nineteenth Century! May it Commence with the Millenium of Universal liberty! (3 *times* 3 *cheers and* 5 *guns.*)[22]

In Rhode Island, Enos Hitchcock bade Americans warmly to wish success to the French Revolution, and to look on the European war as one of kings and despots 'against the dearest rights and most valuable privileges of mankind.' He thought that America might prove to be 'the model of that glorious temple of universal liberty which is about to be established over the civilized world.'[23] In New York, Samuel Miller agreed. The French Revolution was 'a great link in the chain, that is drawing on the reign of universal harmony and peace.'[24] In Pittsburgh, 'Citizen Brackenridge' repeated that 'the great law of humanity' bound Americans to assist France.[25] It was not only gratitude for the French promotion of American independence that made the French cause attractive. In addition, France was now subscribing to the true republican persuasion that

> Political evils never are occasioned by the people, but are caused by the government – How could it be otherwise? The people are interested in the public good: the man in office has a private interest.[26]

Some Republicans saw the downfall of resurgent American aristocrats in the success of the French.[27]

In the face of this Francophilia, Federalists continued to advise Americans to reject the customs 'of older nations,' to strive instead 'to excel in economy, industry and frugality.'[28] They held up that 'road to honors, riches, usefulness and fame,' which 'in this happy country is open equally to all.'[29] They reasserted their vision of an America of agriculture prospering alongside 'great cities,'

> busy hives amassing treasures of wealth, yet enjoying the highest tranquility, the strongest security of their property and peace, under the all-fostering, and all-protecting arm of our glorious CONSTITUTION.[30]

The most that Elisha Lee was willing to grant to the French enthusiasm was that if 'the renovation of France' was 'the design of heaven' it would eventually succeed, despite the efforts of the diplomatic coalition against that country, and 'the crimes of the daemoniacs of Paris.' He had noted that American government was in part an imitation of the British constitution, and he went on to attribute America's present happiness to the Constitution and the fiscal arrangements made under its auspices. With improving agriculture making the wilderness blossom 'like the rose,' with industry 'sure of the reward of opulence,' with enterprise opening 'a thousand avenues of wealth,' with their fabric of government uniting 'the blessings of LIBERTY, the dignity of ORDER, and the energy of POWER,' had not Americans reason to love their country, to glory in its Constitution and to honor its 'illustrious ADMINISTRATORS'?[31]

The leaders of the Republican party were not quite sure what could be made of the renewed ardor for France without sacrificing any of the ground they had gained in the recent elections. In January, Jefferson had been satisfied that the 'successes of republicanism in France have given the coup de grace' to the prospects of America's Anglophile monarchists. The following month, he recorded that Washington was at last feeling the alarming discontents in the South.[32] But when spring brought in complications to foreign affairs, Jefferson had reason to

fear that if this summer should prove disastrous to the French, it will
damp that energy of republicanism in our new Congress, from which
I had hoped so much reformation.[33]

Circumstances abroad were no longer neutral or favorable to the Republican party. War meant that the French government, which had previously tried to back Jefferson's policy of encouraging bonds between
equally reluctant merchants in France and America by means of a
commerical treaty, was now obliged to give America commercial privileges without being able to insist on reciprocity.[34] Republican hopes for
an intensification of the French alliance lost what little they had ever
had of solid foundation. Jefferson, in Philadelphia, could see what
Madison and Monroe in Virginia did not at first see – namely, that a fair
neutrality was indeed true policy, and that the acceptance of this policy
and the antics of Genet, not to mention French military setbacks, could
turn public opinion in America against the Republicans. The realities
of international relations meant that the entanglement of domestic
parties with foreign loyalties might well have an effect opposite to that
counted on by Monroe, for instance, who thought that anything that
precipitated a crisis in American politics, even if it was something
against the Republicans, was good, because as soon as the public was
made to take notice of public affairs it would judge 'the measures of
4 or 5 years together,' and therefore condemn the Federalists, not the
Republicans.[35] Jefferson proved to be the more accurate predictor of
public opinion. He assured Washington that his (Jefferson's) 'intimacy'
with the Republican party in Congress made it possible to predict

> that the manoeuvres of Mr. Genet might produce some little
> embarrassment, but that he would be abandoned by the republicans
> the moment they knew the nature of his conduct; and on the whole,
> no crisis existed which threatened anything.[36]

He cautioned his fellow Virginians that because 'the desire of neutrality
is universal, it would place the republicans in a very unfav[ora]ble point
of view with the people to be cavilling about small points of propriety.'
Public opinion was abandoning Genet, and if the popular leaders did
not have the good sense to do likewise, they would find the peoples'
allegiance 'transferred to the other party.'[37]

By August, yellow fever was beginning to take the place of the French
contagion, helping to verify Jefferson's prediction.[38] Yet Jefferson had
also prompted Madison's writing of the five 'Helvidius' papers, and
these appeared in the press in August and September, keeping alive the
partisan consciousness of the American people and their Congressmen-

elect. In these papers, Madison was concerned to refute Hamilton's generous interpretation of 'executive power.' He asserted 'that the powers of making war and treaty [were] substantially of a legislative, not an executive nature,' since it was a question of making rather than executing laws. Even John Locke[39] had distinguished these federative powers from executive ones, though 'the reason of the philosopher was clouded by the royalism of the Englishman' when Locke supposed that these distinct powers generally rested in the same hands. The American Constitution did not follow Locke's example; it treated the powers of war and peace as legislative powers. Madison adroitly quoted Hamilton's own *Federalist* writings to prove this point. Madison suggested that the neutrality proclamation tended to interfere with legislative prerogative, and that 'the new and aspiring doctrine' of 'Pacificus' had no other source than the dangerous example of British theory and practice.[40] The Republican leaders were beginning to see that identification of their cause with that of France could prove disastrous; they remained confident, however, that they could only gain from the identification of Federalism with Anglophilia and monarchism.

This is apparent in other fruits of Republican party operations that summer. Resolutions were adopted in various counties in Virginia, in opposition to Federalist resolutions published in Richmond, Philadelphia and New York. Archibald Stuart, a political ally of Madison in the 1780s, introduced the resolutions 'unanimously adopted' at a meeting in Staunton:

> That we are attached to our own government – that we are attached to the President – that we are attached to peace so long as it can be maintained on honorable terms – that we hate monarchies, and more intimate connections with them as the worst of evils – and that we most sincerely desire that the imprudence and indiscretion of a servant of France on the one hand, or the ill-judged interference of our own citizens (not in the executive department) on the other, may not disunite two nations, who have embraced the same principles of freedom, and who we believe esteem each other most ardently.[41]

Madison himself was the author of the resolutions of Caroline County, which 'the very respectable old gentleman,' Edmund Pendleton, was recruited to sponsor.[42] Pendleton had supported a proclamation of neutrality, and the Caroline Resolves, like those in Staunton, reproached Genet, and expressed support for the Constitution, a desire for peace and gratitude for the virtuous Washington. But they too did not hesitate to express gratitude for French assistance in the War of Independence, sympathy with the French Revolution and condemnation of those who had attempted to alter the French alliance, for

> a dissolution of the honorable and beneficial connection between the United States and France, must obviously be attempted with a view to forward a plan of a more intimate union and connection of the former with Great Britain, *as a leading step towards assimilating the American government to the form and spirit of the British monarchy.*[43]

Pendleton emphasized the last point when he defended the Resolves in a letter to Washington the day after they were published: from his Reports, Hamilton appeared to have

> made the System of the british Ministry, the model of his conduct as assumed American Primate – chusing rather to trust to a monied Interest, he has created, for the Support of his measures, than to their rectitude.[44]

The Republicans were striving to keep their partisanship alive, so that unregenerate Federalists could expect 'no calms, except those which are portentous of storms.'[45] They had quickly learned the danger of tying their own fate to that of Republican France; but they continued to lament that,

> in a country upon which the Blessings of Heaven were so bountifully poured out...strange as it may appear, sorrowful to relate! almost incredible to tell! there is reason to believe the existence of persons within it strongly disaffected to this beneficent system. Prejudiced in favour of monarchy, they pant for Crowns and Royal Distinctions; or jealous of Republican equality, they wish to establish an Aristocracy.[46]

And Federalists sustained the opposite interpretation of the political ills of America. Hamilton produced an extremely perceptive version of this interpretation in an unpublished draft introduction to his 'Pacificus' papers:

> It is a melancholy truth, which every new political occurrence more and more unfolds, that there is a description of men in this country, irreconcileably adverse to the government of the United States; whose exertions, whatever be the springs of them, whether infatuation, or depravity or both, tend to disturb the tranquillity order and prosperity of this now peaceable flourishing and truly happy land. A real and enlightened friend to public felicity cannot

observe new confirmations of this fact, without feeling a deep and poignant regret, that human nature should be so refractory and perverse; that amidst a profusion of the bounties and blessings of Providence, political as well as natural, inviting to contentment and gratitude, there should still be found men disposed to cherish and propagate disquietude and alarm; to render suspected and detested the instruments of the felicity, in which they participate.[47]

Jefferson thought that 'The war between France and England... brought forward the Republicans and Monocrats in every State, so that their relative numbers' were more visible.[48] But the founders of the Republican party thought that these numbers had already told, in the election of the new and enlarged Congress, so they continued to look expectantly to this Congress, and tried to make more recent trends in public opinion support the mandate of 1792.

When Secretary of State Jefferson retired to Virginia in January 1794, he may have been disillusioned. But perhaps he had in mind ulterior motives, and considerations of his own long-term political interest.[49] And he also retained some of his confidence that the Republic had been set on to the right course by the elections of 1792. Besides, he had left behind him in Philadelphia his Report on America's foreign commerce, and doubtless he was aware that this was the field of legislation in which the new Republican element in Congress was to try its strength. Madison had hinted at this direction of Republican concern in his last 'Helvidius' paper, where he complained that the hasty and unilateral declaration of the irrelevance of the French treaty to the current war must tend to inspire France 'with a disinclination to feed our commerce with those important advantages which it already enjoys, and those more important ones which it anxiously contemplates.'[50] In his Report on foreign commerce Jefferson seconded the confidence of 'Helvidius' that the French republic, if persuaded that America's neutrality was not a British neutrality, could be expected to increase its commercial freedom with the American republic. He added:

> should any nation, contrary to our wishes, suppose it may better find
> its advantages by continuing its system of prohibitions, duties and
> regulations, it behooves us to protect our citizens, their commerce
> and navigation, by counter prohibitions, duties and regulations,
> also.[51]

He meant Britain. Accordingly, in January 1794, Madison introduced in the House of Representatives proposals for commercial retaliation against Britain. News of the British-negotiated truce between Portugal and the Algerian pirates (who constantly harassed American shipping), which had reached America in December 1793, made public opinion more amenable to the idea of retaliation against Britain. Federalists requested arms; Republicans proposed commercial sanctions.[52]

In a letter to Jefferson, James Monroe summarized the Republican motives for these proposals, outlining party strategy for years to come:

> You were aware of the motive in commencing the session by some act, connected with the present state of our affrs. founded on the publick sentiment, and which shod. at the same time, vindicate our rights and interests, and likewise shun all possible pretext for war, on the part of the power it was meant to affect, and that the propositions introduced by Mr. Madison were tho't. best calculated to accomplish this object...whether we succeed or not, they will certainly tend to open the eyes of the eastern people respecting the conduct of their representatives as well as of the motive for it. Information is all they want: an opposition to our carrying trade, by their own members, will affect them, in such a manner, they will all know the fact, and understand the motive.[53]

If the propositions succeeded, Republican policy would at last begin to be implemented. Their failure, on the other hand, would show that the Republicans had not yet captured control of Congress, and therefore that more Republican support was necessary in the Eastern citadels of Federalism; the failure could also help to stir up this additional support. Indeed, Monroe expected that Republican support for these proposals, whether successful or not, would garner support for the Republican party in the East, by demonstrating the corruption of the Eastern Representatives. Madison's commercial propositions were intended to be an alternative to the war against Britain favored by some Americans. At the same time, they were designed to make pro-French and anti-British sentiments support Republican domestic policy.

Madison had made similar proposals to the House of Representatives several times since 1789. They had been laid aside on the grounds that diplomatic exchanges with Britain were in the offing, but with more Republican strength in Congress and a war under way between Britain and France, the proposals were renewed with great vigor.[54] They were now favored, where they had previously been opposed, by many of Madison's fellow Virginians. One of the objects of these proposals was the abrupt elimination of American dependence on British markets and credit. (This was the consideration that induced Hamilton to prefer more direct methods of encouraging American economic development.)

Any stimulation of American manufactures necessitated by this commercial warfare was to be done by the states, not by the United States.[55] As Hamilton pointed out, through William Loughton Smith, the alternative policy to the Republicans', not contemplated by Jefferson's Report, was '*an efficacious system of encouragement to home manufactures.*' Smith expressed Federalist doubt that France, in spite of its recent overtures, had much to offer America in the way of either credit or goods; if it had, and could lessen America's dependence on Britain, this should be secured by treaty, without which the proposed duties on British goods would simply be a subsidy of French merchants by American consumers.[56]

In his reply, Madison set out the Republican dogma that would echo through American politics until its practical refutation by the War of 1812: Britain, the birthplace of the 'paper system,' was a paper lion, more dependent on American 'necessaries' than America was on Britain's manufactured 'superfluities,' and it would follow the dictates of its economic interest. Besides, Britain had great unfunded debts, expensive wars, and a stationary if not diminishing population on its hands, so it could not resort to arms.[57] This faith was hardly shaken by the news of Britain's maritime belligerency of 1793 and 1794;[58] Republicans persisted in their belief that coercive economic measures would produce honorable results. Federalists, however, hastened to put the country on a war footing, and they were able to practice their military virtuosity in their suppression of what they could find of a 'Whisky Rebellion' in western Pennsylvania in the summer and autumn of 1794. Republicans, not believing that war could come, believed that Federalist military measures were simply an extension of the devices of the 'fiscal party'; Jefferson confided to Madison:

> As to the naval armament, the land armament and the marine
> fortifications which are in question with you, I have no doubt they
> will all be carried. Not that the monocrats and paper men in
> Congress want war; but they want armies and debts; and though we
> may hope that the sound part of Congress is now so augmented as to
> insure a majority in cases of general interest merely, yet I have always
> observed that in questions of expense, where members may hope
> either for offices for themselves or their friends, some few will be
> debauched, and that is sufficient to turn the decision where a
> majority is, at most, but small.[59]

The Republicans' persistent preoccupation with the machinations of a fiscal, crypto-monarchist party is evident in Republican pronouncements like Congressman William Findley's anonymous *Review of the Revenue System Adopted by the First Congress*, which offered background to the Republican hope 'that the present Congress, being the first equal respresentation of the people, may adopt different principles of legislation.' Findley explained that, although there had been a few persons with a 'love of courtly grandeur, and privileged orders' at the time of Constitution was adopted, 'republican virtue' had been ascendant. Admittedly, it had received a 'taint' from the necessary tender laws and paper emissions of Revolutionary War days. But this circumstance was only an excuse, not a justification, for the monarchists to seize upon this 'apparent decline of republican virtue' to support their projects. Happily they were too few in the Philadelphia Convention. Unhappily, since then, they had found more devious ways of securing their ends. Ignoring, or ignorant of, Madison's leading role in the organization of the Treasury Department, Findley considered that

> The first proof of a systematic plan for subverting the principles of the government by the instrumentality of fiscal arrangements, was given by the law for establishing the treasury department, by which a transfer is made of the exclusive right to originate money bills, to the Secretary of the treasury, and this proof is rendered indubitable by the use that has been uniformly made of it.

Hamilton's system had

> greatly encreased the spirit and enterprize of speculators, and occasioned in this way the most detestable and enormous frauds, and promoted a depravity of morals and a great decline of republican virtue.

Their activities prepared the way for attempts 'to govern by standing armies, &c,' but the maturity of this plan was checked by 'the discernment of the people,' and the greater opposition it met in the second Congress. Proof of the existence of such a plan was, however, not wanting:

> To render an extensive revenue necessary, and to engage interests and feelings of numbers whom avarice could not influence in favour of an excise, an Indian war was a necessary succedaneum.

On top of all this, the interpretation of the 'general welfare' clause as an amplification rather than a restriction of powers granted by the Constitution (in the Bank adventure) was ominous. These two things showed that the 'monarchical faction' had adopted 'more successful artifices.' They had begun (as 'Helvidius' had noticed) to speak of the administration as the equivalent of the government, and to class Hamilton with Washington. They identified the excesses of the French Revolution with genuine republicanism, and apologized for those of Great Britain. Federalists were mistaken in their belief that the 'fiscal system' nourished economic growth; in fact, it discouraged industry. Findley proposed a large simple direct tax to discharge the national debt, leaving it to each state to levy the tax in its own choice of mode. He also insisted, in agreement with Monroe's summary of the motives of the commercial propositions, that even in New England 'the mass of the people...still retain their republican principles and habits':

> If the channels of public information were pure, or if Congress sat in these states, we would soon hear the same republican language from their members of Congress that is experienced in their town meetings and state legislatures.[60]

Another anonymously published pamphlet, by John Taylor, reflected these same familiar fiscal concerns, which had pre-dated the intensification of Anglo-French differences. He began with the Machiavellian maxim: 'No free government or the blessings of liberty can be preserved to any people, but by a frequent recurrence to fundamental principles.' However, he meant not the original force and fraud of a princely founder, but a 'frequent and firm national inquiry into the measures of government,' designed to 'check political vice, and reward political virtue.' Machiavelli had suggested the usefulness of public indictments as an outlet for the malignant humors which might lead to the kind of partisanship that was dangerous to the rulers of a country if these humors were not defused in this way.[61] Taylor's proposal, on the contrary, aroused partisanship by its assumption that the people rather than the government needed protection. National inquiries were necessary, he said (with Washington in mind), because a 'patriotic magistracy hardly appears to gladden the historic page, once in a century.' That such a one had not prevailed in the United States was apparent from the institution of the Bank alone, 'the master key of that system, which governs the administration,' and which declared that 'a design for erecting aristocracy and monarchy' still existed. The Bank was a 'devouring monster,' consuming the only source of real gain, the labor of the 'agricultural, mechanical, professional and mercantile interests.' Titles had been delayed until a safer time, but the Bank and the funding system, the latter now 'irrevocably passed,' had already fixed upon America the substance of aristocracy. What could be done?

Recourse to the people was the proper remedy. It was a safe one, for 'The many have no motive to oppress the few.' And it was

> the only impartial corrector of unconstitutional political
> designs... Therefore if Liberty is a national object, the nation itself
> must watch over the constitution, preserve it from violation, and
> supply its defects, or admit it to be the Lethe of the community,
> producing an intire forgetfulness of the rights of man.

The people could act in two ways, without resort to a general convention. They could elect unbiassed representatives, or they could work through their state legislatures – 'the people themselves in a state of refinement, possessing superior information, and exhibiting the national suffrage in the fairest and safest mode.' (Taylor referred to the part played by state legislatures in electing Senators and in Constitutional amendment.) The substance of the remedy would be what Taylor had proposed the year before: the exclusion of public creditors from Congress, and the disestablishment of the Bank.[62]

Republicans did not fare nearly as well as they had hoped they would in the third Congress. Their high point was reached in April, when their bill to stop the importation of British goods was passed by the House, but defeated in the Senate by the vote of the Vice-President.[63] In May, following the Senate's expulsion of Albert Gallatin, Monroe despaired: 'the republican party is entirely broken.'[64] In the House, Fisher Ames had reason to rejoice:

> The combat against excises on tobacco turned favorably. Madison
> spouted against excise, in favor of land tax, hoping to prevent any
> thing, or to get only that voted which would raise enemies to the
> government. Taylor, of Virginia, says to King – 'You are strange
> fellows: formerly, you did what you chose with a small majority; now,
> we have a great majority, and can do nothing. You have baffled every
> one of our plans.'
>   I wish he may prove a prophet. The resistance to wild projects
> has risen in its spirit and style, as hope declined. We have banged
> them as hard as we could, and they have been tamer than formerly.[65]

A month later, Hamilton could concur:

> The session of Congress is about to close much better than I
> expected. All mischievous measures have been prevented and several
> good ones established.[66]

Despite their setbacks in Philadelphia, the Republican leaders had probably been wise to fight shy of a French label and to support neutrality. The Democratic-Republican Societies, which flourished in the United States in 1794, were much more willing than the Republican party to declare:

> we are the enemies, the avowed enemies, of him or those who dare to infringe upon the holy law of Liberty, the sacred *Rights of Man*, by declaring that we ought to be strictly neutral, *either in thought or speech*, between a nation fighting for the dearest, the undeniable, the invaluable Rights of Human Nature, and another nation or nations wickedly, but hitherto (we thank God) vainly, endeavoring to oppose her in such a virtuous, such a glorious struggle.[67]

The Republican leaders could easily see that they did not need to cultivate the loyalty of those who shared these sentiments. This circumstance discouraged official Republican 'Gallomania,' though it inhibited neither Republican enthusiasm for France against Britain, nor Federalist perception of Republicans as democrats and Jacobins. A complementary circumstance was the reluctance of Federalists to throw away the independence from Britain that many of them had fought for. This reluctance, coupled with genuine gratitude to the French nation, was relected in orations on the Fourth of July. The remarks by David Ramsay of Charleston – who had challenged William Loughton Smith's seat in the first Congress, on the grounds that Smith (who had spent several years in London) was not an American citizen – were not untypical:

> We trust and hope that the French will discover as great abilities in planning and executing a good new government, as they have hitherto done in destroying an ancient bad one.[68]

Federalists condemned the 'excesses' of France, but as often as not acknowledged that its cause was just, and that reliable information of events abroad was scarce.[69] Again, this did not inhibit Republican accusations of Federalist Anglophobia. Nevertheless, these circumstances were unfavorable to the reduction of Republicans and Federalists to a French party and a British party.

Other pressure against this kind of reduction had been supplied in the spring of 1794 by the decision to send John Jay to London to negotiate the differences between America and Britain. This was the carrot that Federalists hoped the British cabinet would be induced to swallow by the stick of American rearmament. This had been a Federalist decision, but Republicans were compelled to admit negotiation as an alternative, even a preferable alternative, to economic confrontation.[70] The results of Jay's mission would soon provide a party issue intimately connected with foreign policy, but the party electoral battles of 1794 took place while negotiations were under way, and some at least were still fought on the ground first fought over in 1792: the Republican accusation of the insinuation into the government of principles of 'corrupt selfishness.'[71]

The outcome of these battles was judged to be unfavorable to the Federalists. Until 1800, this was the last series of elections in which foreign affairs momentarily receded from the agenda of party debate; it was also the last election before 1800 in which Republicans were clearly victorious. In November, Fisher Ames had thought there were 'hopes of having anti-federalism weeded quite out of the Massachusetts corps' of Congressmen. But December brought disappointing news on this score.[72] Congressman William Vans Murray feared that the fourth Congress (to meet in December 1795) would be

> composed of a majority who will be composed of two sorts of men. A few who were anti in 87 – and are so still – and those also [who] were Federal in 87 – and also think themselves to be so still – men who do not wish to overturn the government – but who by an undue infusion of new fangled disorganizing principles are outrageously wild in their theories & practice, & who wish to make the constitution the post on which they would hang up these new principles.[73]

From the opposite point of view, Jefferson saw that the changes in the House of Representatives were 'going on for the better,' and even the Senate was being purged of its 'impurities.' The Republicans needed only to 'hold on, that we may not shipwreck in the meanwhile.'[74]

1795–6

The 'meanwhile' between this second propitious election and the Congress it produced provided a new topic of party contention, and a new object of Republican party strategy. As early as February 1795, Fisher Ames predicted: 'The success of Mr. Jay will secure peace abroad, and kindle war at home.'[75] In New York, where Jay was a (successful) candidate for Governor, his supporters were obliged to defend this signer of the Declaration of Independence from charges of betraying America to Britain, and to stress that the contents of the treaty he had negotiated were not yet certainly known.[76] But the furious public debate over this treaty did not come until July and August, after the Senate had approved the treaty in June, and a copy of it was leaked to the Republican press.

Meanwhile, Republican propaganda continued to remind Americans of the injustice of the proceedings of the first and second Congresses – the funding system, the Bank of the United States, the debt and the defeat of Madison's commercial propositions.[77] If government were what it ought to be – nothing but 'public opinion, collected to a system'[78] – instead of the corruptly biassed system of fiscal Federalism, these proceedings would be reversed. American commercial intercourse would occur less with nations from which 'we import prejudices more pernicious to the sanity of the body politic, than infection to the body natural.'[79]

Federalist faith in the wisdom of the federal system and the justice of Federalist measures was also declared as firmly as ever. Federalists had retreated to their previous position that the American Revolution was indeed the 'primum mobile' of world revolution, but they insisted that American political success be judged primarily in terms of the increase of population, and 'the effects of industry' in agriculture, building, transportation and manufactures.[80] The American Constitution did not boast of the 'gothic' features lauded by Burke; it was erected instead 'on the broad basis of freedom and equal rights.' The sacred rights of property became more secure in civilization. That, under the 'severely republican' Constitution, 'enterprize has enlarged its sphere, and explored new regions of profit, that our country, every where presents the charms of creative cultivation and diffusive opulence,' owed much to Hamilton's efforts.[81] Federalists continued to desire the national encouragement of manufactures as well as agriculture 'as the natural means of deepening, and spreading the roots of our Independence'; this implied a preference for 'home-made utility' over 'imported elegance.'[82] But neither Federalist minds nor Federalist interests favored a precipitate break from English trade and credit.[83]

When the debate on the Treaty did come, it continued this dialogue of republicanism. For it appeared that Jay and the Federalists were determined upon an ever closer connection with 'the old, corrupt, and almost expiring government of Great Britain.'[84] Even hard-core Federalists were disgruntled with some aspects of Jay's Treaty, which had been negotiated in a climate of French military defeats.[85] In fact, although Britain would have gone to war rather than acquiesce in the old American contention for establishment of the principle that free ships make free goods, it could ill afford war with the United States in 1794, and the Twelfth Article of the treaty was considered, by Jay as well as by the British, quite a remarkable British concession; it offered – albeit on terms that proved to be unacceptable because they required federal regulation of American exports – a wedge into the West Indies trade.[86] However, to the Republicans, the treaty was the poisonous fruit of the doctrines on executive power preached by Hamilton in 1793. The partisans of the treaty were none other than those friends of this 'crusader against Republicanism' (who had a known 'devotion to monarchy'), the 'funding order.' Under the influence of the Machiavellian Hamilton,

> The spirit which animated our country to resist British tyranny and to declare independence, is, alas, paralized by systems, artfully contrived to render the mind pliant to the views of an insidious and ambitious administration. Funding and bank systems, with the speculations which have grown out of them, have substituted an avarice for wealth, for the glory and love of country.[87]

The Senate's approval of the treaty furnished proof of 'the existence of an aristocracy in this country,' which had been

> too often regarded as the chimera of some distempered enthusiast, or the fiction of some demagogue…the funding system has…organized a great aristocracy, which has usurped the dominion of the senate, which has often preponderated in the house of representatives, which proclaims itself in servile addresses to our supreme executive…[and] in monstrous accumulations of debt.[88]

Washington's ratification of the treaty in August 1795 – actually induced by his belief that another war with Britain was the alternative, by Edmund Randolph's intrigues with the French ambassador, Fauchet, and perhaps by Hamilton's decision that exchange of the instruments of ratification rather than ratification itself should be withheld until the Twelfth Article was rescinded[89] – appeared to indicate his intention to support the antirepublican secrecy of the Senate, and to promote a monarchical and aristocratical government 'under the insidious title of *an energetic scheme of government.*'[90] Hamilton's 'political heresies' had acquired a dangerously large influence: many Representatives, two-thirds of the Senate, and now even Washington, whose signing of the treaty confirmed in many eyes the partisan tendency of his recent condemnation of the Democratic-Republican Societies.[91] The people – if they were not enervated by a *'funding system,* aided by *British influence'*[92] – were more than ever required to come to the rescue. The history of the treaty negotiation had the advantage of reminding Americans that government requires surveillance.[93] The governors of America had not fulfilled their role of representatives as 'agents.'[94] The

people had demonstrated their disapproval of administration policy in
the last election to Congress, but the 'system of monarchical policy'
persisted in manifesting 'a contempt for their opinions, and an independence of their authority.'[95] Washington's perfidy left only the re-
cently elected House of Representatives to rally round.[96]

Republican party strategy fell in with this movement of public
opinion. The Republicans in Congress tried to live up to Jefferson's
expectations:

> I trust the popular branch of our legislature will disapprove of it, and
> thus rid us of this infamous act, which is really nothing more than a
> treaty of alliance between England and the Anglomen of this
> country, against the Legislature and people of the United States.[97]

Welding sentiment against the treaty to Congressional resentment
against executive initiative, the Republicans succeeded in passing a
resolution requesting the papers concerning Jay's mission from the
President. But Washington refused to comply with this request, and the
Republicans were unable to maintain a majority in Congress firm
enough to refuse to pass enabling legislation, which was approved at the
end of April by a vote of 51 to 48.[98] The Republican stand against the
treaty was an electoral failure too, probably contributing to Federalist
gains in the Congressional elections of 1796.[99]

The only solace Republicans could find in this latest Federalist victory
was that it relied even more than previous ones on George Washington's
influence. The weaker the Federalist persuasion became, the more Federalists had to rely on a kind of monarchism, thus verifying their critics'
accusations. These critics argued that Federalism was fundamentally
rather than residually monarchical. Jefferson took comfort in believing
that the Federalists saw

> that nothing can support them but the colossus of the President's
> merits with the people, and the moment he retires, that his successor,
> if a monocrat, will be overborne by the republican sense of his
> constituents; if a republican, he will, of course, give fair play to that
> sense, and lead things into the channel of harmony between the
> governers and the governed. In the meantime, patience.[100]

The conclusion was that 'Republicanism must lie on its oars' until
Washington announced his retirement, which he did not do until September. The House of Representatives had proved not to be the supreme
power in the new Constitution. The Republicans therefore turned their
eyes to the Presidency. (They had already discovered that the third

6

branch of government was not going to be an easy channel for Republican policies, by the failure of John Taylor's plea for the judiciary to correct legislative mistakes.[101]) In this line of vision they could find a bit more comfort in the realization that the names of Jay and Hamilton, two otherwise likely Federalists, could not be protected from the unpopularity of the treaty by the aegis of Washington.[102]

While Republicans (spurred on by Thomas Paine's *Letter to George Washington*[103]) tended more and more to inculpate Washington in Federalist heresies, Federalist rhetoric more insistently praised Washington and the treaty he had signed into law, at the same time that it reasserted the philosophical basis of the Federalist persuasion. In Rhode Island, Paul Allen condemned the hypothesis of 'ingenious writers' who 'have done more injury to the cause of freedom by their pens, than tyrants by their swords,'

> that man, when he wanders a savage in the forest, enjoys certain rights incompatible with the very existence of society...Natural rights are those rights which a man can enjoy in a state of society, without injury to others. If we wander further than this in quest of them, we search not among mankind, but in the world our fancy has created.

It was true that the moment representatives violated these natural rights, they were no longer owed obedience. But this was not the case in the altercation between the 'disappointed faction' and the American President. Washington had upheld the Constitution, and the Constitution set the precedent for the exorcism of the spell of aristocracy in the present French Revolution, and, to Burke's chagrin, in the coming British Revolution. The Constitution, recognizing property as 'the very basis of civil jurisprudence,' had ensured America's prosperity.[104] Abraham Ellery concurred: the Constitution was clearing a path 'to unbounded opulence and grandeur,' and to calumniate Washington was to calumniate virtue and patriotism.[105] This theme of the truly republican Constitution and the faithfully Constitutional President was pronounced by several New England Federalists, and was carried into South Carolina by William Loughton Smith.[106]

Congressman John Page of Virginia did not find such an overwhelming approval of Washington in his own state, but he did find it necessary to submit to his constituents a defense of his consistently Republican votes in Congress, from funding and assumption to the treaty. Page argued that his conduct in these matters was calculated not to overthrow the Constitution, but to establish it 'upon a sure and lasting foundation,' and that this rationale

> is evident to those who believe that the constitution is founded on democratical principles; and that vigilance and republican jealousy are necessary to restrain those branches of our government which were intended to resemble the monarchical and aristocratical branches of the British government, (as far as republican principles could permit) from exceeding their constitutional powers, and claiming those which are exercised by the King and House of Lords of Great Britain: and it must be evident to those who think that opposing the funding system, the assumption of the state debts; the establishment of the Bank of the United States, and the excise laws, was opposing a system completely adapted to the taste and practice of a monarchical government; and of that government too, which by such a system has rendered itself despotic, and the scourge of the people: a system utterly incompatible with the principles of a republic standing on the foundation of democracy or the will of the people; being calculated to perpetuate the national debt, and to encrease taxes; to strengthen the hands of the executive, and to weaken and impoverish the people; to excite avarice; multiply sources of speculation, and propagate corruption.[107]

Republican adherence to anti-fiscality was bolstered in 1796 by the pellucid speeches and writings of Albert Gallatin, who, having been refused a seat in the Senate, became a Representative for Pennsylvania in the fourth Congress. Gallatin composed a survey of the country's revenues, expenses and debts, in which he argued that the debt had been unnecessarily increased by assumption, that too much was currently being spent (on military and naval expenses), and that too little was being collected to pay off the useless debt (he suggested the sale of lands purchased cheaply from the Indians, and direct taxes levied by the states). This survey was published in November, the month when Presidential electors were chosen.[108]

Washington opened the partisan Presidential campaign of 1796 with his 'Farewell Address,' published in September, and its famous warning against 'the baneful effects of the spirit of party' in non-monarchical polities.[109] Republicans had already developed a confident justification for their partisanship. The appearance of Madison's essay on parties in 1792 had been preceded by Monroe's bold statement: 'To be passive in a controversy of this kind...is a satisfactory proof that [one] is on the wrong side.'[110] Jefferson was equally insistent:

Were parties divided merely by a greediness for office, as in England, to take a part with either would be unworthy of a reasonable or moral man. But where the principle of difference is as substantial, and as strongly pronounced as between the republicans and the monocrats of our country, I hold it as honourable to take a firm and decided part, and as immoral to pursue a middle line, as between the parties of honest men and rogues, into which every country is divided.[111]

Republicans agreed with Washington that parties ought to be unnecessary in a republic, and tolerable if not desirable in a monarchy. But the Republican party was more than tolerable, it was necessary in order to re-establish a state where open partisanship would again be unnecessary, where governments and peoples could harmonize and sympathize.

To this end, the Republican party sought to elect Jefferson to the Presidency in 1796. Jefferson himself and Benjamin Rush appear to have been among the few Republicans who had doubts about the wisdom of this move. While Monroe, in Paris, thought the election of Jefferson would satisfy French apprehension of an Anglo-American *rapprochement*,[112] Jefferson thought

our foreign affairs never wore so gloomy an aspect since the year 1793. Let those come to the helm who think they can steer clear of the difficulties.[113]

He looked forward to a continuation of his retirement, 'while our eastern friend will be struggling with the storm which is gathering over us; perhaps be shipwrecked by it.'[114] His inactivity in this campaign stands in marked contrast to his active partisanship from 1797 through 1800.

However, Jefferson's suggestion that Madison might become a candidate for the Presidency (a suggestion not repeated in 1800) was not heeded by the Republicans, and Jefferson was widely recognized as the Republican choice. So Republican campaign managers told the voters:

There is (the assertion, alas, is too well founded) a powerful party in the United States, who have, under a variety of disguises, laboured to subvert republicanism, and introduce a system inimical to liberty.

Therefore, it was imperative that they 'analyse the conduct of each pretender.' In the Republican analysis, Hamilton was dismissed as a man of 'unprincipled artifice,' Jay as a man who had betrayed his Revolutionary experience by his recent adulation of 'the tottering tyrant,' George III. Adams, with his 'avowed approbation of the British constitution,' was not 'worthy to be trusted with the guardianship of a system dissimilar not only in fundamental principles, but even in its exterior aspect.' The manifestly unambitious Jefferson, therefore, 'must be the man of your choice.'[115]

In support of John Adams' succession, Federalists insisted: 'we are *all republicans*,' Adams included. They were obliged to defend at some length the republicanism of Adams' *Defence of the Constitutions*.[116]

Yet there was in 1796, as in 1800, a lack of unity in the Federalist party, and the unsuccessful attempt by some Federalists to make Thomas Pinckney President, and to leave John Adams in second place, opened up the possibility that Republicans might (in Jefferson's words) 'come to a good understanding with him as to his future elections.'[117] But Republican leaders soon fell back on the plan of dissociating themselves from Adams' attempts to prevent war between the United States and France, which they believed were likely to fail.[118] Jefferson made his new office of Vice-President constitutionally separate from the President's administration,[119] as if to verify Fisher Ames' prediction:

> In a Senate that will bring him into no scrapes as he will have no casting votes to give, he may go on affecting zeal for the people; combining the *antis*, and standing at their head, he will balance the power of the chief magistrate by his own. Two Presidents, like two suns in the meridian, would meet and jostle for four years, and then Vice would be first.
>
> His Vice-Presidency is a formidable danger. This I say as a conjurer.[120]

1797–8

Jefferson thus took up a position that would allow him to help manage the Republican opposition to Adams' administration – an easier task than opposition to an administration headed by Washington. The 'Anglican monarchical aristocratical party' had prevailed in the elections of 1796. The Republicans' House majority was made, at best, 'equivocal,' and their minority in the Senate became even weaker than before. But in 1797, Jefferson anticipated the effects that Washington's retirement could have on the elections of 1798: the people had been

> lulled into rest and security from a cause which no longer exists. No prepossessions now will shut their ears to truth. They begin to see to what port their leaders were steering during their slumbers and there is yet time to haul in, if we can avoid war with France. All can be done peaceably, by the people confining their choice of Representatives and Senators to persons attached to republican government and the principles of 1776.[121]

The avoidance of conflict with France was necessary for the security of the Republican party and its goals, because anti-French sentiment, incited by anti-republican Federalists, 'has on the minds of our citizens an effect which supplies that of Washington's popularity.'[122] Given peace, there was some prospect

> of the penetration of truth into the eastern States; if the people there, who are unquestionably republicans, could discover that they have been duped into the support of measures calculated to sap the very foundations of republicanism, we might still hope for salvation, and that it would come, as of old, from the east. But will that region ever awake to the true state of things? Can the middle, southern and western States hold on till they awake?[123]

Given peace, 'the matter of finances' would determine the future of the parties, for 'the next step, and it is an unavoidable one, a land tax, will awaken our constituents, and call for inspection into past proceedings.'[124]

Jefferson was certainly correct in thinking that New England was still the most solidly anti-Republican region. However, he was wrong in imputing anti-republicanism to New England Federalists. There were those who followed President Adams in equating good government with social 'balance.'[125] But the more orthodox Federalist science of politics was more pronounced even in Adams' own neighborhood. Federalists agreed with Republicans in the construction of civil society on the natural equality of the state of nature. But they saw in this original state 'universal strife and perpetual war.'[126] In this state, an individual was 'wholly incompetent to the acquisition of more property, than a bare sufficiency for a scanty subsistence.' 'The primary object of civil institutions' was to prevent these evils of the state of nature, evils which were visible during revolutions – even the American Revolution – wherein is illustrated the principle that 'Selfishness is the predominant principle of fallen man.'[127]

> The primary design of government... is not so much to render the subjects of it positively happy, as to prevent their being rendered miserable by the violence, injustice, fraud or negligence of their fellow men. This appears to be in perfect conformity to the apostle PAUL's ideas, when he exhorts that 'supplications, prayers, intercessions, and giving of thanks be made for all men; for kings, and for all that are in authority, *that we may lead a quiet and peaceable life, in all godliness and honesty.*'[128]

To set up a 'system of checks' in a government delegated by popular consent, 'and yet to throw a suitable weight into the scale of government to give it energy and force, is the grand secret of the legislation.' The secret had been discovered by the framers of the federal Constitution, the operation of which 'has evinced the justness of its principles. By a steady adherence to these, United America has become proverbial for prosperity.' Therefore one could expect the current misunderstanding with France to be accommodated 'by the wisdom and integrity' of the federal government.[129] The American experiment in republican government was distinct from the bankrupt regime of Britain, but it was also very different from 'the republic of TYRANTS' which was the regrettable result of the French Revolution. The recent belligerency of the perverted republic had the advantage of demonstrating the Federalist maxim:

> Self interest is no less the ruling principle of nations than of individuals. And we may rest assured, that neither French nor English fraternity will avail us, whenever it shall be incompatible with this principle.[130]

New Englanders were proud of their long record of sober republicanism, and had their own doubts about the republicanism of the slave owners of the South.[131] And the sobriety of their republicanism did not prevent them from wishing its extension throughout the world.[132]

Republican rhetoric remained less censorious of the course of the French Revolution, and more concerned with the 'Political apostacy which has appeared in this Country.' According to Elihu Palmer, the American Revolution had been the unhesitant first step in the establishment of political associations which would not deprive man of the enjoyments resulting from 'the possession of his faculties,' to which he 'is justly entitled by the laws and constitution of Nature.' The proper objects of political institutions went beyond 'the security of the fruits of man's industry,' to include 'his pursuit of happiness in every possible way.' The 'excesses' of French Republicans were deplorable, but there was 'no price too great to pay' to secure 'the liberty and happiness of man.' Those Americans who relinquished their attachment to this cause on this account generally betrayed a 'secret attachment to the British system of government.' They were not helping to bring about that time, which would come, when war between nations would cease, and 'social virtues' become 'the object of the human heart.'[133] They did not see that the state of nature existing between nations was by nature a peaceful state.

In fact, there were probably fewer Federalist hawks in 1797 than there had been Republican ones three years before, when Britain was the object of hawkishness,[134] perhaps partly because news of French victories on the Continent and British troubles in Ireland, in the navy and in fiscal affairs reached America in June 1797.[135] But Republican suspicions of Federalist warmongering were fed by the un-Republican means that Federalists chose to adopt in order to oblige the Republicans with peace. Harboring some doubts about the possibility of universal peace, and in any case not sharing Republicans' persistent faith in commerce as a weapon,[136] Federalists sought to negotiate from strength. The French Directory's refusal to receive the new minister (General Charles Cotesworth Pinckney) and its ill treatment of American shipping had been its answer to the Jay Treaty and the election of Adams.[137] Adams' response was to call a special session of Congress for May, to which he announced his intention to 'institute a fresh attempt at negotiation,' and recommended that, meanwhile, 'effectual measures of defence' be legislated.[138] Within a week, the Senate addressed an answer to the President, expressing 'entire approbation'; only one attempt to tone down the approbation had been made, and quickly defeated.[139] Republicans in the House, disposed to entertain the possibility that the Jay Treaty might have been an understandable cause of French belligerence, succeeded with some effort in inserting in the House's answer a clause suggesting that the negotiators be instructed 'to place France on grounds similar to those of other countries in their relation and connection with us.' (The commercial treaty with France provided that free vessels made free goods, the principle which Britain refused to recognize.) To this Adams encouragingly replied that negotiation would look to 'a removal of prejudices, a correction of errors, a dissipation of umbrages, an accommodation of all differences.'[140] The special mission sent to France (General Pinckney, John Marshall and Elbridge Gerry) was instructed accordingly.

Republicans were also less happy than Federalists to provide the military and naval measures recommended by Adams. The prospect of the peaceful negotiation of foreign disputes made it possible to concentrate more on their domestic aspects, presuming peace rather than war. In the remainder of the special session of Congress, in June and July, Republicans opposed the provisions made for increased defense expenditures. At the beginning of the regular session, Albert Gallatin revealed the Republican party outlook in a letter to his wife:

> The other party have a small majority...Yet...I think that unless the French government shall treat our commissioners very ill, this

session will pass on quietly and without much mischief being done. We will attack the mint and the whole establishment of foreign ministers, and will push them extremely close on both points. Even if we do not succeed in destroying those useless expenses, we may check the increase of the evil.[141]

The news that the French government was treating the American commission very ill indeed did not arrive before March 1798. At the beginning of the year, Republicans thought that an accommodation with the French would be reached, and that the domestic scene could therefore become more accommodating, too. Jefferson could see good omens in all quarters:

It is said, that the people from hence quite to the eastern extremity are beginning to be sensible that their government has long been playing a foul game. In Vermont, Chipman was elected Senator by a majority of one, against the republican candidate. Tichenor chosen Governer of Vermont by a very small majority. The House of Representatives of this State [Pennsylvania] has become republican by a firm majority of six...It is thought that the republicans have also a majority in the New York House of Representatives...In the House of Representatives of Congress, the republican interest has at present, on strong questions, a majority of about half a dozen, as is conjectured, and there are as many of their firmest men absent.[142]

Until March the Republicans in Congress concentrated on an 'attempt to bring back the establishment of the diplomatic corps to the footing on which it was settled at the commencement of the Government, and continued down till the year 1796.'[143] In this attempt at financial retrenchment and curtailment of executive patronage, they were able to evoke most of the fundamental issues on which their party was built. These issues pointed away from the foreign conflicts, towards the domestic regime. If the Republicans did not find advantage in identification with France in 1794, when public sentiment was anti-British, they could hardly allow such an identification now, when sentiment was often anti-French.

Albert Gallatin's long speech against the Foreign Intercourse Bill (authorizing a two-year continuation of expenditure on the diplomatic establishment) illustrates Republican ideas and rhetorical strategy. (The speech was published in pamphlet form, as was the reply to it by Congressman Robert Goodloe Harper, a Federalist from South Carolina.) Gallatin urged:

May we not hope that a fixed determination to prevent the increase of the national expenditure, and so far as our present engagements will permit, to detach ourselves from any connection with European politics, will tend to reconcile parties, and that our own united efforts may then prove not altogether unsuccessful in promoting the happiness of America, and conciliating the affections of every part of the Union?

Expenditure which involved executive patronage was particularly dangerous. So was the doctrine (originally developed by 'Pacificus') of certain Federalists who, in support of the bill, claimed that the House was obliged to appropriate money whenever the President and Senate exercised their nominating and treaty-making powers. These methods of executive aggrandizement, in accord with 'such systems as the plan of Government which the late Secretary of the Treasury (Mr. Hamilton) had proposed in the [Philadelphia] Convention,' had justly raised Republican apprehension of 'a Monarchico, Aristocratic Faction, who would wish to impose upon us the substance of the British Government.' In Britain, since the Revolution of 1688, 'a progressive patronage, and a systematic, corrupting influence have sunk Parliament to a nominal representation, a mere machine.' And

> Wherever the Executive have acquired an uncontrolled command over the purse of the people, prodigality, wars, excessive taxes, and ever progressing debts have unavoidably ensued. Not to speak of Spain and Holland, weakened by those causes; not to speak of France, whose example is still more awful, the fate of England is sufficient to warn us against the dangers of that system.[144]

The Federalist response was to point away from the 'money systems' that Gallatin arraigned, which commenced in 1789, to the Republicans' 'system of measures...so zealously and perseveringly pursued, since the commencement of the war between France and England.' The 'main object of those gentlemen' appeared to Federalist eyes to be 'that concentration of powers in one popular body, which it was the main object of the constitution to prevent.'[145] This characterization of the Federalist purposes of the Philadelphia Convention, which had been concerned to marry republicanism and administrative energy, was fairly accurate, though it was and is very often forgotten or denied by men preoccupied, as were the Republicans, with administrative malfeasance and corruption.[146]

The passage of the Foreign Intercourse Bill without amendment indicated that the Federalists could count on a majority of five or six in the 106-member House of Representatives at the beginning of March 1798. March and April brought a sizeable increase in Federalist power in the House, because of the Senate's publication of the XYZ papers. These papers revealed, to Republican dismay, the French government's demands for an apology, a bribe and a loan as conditions for negotiation. The negotiators had refused, and war against the offending French seemed unavoidable.

Republicans, however, still chose to disbelieve in the necessity of war. A scientific paper by Vice-President Jefferson, who was also President of the American Philosophical Society, was read to that learned gathering in May. As the now unequivocally Federalist Congress was busy appropriating even more millions for defense than the indignant President Adams had called for, the philosophers heard the Vice-President's sad but hopeful reflections:

> I am fixed in awe at the mighty conflict to which two great nations [Britain and France] are advancing, and recoiling with horror at the ferociousness of man...We see numerous societies of men (the aboriginals of this country) living together without the acknowledgement of either laws or magistracy. Yet they live in peace among themselves, and acts of violence and injury are as rare in their societies as in nations which keep the sword of the law in perpetual activity. Public reproach, a refusal of common offices, interdiction of commerce and comforts of society are found as effectual as the coarser instrument of force. Nations, like these individuals, stand towards each other only in the relations of natural right. Might they not, then, be peaceably punished for violence and wrong?[147]

George Logan, speaking to the Tammany Society a week later, offered similar reflections, repeating his argument of 1792:

> Man was formed by Nature for Society...This comprehensive rule was in all ages respected, until Hobbes, and other devoted slaves to Tyrants, broached the detestable opinion, that the state of Nature, in respect to Man, is a state of war; that consequently all Men are enemies to each other, and that they are only to be governed by fear.

More enlightened men, perceiving 'the wonderful regularity of all Nature,' had taught that the

> degraded state of Man had been affected by the Executive Magistrates of all Countries...Wars created by ambitious Executives have been undertaken more to their own aggrandizement and power, than for the protection of their Country...The present

gloomy appearance of our public affairs has no doubt been
occasioned by the Citizens of the United States having too much
neglected the representative principles of the federal government,
and looking up to one man for the salvation of the country.[148]

Republicans feared, or hoped for, a successful French invasion of
Britain, so that their warnings against war with France could present
themselves as solid calculations of national interest. But they also maintained that French victories were 'triumphs of benevolence' over
corruption.[149] Jefferson reflected: 'I do not indeed wish to see any nation
have a form of government forced on them; but if it is to be done, I
should rejoice at its being a free one.'[150] At the same time, Republicans
insisted that the United States was in a happy position in which a navy,
to say nothing of a war, was not worthwhile, since it would only 'serve
a few bold mercantile speculators...foreign or domestic.'[151] They used
the words of Washington's Farewell Address to appeal to Jefferson's
idea that America follow the example of China, eschewing all foreign
connections.[152] Above all, they contrasted the truth that 'The first and
most essential support of republican government is the virtue of the
people,' with the legislative record of the Federalist party:

> National debts should ever be considered as national evils: they are,
> in their operative consequences, both unjust, and impolitic, and
> hostile to the interest of republics; they load posterity with burthens
> which have generally been accumulated by the folly and
> extravagance of the preceding governments; and without
> purchasing a single benefit. They create a baneful spirit of
> speculation; they poison the morals of the people; they naturally
> accumulate, and will either finally destroy the government, or be
> fraudulently destroyed by the government. They add an artificial
> support to the administration, and by a species of bribery enlist the
> monied men of the community on the side of the measures of
> government, however corrupt or ruinous to the general weal. Look
> to Great Britain.[153]

Federalists reacted to the French insults by preparing for war, and by
condemning the Republicans as 'a faction avowedly devoted to a foreign
nation, exciting strife, contention and division, in order to throw us into the arms of France.'[154] Against the Republican conviction that society
could be based on the truth that man was naturally social (and that
nations, therefore, although still in a state of nature, could resolve differences pacifically), Federalists proposed

that man is but a composition of nature and habit. – Habit is but a
collection of the biasses, prejudices, and warpings of opinion,
impressed and riveted in our minds by a long course of education. –
All the rest is savage nature. Destroy habit and you deprive us of all
social affectations.

The hints of Burke were studied. The French crisis, and perhaps Burke's
death (in 1797), brought Federalists to peruse again – or perhaps for the
first time – their dusty volumes of Burke. Whereupon, they felt
constrained to acknowledge, they discovered that he had been more
correct than they had believed.[155] They began to pay more heed to 'what
the combined wisdom of ages had erected,' and to see in the French
Revolution not a justifiable if perverted rebellion against monarchy, but
a conspiracy of atheists against all religions and all governments.[156] The
French Revolution was now clearly revealed as a thing apart from the
American Revolution, perhaps from its outset, and surely in its present
issue as a quest for '*despotic and universal dominion.*' American independence, after all, had been based only on the 'cruel necessity' of 'self-
preservation.' The same necessity now dictated that America be prepared to throw its weight against France, to maintain the European
balance of power. France had shown that republics could be as oppressive as monarchies, and had forfeited any remaining debts of American
gratitude.[157]

Republicans stubbornly demurred to the Federalists' reassertion of
realism in international relations. James Sullivan, while calling for a
'strict neutrality,' and holding that no nation had a right 'to interfere
in the form of government in another,' held nonetheless that 'each
nation has an interest in the examples and morals of another.' He
proceeded to attack the British and European monarchies for their
inherent corruption, lamenting that, in them,

> vice has its full career, and under the appellation of artificial, or
> political virtue, is cherished and supported. Machiavellian policy, is,
> to render *vice*, as *vice*, subservient to the purposes of virtue...
> But...natural genuine virtue exceeds all the artificial substitutes,
> which a corrupted and abandoned set of politicians can produce.

Such virtue was the correlative of 'free popular governments.' And when
a revolution from a vicious, hereditary government to a virtuous republic
was attempted, 'it must of necessity produce convulsions, ravages and
bloody carnage. But is this a reasonable objection to making the
attempt?'[158]

With the blow dealt to Republicans in Congress by French affairs, many Republican Congressmen retired to their homes, hoping to make Congress less of a forum for anti-French rhetoric. Federalists were returned to the position they had enjoyed before 1793, with certain control of all branches of the federal government. They now had the opportunity to use their strength to try to prevent the Republicans from plaguing them and the Republic again. Fisher Ames advised Federalists to act quickly, to put the nation into a state of undeclared war and to pass a sedition act.[159] His Republican brother, Dr. Nathaniel Ames, could soon record in his diary:

> All connexion with the French forbid by Traitors in Congress...
> Gen. Lloyd brought in a bill defining treason and for publishing
> sedition, etc., the boldest traitor of any![160]

Deprived of their foothold in the federal government, Republicans despaired of their plan to obtain support in the East through Congressional debates. Monroe judged that this support and changes in federal policy would now have to wait for a change in 'the course of publick events' either foreign or domestic. By foreign events, he referred to the possibility of British setbacks – a possibility soon made unlikely by the failure of France to invade Britain, and by Nelson's victory at the Battle of the Nile in October 1798. By domestic changes, he meant 'a more thorough disclosure of the views of the preponderating party,' coupled with the 'encreased pressure of distress, which the policy of that party must produce.'[161] Monroe's call for 'a more thorough disclosure' of Federalist views signaled the beginning of the campaign of 1798, which, when extended almost continuously through 1800, would result not only in a commanding Republican majority in the House, but also in Jefferson's elevation to the Presidency and a 'safe majority in the Senate.'[162]

This campaign was staged from the 'last citadel' of Republicanism,[163] the Southern state legislatures. As the New England Federalists would soon do when their party had been turned out of the federal government, and as John Taylor had already done in 1794,[164] many Republicans now used states' rights language in connection with their partisan efforts. Yet these efforts were still thought to be national in scope; for the Republican leaders thought that they could still rely on the anti-Hamiltonian republicanism of 'the body of our countrymen...through every part of the Union.'[165] Jefferson's Kentucky Resolutions of 1798 asserted a doctrine of nullification, and attacked the constitutionality of the Federalists' Alien and Sedition Acts; but they culminated in a rejection of the Federalist notion of popular confidence in governors:

it would be a dangerous delusion were a confidence in the men
of our choice to silence our fears for the safety of our rights:
...confidence is everywhere the parent of despotism: free government is founded in jealousy and not in confidence...In questions
of power then, let no more be said of confidence in man.[166]

Madison's Virginia Resolutions of 1798 did not even justify nullification;
in citing the bill of rights, he was making 'an appeal to the sense of the
community,' one of the main uses of a bill of rights in a popular
government, according to Madison's reflections of 1788.[167] In support of
the Virginia Resolutions in the House of Delegates, William Branch Giles
was not alone in depicting the Sedition Act not as a measure dictated
by war, but as an integral element in the Federalist system which had
begun with funding and the Bank of the United States, and would end,
when Republicans had been repressed, in 'the establishment of
monarchy limited or absolute.'[168] It is fair to say that the immediate
importance of the Kentucky and Virginia Resolutions 'as a political
attack on the Federalist administration was far more significant...than
the doctrine of states rights' which they advanced.[169] Similar protests
were made by individuals and by groups other than state legislatures
in the South, against what was perceived as a Federalist system of
standing armies, a large navy, foreign alliances with extensive diplomatic
patronage and large debts with a funding system – all justified by the
unnecessary war with France.[170] In Vermont, where party alignments
were skewed by the Canadian connection,[171] James Lyon nevertheless
thought it useful to reprint Republican speeches of Virginia and New
York provenance, and added his own caricature of the 'Federal Aristocratic Creed':

I BELIEVE in J— A—, the greatest captain and mightiest Monarch
under Heaven, and in T—y, his only Minister, our LORD, who
sit[t]eth above the Treasury.
   I believe in blind submission to the powers that be,
   In passive obedience and non-resistance,
   In the infallibility of the President,
   In the independence of the Senate,
   In Jay's British Treaty,
   In Alliance with Britain,
   In the expediency of a Nobility,
   In the equity of a Funding System,
   In the mysteries of Civil Government,
   In the raising Lawyers only for Legislators,

In a war with the French Republic, – and
In the blessings of a National Debt everlasting. AMEN[172]

New England Republicans were more democratic than their colleagues
to the south, and not so fond of states' rights; what united the Republican
party was its universal detestation of the monarchical tendencies of
Federalism.

By insisting on the continuity of the issues from 1790 onwards, the
Republican electoral campaigns of 1798 had anticipated the strategy
employed by Republican Congressmen:

> We have thought better to let the answer to the address [of the
> President] go without debate, as we mean, if possible, to avoid fighting
> on foreign ground. Their clamor about foreign influence is the only
> thing we have to fear, and on domestic affairs exclusively we must
> resist them.[173]

Many of the Congressional elections of 1798 occurred while the reaction
to the XYZ affair was at its height, and increased the Federalist majority
in the House for the sessions of 1799–1801 to twenty. However, although
Federalists made heavy gains in the South, where the Kentucky and
Virginia Resolutions excited unionist sentiment,[174] Republicans made
slight advances in New York and New Jersey.[175] In Pennsylvania, the
election increased the Republican majority by three, returning ten
Republicans and three Federalists.[176] In Maryland, even in Massachusetts, Federalists had reason to fear that the elections were going 'ill.'[177]
These advances, and the greater confidence that the Republicans in
Congress were soon able to have, indicated 'that a change of public
opinion in the people and of confidence in the Executive party has taken
place.'[178] The Republican response to the Federalist exploitation of the
quarrel with France was beginning to bear fruit.

1799–1800

Sensing this alarming turn of political fortune, Federalists began to seek
some electoral appeal less contingent on emergencies created by non-
British foreign powers.[179] Hamilton observed, rather belatedly, 'The
first thing in all great operations of such a government as ours is to secure
the opinion of the people.' But what followed? No more and no less than
that a committee should be appointed to deal with the Kentucky and
Virginia Resolutions, to explain with pathos and calm dignity the government's case and the detrimental tendency of such anti-government
acts. This brilliant administrator naturally suggested a committee, a

committee of reasonable men – supported in their reasonableness, of course, by the knowledge that an army could be sent to overawe the Virginians, as the Whisky rebels had been (and John Fries soon would be)[180] 'put...to the test of resistance.'[181] Unlike Hamilton, Fisher Ames had a reputation for oratory; everyone remembered his passionate plea for the House to approve the operation of the Jay Treaty. Yet Ames too now illustrated the incompatibility of Federalist political science with a deep popular political persuasion. Even as he tried to rally support for the government's case, Ames reflected:

> It is however difficult, if not impossible, to excite and maintain as much zeal and ardor in defence of government, as will animate the jacobins for its subversion; for to them action is ease, to us it is effort; to be at rest costs them more constraint, than us to stir...sober duty and a timorous forecast are feeble antagonists against jacobinism; it is flat tranquillity against passion; dry leaves against the whirlwind; the weight of gunpowder against its kindled force...To weight we must impart motion, correct good sense must acquire the energy of zeal. It must be remembered, too, that public opinion is the great auxiliary of good government. Where can its weight fall so properly as on the conspirators who disturb its tranquillity and plot its subversion?[182]

Ames was still arguing for 'republican liberty'[183] as it was understood in Federalist political science. Federalist republicanism, which assumed popular tranquillity, was less akin than Republican republicanism to the energy of popular zeal. In this way, Federalist political science was 'self-defeating.'[184] The 'well-informed, and well directed zeal'[185] now sought by Federalists was not an easily bred hybrid. When the people were called to the government's rescue, they brought with them confidence in themselves – confidence which was denied them in the Federalist science of politics, but charged to them by the Republican persuasion. Even if they had not been internally disunited, the Federalist party were unable to produce a winning rhetoric. They could make 'the spirit of 1776' a part of the Federalist appeal only by attaching it to resistance against France.[186] Their loyalty to Federalism compelled them to rely on coercion, rather than moral suasion, abroad and now at home. John Marshall discerned the useless and counterproductive nature of the Alien and Sedition Acts. But, Federalist that he was, he produced no less bankrupt rhetoric; indeed, he led the Federalist retreat into the judiciary, the non-political, constitutionalist branch. John Adams was also aware of the impolitic politics of the Federalists; but his contrasting moderation did not save his chosen party. His purge of the cabinet, which brought Federalist disunity into the open in a violent way, occurred only after unified Federalism had been defeated in elections in New York.[187] It is true that Adams ran better in 1800 than he had in 1796.[188] But even if he had been re-elected in 1800, he would have faced a hostile Congress. A victorious moderation would not have carried the Federalist party on its coat-tails.

Republicans themselves had feared that war with France could only redound to Federalist advantage, but as the quasi-war with France proceeded, and its burdens of taxation were felt, the Republican cause advanced. There had been indications for some time that France did not intend a full-scale war with America, and was finding even a half-war less lucrative than it had expected, when President Adams, having perceived or guessed French intentions, and having boggled at Hamilton's new use of Washington's reputation to ride to military glory, announced a third diplomatic mission to France.[189] The beginnings of these negotiations proclaimed the end of the Federalist party's desperate electoral strategy, or rather, it demonstrated their desperate want of an electoral strategy, a deficiency which had made their political extremes seem eligible.

With the Presidential candidacy of the Virginia philosopher proceeding apace (the elections of 1799 determined the Presidential electoral vote in many states), Federalist students of Burke toyed with the idea of replacing their political science with a political history. In their very celebrations of the anniversary of the appeal (penned by the philosopher) to 'the Laws of Nature and of Nature's God,' even while distinguishing American from British government, they deplored 'political speculatists' and appealed to 'the experience of ages.'[190] In sage admonitions against mixing theory and practice, they suggested that the blessings enjoyed by Americans – a growing population and a commerce second only to Britain's – were based not on any political, moral or economic theories, but on the virtuous industry of Americans' ancestors.[191]

But the majority of Federalist spokesmen adhered to the anti-Burkean 'liberal tradition' of America, and took pains to defend the Federalist administrative record in terms of Federalist political theory. Thus Thomas Beedé defended the martial measures:

> Previously to the formation of civil society, the law of nature
> authorized men to defend themselves against the unjust attacks of
> enemies. In a civilized state the same law justifies the sovereign of a

nation in collecting his forces to repel any combination of invaders. The sovereign has a right to compel his subjects to action whenever the public good renders it expedient.[192]

Defending the federal Constitution's unique political solution, Amos Stoddard declaimed against 'political errors and heresies' like the programmatic popular jealousy recommended by Republicans:

> when they imagine, that our Government *naturally* inclines to corruption, and to a dangerous accumulation of power, they manifest inaccurate conceptions of its structure and principles. No political truth is more evident than that foreign Governments are pregnant with danger – while the greatest danger to be apprehended in *America*, is from the wicked disposition, and blind credulity of certain portions of the people.[193]

Republicans agreed that the American political experiment was unique, but they held that it was in danger of failing, because of its monarchical perversion by Hamilton's program. Madison repeated this charge in January 1799, in an 'Address of the General Assembly to the Commonwealth of Virginia.' With 'fiscal system and arrangements, which keep a host of commercial and wealthy individuals imbodied, and obedient to the mandates of the treasury'; the transfer to the executive of important powers (borrowing money with no apparent limit to interest rates, raising armies, and expelling 'aliens'); the construction of the Constitution in such a way as to remove all restraints on federal power – with all these, Madison prayed, 'let the artificers of monarchy be asked what further materials they can need for building up their favorite system.'[194] Henry Lee, Governor of Virginia while Hamilton's program was being implemented, and soon to be elected to the last Federalist-ruled Congress, replied to these 'heavy charges.' The holders of the debt, he claimed, were independent of the Treasury; had Virginia's payment of the interest on the debt – before it was assumed – resulted in such a dependence, or tended to monarchy? As for the 'swarms of officers, civil and military,' the more numerous existence of such officers in the state's government showed that they were necessary agents of government,

> inseparable from the very existence of government, and the execution of its laws. If it be a measure leading to monarchy, then monarchy is only to be avoided by dissolving government.[195]

Apart from such feckless objectivity, Federalist rhetoric could only appeal from the burdens of the 'free, wise and efficient government' to its benefits: 'the general prosperity of the Nation, and...the security and happiness of individuals.'[196]

The Republicans pressed home their advantage, giving special attention to New England and South Carolina. In a letter which served as his party's platform in the Presidential election of 1800,[197] Jefferson presented to Elbridge Gerry of Massachusetts a 'profession of my political faith.' Here, in addition to expressing support for civil liberties and lack of support for political connection with any foreign nation, he condemned the 'hue and cry against the sacred name of philosophy'; wished for 'an inviolable preservation of our present federal Constitution'; rejected the institution of a standing army, a navy and a large diplomatic establishment; called for 'a government rigorously frugal and simple'; and opposed the consolidation and 'monarchising' of the Constitution and the 'multiplication of officers and salaries merely to make partisans, and for increasing, by every device, the public debt, on the principle of its being a public blessing.' The funding system could not be repudiated, Jefferson granted, but he was 'religiously principled in the sacred discharge of it to the uttermost farthing.'[198] Jefferson may have guessed that he was already composing his first Presidential inaugural address, more than two years in advance; he was certainly aware that most of the issues he raised were present in the foundation of the Republican party, eight years before.

Jefferson recruited his venerable neighbor, Edmund Pendleton, who had hitherto been reluctant to suffer his name to come before the public, to publish a widely reprinted[199] discussion of American political affairs. Pendleton criticized Federalist bellicosity for its anti-republican tendency:

> The measures recommended by the Secretary of War, and
> Commissioner of the navy, for an augmentation of the army and
> navy of the United States, and now under the consideration of
> Congress are truly alarming; since their adoption would create a
> ruinous debt...An army of 50,000 mercenaries, at the devotion of
> some future enterprising President, aided by a sedition bill and other
> accumulated terrors, with the influence of hope from an enormous
> patronage, will subject America to executive despotism, instead of a
> representative republican government.[200]

Virginians of both parties were surprised to hear that the state elections in the spring of 1799, while giving the anti-disunionist Federalists large gains in the tidewater counties, showed Republican gains in the transmontane counties;[201] anti-entrepreneurial and anti-imperialist rhetoric seemed to be successful in the least likely places.

In Pennsylvania, Thomas Cooper recommended moderation to both Federalists and Republicans, but he judged that there did seem to be more justice on the Republican side, for there was a discernible 'tendency to stretch to the utmost the constitutional authority of our executive, and to introduce the political evils of those European Governments whose principles we have rejected.'[202] He was sympathetic with the suspicions raised by Gallatin in the House of Representatives, that Federalist military and naval expenditures were designed not as emergency measures, but as long-term imperialistic projects.[203] In a defense of Jefferson's candidacy, John Beckley listed the elements of the Federalist conspiracy:

> our executive functionaries have not been slothful in pursuing,
> under colour of law, persecutions and proscriptions of personal
> disqualifications for political opinions, and restraints on the liberty of
> the press – Or in promoting, by every faculty they possessed, systems
> of extended influence and wasteful expenditure, to the creation of
> heavy and oppressive public burdens, in numerous and unnecessary
> appointments to office, a standing army, a permanent navy,
> augmentation of public debt, loans at excessive and exorbitant
> interest, and finally, additional and aggravated impost duties,
> excises, salt tax and land tax.[204]

In the Philadelphia *Aurora*, the main Republican newspaper in the capital since yellow fever and lack of funds had brought an end to the *National Gazette*, Philip Freneau attacked the Federalist candidate for Governor of Pennsylvania, who had

> advocated the British treaty...[and] the alien and sedition
> laws...His warmness on the bill for a standing army, calls loudly on
> the independent farmer and true American – They may easily
> discern that, as soon as a standing army is strong enough, their
> liberty is no more; and by voting for him, they openly approve of all
> these laws, and many others, equally hurtful; as the stamp act, eight
> per cent loan, funding system, bank schemes, &c.[205]

The reaction to the suppression of the 'Fries Rebellion' against the Federalists' direct tax helped to secure a Republican victory in the elections of the governor and the legislature of Pennsylvania in 1799, although Federalist retention of control of the state Senate and gerrymandering *avant la lettre* led to a stalemate and finally to a compromise that limited the Republican share to eight of Pennsylvania's fifteen Presidential electoral votes in 1800.[206]

Federalists having stolen seven Pennsylvania votes, Republicans could feel more courageous in stealing them back, by securing South Carolina's eight electoral votes through Charles Pinckney's offer of patronage to members of the state legislature, an action which probably decided the outcome of the Presidential election of 1800.[207] In 1799, however, Pinckney ('Blackguard Charlie' to his Federalist cousins) was busy propagating Republican views on American politics, and his labors in this field were no doubt as important as his partisan chicanery, in Jefferson's appointment of him as ambassador to the court of Spain.[208]

The strength of Republicanism in New England continued to grow. The Republican persuasion challenged Federalism more frequently and more tellingly. Republican newspapers from the Middle and Southern states circulated with some freedom, and a few native Republican presses were founded.[209] Like their allies, New England Republicans believed that there was no need for a strong government and a standing army in America, because the American polity contained none of the elements that traditionally demanded governmental enforcement of peaceful coexistence. There was no cold warfare between plebeians and patricians, because there were no such classes, and there was no discord between private citizens and public servants, because the interests of both were identical. The need for energy in government was in inverse proportion 'to the vices which it creates.' In a natural state, human vices were 'thinly sown'; moral ugliness was generated by ill-suited laws. Government should be 'a superstructure built upon the natural relations of man,' a 'means of erecting the happiness of man on the social affections of his nature.' A national debt was bad; it encouraged a large and secretive government which enslaved a people by means of influence and favoritism, as in Britain. Obedience to such a government did not arise 'from open examination into the motives of the Legislature,' which alone 'can accord with the dignity of man.'[210] New England Republicans followed their Southern colleagues in protesting their loyalty to the Constitution properly understood, and identifying the Republican party of the 1790s with the Patriots of 1776. They discerned a likeness between the standing armies established by the Federalists and those put down by the Declaration of Independence as acts of a tyrannical king, and wondered whether American government was truly immune to those 'sins so easily besetting all established governments,' so that 'there is even now no security, but in the caution, the spirit, and the unceasing vigilance of the people.' They said, 'let us not be intimidated' by our own government:

> Whether in its past administration, there are already discoverable any symptoms of such a declension from first principles; whether it has sought to establish its measures, by a system of terror, compulsion and alarm; rather than upon the broad basis of the people's affections; whether its organization has been laid, in principles of frugality, moderation, and virtue; or in principles of profligacy, imprudence and venality, are questions, on which those who must feel their effects, have a right freely to judge; and the result of that opinion, they have a right as freely to declare.[211]

Well might Fisher Ames fear that such 'nonsense,' such theory 'tinctured with fanaticism,' was being 'inhaled in every breath,' and that these 'errors...will have vent, and then all will shake to the Alleghany ridge.' Among these 'errors' Ames reckoned

> the dreams of all the philosophers who think the people angels, rulers devils; information will keep all right, quell riots and rebellions, and save the expense of armies; the people always mean right, and if the government do not oppress, the citizens will not resist; that man is a perfectible animal, and all governments are obstacles to his apotheosis[212]

– a perceptive, though exaggerated, description of the persuasion confounding Ames and his Federalist friends.

Not even the apotheosis of George Washington (who died of laryngitis and doctors in 1799) could stave off the blow dealt to the Federalists in 1800. Some had hoped to bring Washington out of retirement to head the army and to galvanize the nation behind Federalist policy.[213] Their disappointment was not soothed by anything like a Federalist revival rising out of the nation's mourning. The Federalist-dominated sixth Congress, until it became the reluctant arbiter between Jefferson and Burr in 1801, was little more than 'a conclave of cardinals, intriguing for the election of a Pope.'[214] With the second contest between Jefferson and Adams (or Jefferson and General Pinckney, to Hamilton and a few other anti-Adams Federalists) holding everyone's attention, and the Congressional elections reflecting even more than the Presidential contest the growing ascendancy of Republicanism, the propagation of the Republican persuasion hardly paused.

In January 1800, the Virginia House of Delegates printed 5,000 copies of Madison's Report on the Resolutions of 1798, a reply to other states' failure to accede to these Resolutions. The Virginia leaders of the Republican party were still ringing the changes on their accusation that Federalist policies aimed at consolidation of American government, and that the 'inevitable result of a consolidation...would be to transform the republican system of the United States into a monarchy.'[215] A new tract on the national debt by Gallatin, published in Philadelphia and New York, made clear the alleged basis of the alleged consolidation, and suggested that the most lasting achievement of Federalist measures from 1798 to 1800 was an increase in the debt to some $11½ million.[216]

In May, the Republicans' acquisition of the Presidential vote of New York imparted a momentum to their cause which the Federalists' reduction of military expenditures[217] failed to diminish. Independence Day could be celebrated by some men with more peace of mind than had been possible for several years:

> In our country some Liliputian efforts have been made to annihilate the glorious effects of the American revolution, but they are like to terminate in smoke, and fall sacrifice to the just resentment of an injured people. The unconstitutional and arbitrary measures of the federal government, have been partially abandoned, by those who were their first abettors, and the political temperament of the high toned monarchist is ameliorated, and begins to coincide with the republican sentiments of the great body of the people.[218]

Federalists still agreed that 'the great body of the people are as firmly attached to a republican government, as they ever were'; but they also still insisted in no uncertain terms that the representative republic of America, a kind of meritocracy, was not to be confused with direct democracy in the ancient style.[219] This may have been good political science, but it was bad rhetoric. Fisher Ames perceived as early as August: 'The question is not, I fear, how we shall fight, but how we and all federalists shall fall.'[220]

The Federalist persuasion had originally been voiced by several political parsons; it was natural, then, when it proved unable to persuade, that an appendix to the Federalist science of politics should be suggested:

> in the opinion of some, our greatest danger at present consists in our depending too much on the perfection of our constitution and resolution to maintain our liberty, to the neglect of those institutions, calculated to inspire the republican virtues and form good citizens, on which the ancients seemed chiefly to rely. But in what nation was

there an institution superior to the Christian Sabbath – O! may it never pass into general neglect.[221]

The attempt to shore up Federalism with Christianity took its most common form in the publicity given to Jefferson's deism.[222] The proper response to this slur was made by a Connecticut Republican, Abraham Bishop. Bishop did not deny (it was, after all, perfectly true) that Jefferson was a deist; he simply pointed out that there were deists in both parties.[223] This was equally true; the voice of Federalism often spoke in deist accents. Federalism was justly denied the monopoly of Christian support it now bid for. The weakness of the Federalist persuasion had provoked this bid. But the Federalist science of politics was if anything more opposed than the Republican persuasion to the mixture of religion and politics. Christianity could only render last rites to the Federalist party.

By the time the new federal capital was being officially occupied for the first time (Congress first met in Washington in November 1800), it was evident that the Republicans would soon become the keepers of the temple now removed from the moneychangers of Philadelphia (where the Bank and the Mint remained). The Presidency was secured – for one Republican or another – by the South Carolina vote in December. However, the extent of the 'victory . . . by virtue over vice, republicanism over aristocracy, and the consequent downfall of Hamiltonians, Pickeronians, British Agents and Old Tories,'[224] became clear only when the elections of the seventh Congress were completed in the spring of 1801. These elections produced a Republican majority of twenty-six[225] – a greater majority than the one given to the Federalists at the height of the XYZ affair. Among this majority were several members from Rhode Island, Vermont and Massachusetts; Republicanism was beginning its conquest of New England.[226]

EPILOGUE

7

Party politics and party government

In 1808, with the Federalist party enjoying a revival, John Adams observed that

> it seems to be established as a principle, that our government is forever to be, not a national but a party government...While it lasts, all we can hope is, that in the game at leap frog, once in eight or twelve years, the OUTS will leap over the head and shoulders of the INS.[1]

But party government in the United States did not take the form that Adams expected. That his son would take office in 1825 as a Republican President, with other Republican candidates as losers epitomizes the kind of triumph that the Republican party enjoyed in spite of Federalist tenacity and survival through the War of 1812. In 1801, Federalists might cry 'we are not dead yet,'[2] but they were moribund as far as national politics was concerned.[3] They survived long enough to aid the advance of the democratization of American politics, but only as a minority at the national level. The Republican leadership succeeded in placing them in course of ultimate extinction, in spite of the great organizational momentum behind Federalism, and of the contrary wishes of John Adams and many political scientists today.[4]

Jefferson and Madison admitted that Federalism was based on a fault in human nature, and that it could therefore never be entirely expunged; 'whigs' and 'tories' were natural parties, not to be eliminated by man's art. But they never envisaged political toleration of the Federalist disease. In their policy toward Federalists, they agreed with the amalgamation policy of Monroe, who even denied that human nature furnished an excuse for hard-core Federalism. Republicans held that the party division in America was fundamentally between those who 'cherished' and those who feared and distrusted the people.[5] In Republican eyes, the Federalists had displayed a toryish pessimism by policies that depended on legislative and popular corruption. The Federalists' lowered expectations of the people, which were clear, caused Republicans to doubt the Federalists' adherence to republicanism, which is indubitable. The Republicans' more idealistic approach to the people explains their characterization of the Federalists as monarchists.

Federalist reflections on the natural basis of political parties which was revealing itself in America were naturally somewhat different from the Republican formulation. Like Jefferson and Madison, Fisher Ames had become convinced that 'the causes of opposition to free republican systems are in the heart of man and not to be eradicated.'[6] But Ames was more likely to agree with the *Massachusetts Mercury* than with the Republican leaders from Virginia on the natural foundation of partisanship:

> Naturally there can be but two parties in a Country; the friends of order and its foes. Under the banners of the first are ranged all men of property, all quiet, honest, peaceable, orderly, unambitious citizens. In the ranks of the last are enlisted all desperate, embarrassed, unprincipled, disorderly, ambitious, disaffected, morose men.[7]

As a description of the social constituency of the Republican party, this was probably at least as accurate as the Republicans' description of the political convictions of the Federalist party. For Republican electoral strength resided precisely in those 'new towns and counties' the proliferation of which the Federalists were so proud to have promoted[8] – towns and counties full of ambitious 'new men.'[9] However, the rhetoric of Republicanism, throughout the country, countered Federalist disenchantment with popular virtue by a reassertion of the necessity of popular virtue in republics. The political economism of Federalism demanded stern virtues, for acquisitiveness had to be kept honest; but it had little use for virtues that denied the desirability and humanity of acquisitiveness and 'possessive individualism.' With hard-headed, 'realistic' Federalists relying on a rhetoric of self-interest rightly understood, Republicans could pay homage to virtue with resounding success. They could condemn the corruption of capitalism even while they or their supporters exploited the equality of capitalistic opportunity lauded (if not particularly well-established) by Federalists. The relationship between rhetoric and reality in the origins of American party politics is surely evident enough to satisfy the most credulous idealist, yet devious enough to satisfy the most cynical realist.

The reflexive nature that was the strength of the Republican persuasion also found expression in the ambiguous feelings of Americans towards their 'mother country.' In 1787, Jefferson warned a Frenchman that on visiting America, he would 'find the affections of the Americans with France, but their habits with England. Chained to that country by circumstances, embracing what they loath, they realize the fable of the living and dead bound together.'[10] Fisher Ames reflected on the same phenomenon:

> Why should we expect that nations will see, or prefer their interests to their passions, when very wise individuals every day make a sacrifice of the former to the latter? We are like the English; the comparison is to be made between us and them, and in *that*, national pride takes an interest and feels a wound. Our envy, hatred, and revenge, naturally point against England, therefore, because we resemble them, and not against France, whom we do not resemble. Like two rival beauties, we are in danger of hating each other, because both are handsome... While France had so many partisans, no Frenchman here had many friends. England, on the contrary, was hated, yet every Englishman was courted, trusted, and preferred. From our love and hatred of these two nations, we took care, as often as we had opportunity, to make exception of every individual belonging to the one or the other.[11]

Ames remarked that a Chinese-style isolationism was being advocated 'by persons clad in English broadcloth and Irish linen.'[12]

It would be unfair to limit the causes of the decline of the Federalist party to the rhetorical shortcomings of Federalism. Yet the practice of Federalists themselves after the Revolution of 1800 demands that this defect of Federalism be considered as one of the most important causes of the party's undoing. Even as hard experience was compelling the Republican party to appropriate Federalist policies, the Federalist party endeavored to adopt the electoral tactics of the Republicans, and at length their very name and organization as well. If the Republicans in power 'out-Federalized the Federalists,' the Federalists, to retain or to obtain power where they could, had to out-Republicanize the Republicans,[13] for Federalism was 'too true to be good.'

What was the substance of the Revolution of 1800? Were there changes in policy as well as in rhetoric? It is often contended that it 'was not a political and moral revolution because Adams had inaugurated the return to responsible government by his peace decision in February 1799'; that the results of the elections did not reflect a choice of political persuasions but that 'the voters were concerned with the record: with the Alien and Sedition Acts, high taxes, the standing army, and the possibility of future peace.'[14] But the political arguments of the 1790s show how intimately the items in this record were connected with the political persuasions and philosophies of the two parties. The pacific policies of Adams, however noble in themselves, made the choice of Republicanism over Federalism possible, by making domestic policy rather than foreign crises the primary consideration.

The premise of this study has been that American party government is based on – and therefore can be understood only with reference to – party politics; in other words, that the origins of American party government are found in the origins of American party politics. Henry Adams suggests that the party government of the Jeffersonian Republicans in power 'attempted to reduce to practice' the political theory which they had expounded in opposition. 'They failed, and although their failure was due partly to accident, it was due chiefly to the fact that they put too high an estimate upon human nature'[15] – that is, to the fact that their policies were actually based on their theory. The attempt was a part of party government, and it is therefore important to understand the theory, which was most clearly articulated in the Republican party politics of the 1790s. The failure showed that the reality of modern government is interpreted better by Federalist theory than by Republican theory, and it helped to produce the disillusionment with party ideals that underlies the case for a practical, accommodationist party system.

Even if the attempt to govern with reference to the fact that 'the election was one of principle'[16] had not been made, it is clear that the idealistic rhetoric of Republican party politics played an important role in establishing the party in government, so that even when resort was had to Federalist policies, it was Republicans who reintroduced them. Moreover, this neo-Federalism received a neo-Jeffersonian response, in the form of the Jacksonian persuasion.[17] The idealistic rhetoric of American party politics, supporting causes both noble and ignoble, in the twentieth century as well as the nineteenth, follows the Republican rather than the Federalist model.[18] It would be worth studying this rhetoric for this reason alone, even if it were not made more worthwhile by the complex but nevertheless evident relationship between rhetoric and policy, between party politics and party government. The apolitical ideals of the Republicans seem to go well with the apolitical nature of modern political partisanship. The classical art of rhetoric teaches that appeals to passion are necessary even in the best polity; the modern rhetoric of American party government demonstrates the corollary that appeals to virtue are necessary even in a realistic regime, if only in order to elicit 'just so much solicitude as the human mind can never do comfortably without.'[19]

NOTES

Most the works cited here which were published in America from 1789 to 1800 appear in the American Antiquarian Society's *Early American Imprints* microprint collection. In these cases, any attribution of author or place or date of publication – indicated by square brackets – is that of Charles Evans, whose bibliography is the basis of that collection, or of Clifford K. Shipton and James E . Mooney, the editors of that collection and its index (*National Index of American Imprints Through 1800*, 2 vols. [Worcester, Mass., 1969]). Full titles of works cited here only by short titles can be found in Evans' *American Bibliography*, 13 vols. (Chicago, 1903–34; vol. 13 [by Shipton], Worcester, 1955).

Two editions of Jefferson's *Writings* are cited here; unless otherwise noted, the one edited by Lipscomb and Bergh is referred to.

Chapter 1. Party government and party politics

1 John C. Miller, *The Federalist era* (New York, 1960), 69, 277.
2 Everett C. Ladd, Jr., *American political parties: social change and political response* (New York, 1970), 38–39. This picture also emerges from Morton Borden, *Parties and politics in the early Republic, 1789–1815* (London, 1968), 58; Lisle A. Rose, *Prologue to democracy: the Federalists in the South, 1789–1800* (Lexington, Ky., 1968); Roy F. Nichols, *The invention of the American political parties* (New York, 1967); William N. Chambers, *Political parties in a new nation: the American experience, 1776–1809* (New York, 1963) and 'Party development and party action: the American origins,' *History and Theory*, 3 (1963), 91–120; James Sterling Young, *The Washington community* (New York, 1966); Seymour M. Lipset, *The first new nation* (London, 1963); Paul Goodman, 'The first American party system,' in *The American party systems: stages of political development*, ed. W. N. Chambers and W. D. Burnham (New York, 1967), 56–89; Richard Hofstadter, *The idea of a party system: the rise of legitimate opposition in the United States, 1780–1840* (Berkeley, Calif. 1970);

E. E. Schattschneider, *Party government* (New York, 1942), Chap. 1; and William Goodman, *The two-party system in the United States* (2nd ed., Princeton, N.J., 1960), 6–13.

Scholars have not always been so sanguine about the connection between party government and democracy; many have agreed with the argument made by Moisei Y. Ostrogorsky's *Democracy and the organization of political parties*, tr. F. Clarke, 2 vols. (London, 1902), that parties are detrimental to democracy. But it is not doubted that the connection exists, and that parties, whether they are good or bad, must be studied if modern democracies are to be understood. And in studying parties, it is often thought (as is indicated by the title of Ostrogorsky's book) that their organization is all-important. George D. Luetscher, *Early political machinery in the United States* (Philadelphia, 1903), argued that the Republicans owed their victory over the Federalists to superior organization, the Federalists being ideologically opposed to such extra-legal machinery. The organization of the first parties in America has been explored by several other historians, most notably Noble E. Cunningham, *The Jeffersonian Republicans: the formation of party organization 1789–1801* (Chapel Hill, N.C., 1957). The history written to highlight the organization of the first parties has documented entrances and exits, but has paid little attention to the lines that were spoken. It has outlined the body of these parties without accounting for their animation. It has been suggested that if parties are to be defined as party organization and the concomitant professional party ethos, 'the "first party system" may well become a casualty of subsequent research.' (Ronald P. Formisano, 'Deferential-participant politics: the early Republic's political culture, 1789–1840,' *American Political Science Review*, 68 [1974], 473–87; see also James M. Banner, *To the Hartford Convention: the Federalists and the origins of party politics in Massachusetts 1789–1815* [New York, 1967], Chap. 6.) On the other hand, while, for example, Harry Marlin Tinkcom, in his study of *The Republicans and Federalists in Pennsylvania, 1790–1801* (Philadelphia, 1950), claims (p. 52) that 'the crux of the matter and the principal reason' for partisan heat was the friction caused by 'structural lack', it is clear from his account (pp. 61 ff.) and others that the partisans of the 1790s had organizational devices more or less sufficient to their needs, which were considered to be more or less temporary. It seems unlikely that the lack of party machinery was the fundamental cause of party struggle.

3 Ladd, *Parties*, 16–44, 53, 311.

4 Samuel Eldersveld, *Political parties: a behavioral analysis* (Chicago, 1964), 18–22, 526, 543, worries about the undemocratic ways of American parties, but insists that parties do at least provide potential means of participation by citizens in the political process. However, if the analysis that follows is sound, it would seem that the party system is most democratic in issue-oriented, critical elections, when intra-party democracy might be discouraged (see

James Q. Wilson, *The amateur democrat* [Chicago, 1966], 351; but compare James L. Sundquist, *Dynamics of the party system: alignment and realignment of political parties in the United States* [Washington, D.C., 1973], 296, which sees amateur politics increasing in times of crisis.)

5 Wilson, *Amateur democrat*, 359.

6 Harvey C. Mansfield, Jr., *Statesmanship and party government: a study of Burke and Bolingbroke* (Chicago, 1965), 65, 181–88.

7 *Ibid.* 10–11, 113–20. Hofstadter, *Idea*, notices (pp. 34–35) that there was no Burkean defense of parties in America in the eighteenth and early nineteenth centuries, but under-estimates (e.g. pp. 22–23, 121, 242) the cogency of the defense of party (as opposed to parties) by partisans.

8 A theory developed by Arthur W. Macmahon, 'Conflict, consensus, confirmed trends, and open choices,' *American Political Science Review*, 42 (1948), 1–15; Samuel Lubell, *The future of American politics* (New York, 1951), 3, 7, 200–4 (and preface to 3rd ed., 1965); V. O. Key, Jr., 'A theory of critical elections,' *Journal of Politics*, 17 (1955), 3–4; Angus Campbell, Chap. 4 in Campbell and others, *Elections and the political order* (New York, 1966); Harry V. Jaffa, *Equality and liberty* (New York, 1965), 32–41; Charles G. Sellers, Jr., 'The equilibrium cycle in two-party politics,' *Public Opinion Quarterly*, 29 (1965), 16–38; Gerald M. Pomper, *Elections in America* (New York, 1968), Chap. 5; Walter D. Burnham, *Critical elections* (New York, 1970), 1–10; and Sundquist, *Dynamics*, 5–10, 275–98. See also Jerzy J. Wiatr, '"One-party systems" – the concept and issue for comparative studies,' *Transactions of the Westermark Society*, 10 (Helsinki, 1964), 284.

9 *The revolution of American conservatism: the Federalist party in the era of Jeffersonian Democracy* (New York, 1965).

10 'The New South,' speech at Richmond, Virginia, September 20, 1952, in *Speeches of Adlai Stevenson* (New York, 1952), 85.

11 Sundquist, *Dynamics*, 5–6.

12 *Ibid.* 214–15.

13 Alison Gilbert Olson, *Anglo-American politics 1660–1775: the relationship between parties in England and Colonial America* (London, 1973), v–viii, 75–80, notices the important changes in the character of political parties made possible by the secularization of politics after 1688; see also Harvey C. Mansfield, Jr., 'Party government and the settlement of 1688,' *American Political Science Review*, 58 (1964), 945, and 'Hobbes and the science of indirect government,' *American Political Science Review*, 65 (1971), 97–110.

The fate of the Church in this development is felt by Alexander Solzhenitsyn: '"What makes you think the Church is being persecuted?" Yakonov protested. "Nobody stops them ringing their bells, baking their communion bread, holding their Easter processions – as long as they keep out of civic affairs and education."' *The first circle*, tr. Michael Guybon (London, 1970), 158.

14 This consideration makes questionable the parallels drawn be-

tween ancient and modern liberalism by legal scholarship, in accounts like F. A. Hayek, *The constitution of liberty* (London, 1960), 164–6. Hayek quotes with disapprobation Thomas Hobbes' criticism of Aristotle's support for the idea of the rule of law. But in the Aristotelian analysis, laws were made to agree with the regime, the politeia; therefore they encouraged a particular way of life and a particular notion of justice. The controversial and divisive possibilities of this Aristotelianism drove Hobbes to support impartial government, by an 'Arbitrary' sovereign, which acts 'as the Publique Representant.' (*Leviathan*, ed. C. B. Macpherson [Harmondsworth, Mdx., 1968], Chap. 46, p. 699.) In this way, Hobbes rather than Aristotle was a modern liberal.

15 A particular neglected by most of the studies of critical elections; for example, in spite of its subtitle, Sundquist's book on the *Dynamics of the party system* is concerned more with 'the realignment process' than with the very idea of alignment.

16 Joseph Charles, *The origins of the American party system* (Williamsburg, Va., 1958), 139–40; see also Henry Jones Ford, *Washington and his colleagues: a chronicle of the rise and fall of Federalism* (New Haven, Conn., 1918), 173–4; Marshall Smelser, 'The Jacobin phrenzy,' *Review of Politics*, 13 (1951), 257–82, and 21 (1959), 239–58, and 'The Federalist period as an age of passion,' *American Quarterly*, 10 (1958), 391–419; and John R. Howe, Jr., 'Republican thought and the political violence of the 1790s,' *American Quarterly*, 19 (1967).

17 James Albert Woodburn, *Political parties and party problems in the United States* (New York, 1903), 26–30; Claude Bowers, *Jefferson and Hamilton: the struggle for democracy in America* (London, 1925); John Spencer Bassett, *The Federalist system* (New York, 1906); Alexander Johnston, 'Early political parties,' in Johnston and Woodburn, *American political history 1763–1876* (New York, 1905), 203–33; Vernon Louis Parrington, *Main currents in American thought*, 3 vols. (New York, 1927), Vol. 1, Book iii, Chap. 2: 'Political democracy gets under way – 1787–1800;' and Stuart G. Brown, *The first Republicans* (Syracuse University Press, Syracuse, N.Y., 1954).

18 V. L. Parrington, introduction to J. Allen Smith, *Growth and decadence of constitutional government* (London, 1930), x.

19 *The economic origins of Jeffersonian Democracy* (New York, 1915); see also Whitney K. Bates, 'Northern speculators and Southern state debts: 1790,' *William and Mary Quarterly*, 19 (1962), 30–48; Wilfred E. Binkley, *American political parties* (4th ed., New York, 1962); and Manning J. Dauer, *The Adams Federalists* (Baltimore, Md., 1953), which argues that the party division was between mainly commercial farmers and remote subsistence farmers. In *The American party battle* (New York, 1928), Beard indicated that his orientation was inspired by his reaction to the interpretation of American parties in terms of the states' rights debate and the conflict between strict and loose Constitutional construction (see also Binkley,

Parties, x). But, as Henry Adams wrote in 1882, 'the doctrine of States' rights was but a fragment of republican dogma in 1800' (*John Randolph* [Boston, 1897], 32; see also Dumas Malone, *Jefferson and his time* [Boston, 1948–], III, 395–424).

20 Paul Goodman, *The Democratic-Republicans of Massachusetts* (Cambridge, Mass., 1964), xi; see also William A. Robinson, *Jeffersonian Democracy in New England* (New Haven, Conn., 1916); Anson E. Morse, *The Federalist party in Massachusetts to the year 1800* (Princeton, N.J., 1909); Roland M. Baumann, 'The Democratic Republicans of Philadelphia' (Ph.D. thesis, Pennsylvania State University, 1970); and Norman K. Risjord, 'The Virginia Federalists,' *Journal of Southern History,* 33 (1967), 486–517. Reviewing current scholarship, Risjord comments, 'It seems likely that present and future research will concentrate on the social origins of political conflict,' in all their 'amazing variety'; *The early American party system,* ed. N. K. Risjord (New York, 1969), 2–12.

21 Letters to John Adams, August 16, 1792, and to James A. Bayard, April 1802, *The Works of Alexander Hamilton,* ed. H. C. Lodge, 8 vols. (New York, 1886), VIII, 280–1, 597.

22 Gordon S. Wood, *The creation of the American Republic, 1776–1787* (Chapel Hill, N.C., 1969), 484–5, 562, 615. In Wood's account, the Federalists' 'American science of politics' seems broad enough to include the thoughts of John Taylor. But Taylor, 'the philosopher' or at least the publicist of Jeffersonian Republicanism, attacked not only John Adams' rather un-Federalist thinking but also more orthodox Federalists, even *The Federalist* itself. Taylor did adopt the Federalist-sounding notion that republican government could be adapted to a people pursuing their own interests (Wood, p. 591; see also Lance Gilbert Banning, 'The quarrel with Federalism: a study in the origins and character of Republican thought' [Ph.D. thesis, Washington University, St. Louis, Mo., 1972], 312). But he never shared the Federalist expectation that political virtue would be more evident in government than in society. He took issue with those who overlooked the good potentialities of human nature, and the possibility of suppressing bad ones. See Eugene Tenbroeck Mudge, *The social philosophy of John Taylor of Caroline* (New York, 1939), 10–16; and J. G. A. Pocock, 'Virtue and commerce in the eighteenth century,' *Journal of Interdisciplinary History,* 3 (1972), 133–4.

23 Richard Buel, Jr., *Securing the Revolution: ideology in American politics, 1789–1815* (Ithaca, N.Y., 1972).

24 *Ibid.* xi–xii, 81 (see the review by Eric Foner, *New York Review of Books,* 20 [February 22, 1973], 36); Wood, *Creation,* 15, 604, 606, 608, 615 (cf. 47, 119, 467). The sensitive analysis of Banning's 'Quarrel with Federalism' is also marred by the refusal (pp. 8, 10, 77, 103–6, 413 n.) to consider these substantive moral issues and their psychological foundations. The weakness of this approach is especially clear in the interpretation of foreign policy; trying to place Republican policy in the paradigm of opposition ideology, Banning explains the disparity between the military sense of

opposition ideologists and the faith in peaceful measures of Republican thinkers by pointing to differences in circumstances rather than differences in principles (pp. 349, 319 n. 17). Banning's emphasis on an all-encompassing orthodox ideology stresses common ground rather than distinctions between Republicans and Federalists (pp. 154 n. 44, 172–81; cf. 211). His thesis (summarized in 'Republican ideology and the triumph of the Constitution, 1789 to 1793,' *William and Mary Quarterly*, 3rd ser., 31 [1974], 167–88) is that the essence of Republican thought was a revision of the traditional British opposition appeal to the 'classical theory of balanced government.' But this theory itself was, as Ernest Barker said, a 'barren formula' at its very origins, because it ignored the 'moral training' associated with constitutions. ('Greek political thought and theory in the fourth century,' *The Cambridge Ancient History*, 12 vols. [Cambridge, 1923–39], VI, Chap. 16, pp. 533–4.) As noted above (note 19), Beard's 'realistic' interpretation of American political parties was partly a reaction to a narrow constitutional interpretation.

25 *Pace* Banning, 'Quarrel,' 10.
26 *The Federalist*, No. 72. Tacitus (*The Histories*, IV, vi) called it 'the last infirmity cast off even by the wise.'
27 See Jaffa, *Equality and liberty*, 36–40. On Lincoln's (necessarily post-Jeffersonian) addition of piety to the Jeffersonian elements of American political religion, see the same author's *Crisis of the House Divided* (Seattle, Wash., 1973), 225–43.
28 Quoted in Sundquist, *Dynamics*, 194.

Chapter 2. The Federalist science of politics

1 Bernard Bailyn, *The ideological origins of the American Revolution* (Cambridge, Mass., 1967), 299–301.
2 *Ibid.* 301–19.
3 Gordon S. Wood, *The creation of the American Republic, 1776–1787* (Chapel Hill, N.C., 1969), 197–255, 553–62, 596–600; [Alexander Graydon], *Memoirs of a Life, Chiefly Passed in Pennsylvania, within the Last Sixty Years* (Edinburgh, 1822; first published 1811), 361–6; Noah Webster, Jr., 'A Federal Catechism', *The Little Reader's Assistant* (2nd ed., Hartford, Conn., 1791), 104, 110; but compare [Zephaniah Swift], *The Security of the Rights of Citizens in the State of Connecticut* (Hartford, Conn., 1792), 24–37, where the U.S. Senate is connected with 'property' and the 'aristocratic interest', and the House of Representatives with 'the people.'
4 J. R. Pole, *Political representation in England and the origins of the American Republic* (London, 1966), 224, 342.
5 Hamilton, *Federalist*, Nos. 35 and 36 (see below, note 40). Josiah Bridge suggested that unequal abilities and superior education – both due to unequal providence – produced the best rulers; *A Sermon...Massachusetts, May 27, 1789, Being the Day of General Election* (Boston, 1789), 17.
6 However much Federalists and Republicans differed in their

public pronouncements on deference, both parties relied on it.
Madison thought that the 'great body of those who are both for
and against' the new Constitution 'must follow the judgment of
others, not their own'; ratification would depend on widespread
'confidence' in certain 'leading opinions,' for this was one of those
'subjects to which the capacities of the bulk of mankind are
unequal, and on which they must and will be governed by those
with whom they happen to have acquaintance and confidence.'
Letter to Edmund Randolph, January 10, 1788, *The debates in the
several state conventions, on the adoption of the federal Constitution*, ed.
J. Elliot, 2nd ed., 5 vols. (Philadelphia, 1861), v, 571. Madison did
not have to alter this opinion in order to alter his Federalist
allegiance. When Jefferson sent political pamphlets to be distri-
buted in Virginia, he asked that they be given 'to the most
influential characters among our countrymen, who are only
misled, are candid enough to be open to conviction, and who may
have most effect on their neighbors.' Letter to Colonel James
Monroe, February 11, 1799, *The writings of Thomas Jefferson*, ed.
A. A. Lipscomb and A. E. Bergh, 20 vols. (Washington, D.C.,
1903–5), x, 98. See also Noble E. Cunningham, *The Jeffersonian
Republicans: the formation of party organization 1789–1801* (Chapel
Hill, N.C., 1957), 105; and Thomas P. Abernethy, *Three Virginia
frontiers* (Baton Rouge, La., 1940), 84–5.

7 Pole, *Representation*, 363–4.
8 This is indicated by the contradictory interpretations of 'consensus' historians themselves. For example, to Louis Hartz, in *The
liberal tradition in America* (New York, 1955), the 'liberal formula'
(p. 141) is a Lockean 'entrepreneurial ethos' (p. 126). Federalists
would have been more content with this than Republicans. Indeed,
Hartz's analysis, which follows Tocqueville's, is equally congenial
to Federalism, even while chiding Federalists for their lapses into
Old World conservatism. To Yehoshua Arieli, on the other hand,
Individualism and nationalism in American ideology (Cambridge,
Mass. 1964) are fundamentally Jeffersonian. Thus his difficulty
in comprehending in this picture the politics of Abraham
Lincoln, with whom he says that 'Government as a regulative
force...became an integral part of the Jeffersonian theory' (p.
316). Was not the 'optimistic universalism of Jefferson' (p. 302)
thereby diminished, and the 'Jeffersonian theory' therefore
abandoned?
9 Bailyn, *Origins*, 301.
10 *Ibid.* 48, 59–60, 124; Staughton Lynd, *Intellectual origins of American
radicalism* (London, 1969), 24, 67, 163.
11 Bailyn, *Origins*, 48, 59.
12 *Federalist*, No. 9.
13 *An Introductory Lecture to a Course of Law Lectures* (Philadelphia,
1791), 64–5. Daniel Foster expressed the more traditional view
when he claimed that the nature of man 'would, no doubt, have
led him to some sort of government had sin never entered the

world'; Foster pointed out that angels *did* have government: 'In Heaven there are thrones, dominions, principalities and powers, angels and arch-angels.' *A Sermon...Commonwealth of Massachusetts, May 26, 1790* (Boston, 1790).

14 *Federalist*, Nos. 51, 1, 85, 2 and 10; Martin Diamond, 'The Federalist,' *History of political philosophy*, ed. L. Strauss and J. Cropsey (Chicago, 1972), 631–51.

15 *Federalist*, Nos. 10, 51, 6 and 57; Stanley Rothman, 'Systematic political theory: observations on the group approach,' *American Political Science Review* (1960), 32–3.

16 'A Citizen of the United States,' *Political Sketches, Inscribed to His Excellency, John Adams, Minister Plenipotentiary from the United States to the Court of Great Britain* (London, 1787), No. 2 ('Virtue'); reprinted in *The American Museum*, 2, no. iii (Philadelphia, September 1787), 231.

17 *Defence of the Constitutions...the works of John Adams*, ed. C. F. Adams, 10 vols. (Boston, 1850–56), VI, 206–7.

18 *The Spirit of the Laws*, Book V, chap. ii.

19 *Federalist*, No. 10.

20 *The papers of Alexander Hamilton*, ed. H. C. Syrett and J. E. Cooke (New York, 1961–), V, 85.

21 Madison to James Monroe, October 5, 1786, in Gerald Stourzh, *Alexander Hamilton and the idea of republican government* (Stanford, Calif., 1970), 80.

22 Of course, there were men who supported Federalism while maintaining their allegiance to the political science which Federalism was intended to supersede. There were some Americans who saw the desirability of an effective national government, but failed to see or to adopt the move to a scheme of republican government based on the unreliability of republican virtue. They spoke the language of the republican tradition, insisting on the need for republican virtue, or even moral virtue, the distinction being unknown to many, and contradicted by a few. See, for example, Nathan Strong, *A Sermon...May 13th, 1790* (Hartford, Conn., 1790), 14–15; Timothy Stone, *A Sermon...at Hartford...May 10th, 1792* (Hartford, Conn., 1792), 9–10; Timothy Dwight, *Virtuous Rulers a National Blessing – A Sermon...May 12th, 1791* (Hartford, Conn., 1791) and *A Sermon...7th of July, 1795...Connecticut Society of Cincinnati...* (New Haven, Conn., 1795); and Samuel Williams, *A Discourse...Vermont...October 9th, 1794...General Election* (Rutland, Vt., 1794), 24–5. This language did not set the tone of Federalism in the 1780s and early 1790s. It was more significant in later years, after Federalists suffered the challenge of Republicanism. It even helped some old Federalists into the camp of Jacksonian Democracy. See Marvin Meyers, *The Jacksonian persuasion* (New York, 1960), 164–5.

23 Noah Webster, Jr., *The Little Reader's Assistant* (2nd ed., Hartford, 1791), 120.

24 [William Pitt Beers] ('A Citizen of Connecticut'), *An Address to the*

Legislature and People of the State of Connecticut, On the Subject of dividing the State into Districts for the Election of Representatives in Congress (New Haven, Conn., 1791), 17.

25 *Federalist*, No. 76.

26 *Ibid*. No. 9. Hamilton's fear of sectional rivalries led him to discount the importance of the Madison-Hume model of an enlarged republic. The integrity of 'Publius' was saved by the delegation of the sociological argument to Madison, and Hamilton's preoccupation with energetic government, which was not opposed to but rather complemented Madison's sociology.

27 *Federalist*, Nos. 57 (Madison) and 72 (Hamilton).

28 [John Trenchard and Thomas Gordon], 'Considerations on the restless and selfish Spirit of Man' (No. 40, August 5, 1721), *Cato's Letters*, 4 vols. (6th ed., London, 1755), II, 52–3.

29 The classical notion: Aristotle, *Nicomachean Ethics*, IX, IX.

30 *Federalist*, No. 76.

31 See Herbert J. Storing, 'Introduction,' pp. x–xii, in Charles C. Thach, Jr., *The creation of the Presidency 1775–1789* (Baltimore, Md., 1969; first published 1923).

32 'The Constitutionalist, No. VI,' July 4, 1782, *Papers*, III, 103.

33 *Federalist*, No. 73.

34 *A Sermon...Vermont...October 11th, 1792, Being the Day of General Election* (Rutland, Vt. [1792]), 28.

35 Noble E. Cunningham, Jr., *The Jeffersonian Republicans in power: party operations, 1801–1809* (Chapel Hill, N.C., 1963), 232.

36 Speech on June 5, 1788, *The writings of James Madison*, ed. G. Hunt, 9 vols. (New York, 1900–10), V, 126. Madison's writings of the 1780s must have contributed to – they certainly reflected – the truncation of the meaning of 'candid.'

37 Letters to Jefferson, October 24, 1787, and October 1788, *The papers of Thomas Jefferson*, ed. J. P. Boyd (Princeton, N.J., 1950–), XII, 274–9, XIV, 19.

38 Letter to Jefferson, October 17, 1788, *Papers of Jefferson*, XIV, 16–20. Late in life, Madison interlined the word 'existing' between 'the' and 'Governments' (*ibid*. 22 n. 6), in accord with his subsequent opposition to the continued Federalist use of this formulation of the relationship between power and liberty. (Hamilton was to use remarkably similar language to describe his perception of the political tendencies of the 1790s.) On March 15, 1789, Jefferson responded to Madison's remarks by suggesting that an executive tyranny would come in its turn 'at a remote period' (*ibid*. 661). Three years later he would argue that this period was not so remote.

39 Speech on June 20, 1788, *Writings*, V, 223; compare the interpretation of this speech by Douglass G. Adair, 'The intellectual origins of Jeffersonian Democracy' (Ph.D. thesis, Yale University, 1943), 272. Governor Edmund Randolph had made a similar remark, although applying it to state politicians rather than to 'the people,' on June 15: 'The twenty-six senators...will not be those despera-

does and horrid adventurers which they are represented to be. The state legislatures, I trust, will not forget the duty they owe to their country so far as to choose such men to manage their federal interests.' *Debates in the several state conventions*, ed. Elliot, III, 470–1.

40 Hamilton was more specific than Madison in his estimate of the classes of Americans who would be representatives: they would be those men (namely, 'opulent' or 'moderate proprietors of land,' 'merchants, and...members of the learned professions') whose 'habits of life' had 'been such as to give them those acquired endowments, without which, in a deliberative assembly, the greatest natural abilities are for the most part useless.' (Equivalent strictures applied to members of the executive and judiciary.) Hamilton, like Madison, thought that the 'good sense' of the other classes generally made them sufficiently 'discerning' to see that they were best represented by such men. Hamilton allowed that there were politically able men who might rise from 'every walk of life.' But he guessed that, aside from 'occasional instances,' both state and federal representatives would owe their abilities to the advantages 'of situation.' (*Federalist*, Nos. 35 and 36.)

41 *Federalist*, No. 51.

42 Letter to Jefferson, February 4, 1790, *Papers of Jefferson*, XVI, 150.

43 The phrase is Professor Wood's (*Creation*, Chap. XIII). Perhaps the weaknesses that characterized Federalist rhetoric make the term 'science of politics' more appropriate for Federalism, reserving the more animate 'persuasion' for Jeffersonian Republicanism.

44 *Federalist*, No. 39.

45 August 15, 1789, *Annals of the Congress of the United States*, 42 vols. (Washington, D.C., 1834–56), I, 731. The House of Representatives followed the precedent of the House of Commons in tacitly allowing its debates to be published, without any official authorization. The shorthand writers encountered some censure for their errors, but they were nevertheless generally permitted to sit in the House itself rather than in the gallery. (See the debates of September 26, 1789. and January 15, 1790.) The debates were published in the press, and in a three-volume collection, *The Congressional Register* (New York, 1789–90). See also Donald H. Stewart, 'Jeffersonian journalism: newspaper propaganda and the development of the Democratic-Republican party, 1791–1801' (Ph.D. thesis, Columbia University, 1950), 852.

46 John C. Miller, *The Federalist era* (New York, 1960), 117; see also Robert Allen Rutland, *The ordeal of the Constitution: the Antifederalists and the ratification struggle of 1787–1788* (Norman, Okla., 1966), 34.

47 Perhaps David H. Fischer exaggerates, but not pointlessly, when he points to 'the libertarian language which has dominated American political rhetoric since 1800.' *The revolution of American conservatism* (New York, 1965), 378.

48 W. Paul Adams, 'Republicanism in political rhetoric before 1776,' *Political Science Quarterly*, 85 (1970), 397–421, sketches the genesis of this condition; see also Cecelia M. Kenyon, 'The political theory of the Antifederalists,' Introduction to *The Antifederalists*, ed. C. M. Kenyon (New York, 1966), xxv–vi.

49 Wood, *Creation*, 621.

50 June 10, 1788, *Debates in the several state conventions*, ed. Elliot, III, 222.

51 *Federalist*, Nos. 39, 10, 14 and 63 (original emphasis).

52 Stourzh, *Hamilton*, 49–52.

53 *Federalist*, No. 78; see also No. 17, where the administration of justice is seen to inspire 'popular obedience and attachment' to government.

54 *Defence*; *Works*, V, 453.

55 *Rights of Man*, ed. H. Collins (Harmondsworth, Mdx., 1969), 206, 200.

56 *Federalist*, Nos. 6 and 78.

57 Letter to J. B. Colvin, September 20, 1810, *Writings of Jefferson*, XII, 418–22.

58 Letter to John Jay, May 7, 1800, *The works of Alexander Hamilton*, ed. H. C. Lodge, 8 vols. (New York, 1886), VIII, 459.

59 Harvey C. Mansfield, Jr., *Statesmanship and party government: a study of Burke and Bolingbroke* (Chicago, 1965), 128–32.

60 *Federalist*, No. 1.

61 *Federalist*, No. 10.

62 James P. Scanlan, 'The Federalist and human nature,' *Review of Politics*, 21 (1959), 657–77.

63 But by no means sufficient in the crucial ratification campaign in New York, where the convention voted 30–27 in favor of ratification only after a threat of secession by New York City and eleventh-hour support from several Antifederalists. Young, *Democratic Republicans*, 109–19.

64 Letter to Jefferson, October 24, 1787. *Papers of Jefferson*, XII, 277.

65 Urging credit for Madison's originality, Marvin Meyers has noted that Hume's 'Idea of a Perfect Commonwealth' 'does not touch the crucial Madisonian argument from the number and diversity of social-economic interests.' ('Beyond the sum of the differences: an introduction,' *The mind of the founder* [Indianapolis, 1973], xxix n. 8.) Certainly Madison's appreciation of commerce and commercial motives, whether learned from Hume or not, contributed to his alteration of Hume's own views on parties (Essay I, viii: 'Of Parties in General'), an alteration noticed by Douglass G. Adair, 'That Politics May Be Reduced to a Science: David Hume, James Madison, and the Tenth *Federalist*,' *Huntington Library Quarterly*, 20 (1957), 343–60: 'while James Madison compressed the greater part of Hume's essay on factions into a single sentence, he greatly expanded the quick sketch of the faction from "interest" buried in the middle of the philosopher's analysis.'

66 Speech on June 6, 1787, *The records of the federal convention of 1787*, ed. Max Farrand, 4 vols. (New Haven, Conn., 1966), I, 135–6.

67 This is not to say (as is said by Lee Benson, *Turner and Beard* [Glencoe, Ill., 1960], 102–3, 139) that Madison advanced an economic determinist theory of politics. Men in society, not men in government, were expected to be motivated most commonly and most durably by economic considerations.

68 Joseph Dorfman, *The economic mind in American civilization*, 4 vols. (New York, 1946–59), I, 432.

69 'A Summary View of the Politics of the United States from the Close of the War to the Year 1794,' *Porcupine's Works*, 12 vols. (London, 1801), I, 91 (original emphasis).

70 Speaking of his massive *Defence of the Constitutions of Government of the United States* (1787); Letter to James Warren, January 9, 1787, *Warren–Adams Letters*, 2 vols. (Massachusetts Historical Society, 1917–25), II, 281.

71 *Defence*, 'Conclusion;' *Works*, VI, 218 (cf. 241, 245, 274, and 402–3).

72 'Discourses,' II, IV, V, VI and VII (*Works*, VI, 232–53).

73 Since all three methods were essentially passionate, the last had no truer relation to honor than the first two: 'no appetite in human nature is more universal than that for honor.'

74 'Discourses,' *Works*, VI, 263.

75 'Discourses,' VI (*Works*, VI, 249). The motto of these 'Discourses' was '*Felix, quem faciunt aliena pericola cautum.*' But the overwhelming majority of Americans had little but praise for the French Revolution in 1791, when Adams' 'Discourses' were published.

76 *Correspondence between the Hon. John Adams and the Late William Cunningham, Esq., beginning in 1803, and ending in 1812*, ed. E. M. Cunningham (Boston, 1823), Letter VI (February 24, 1804). Adams to Jefferson, November 15, 1813, *The Adams–Jefferson letters*, ed. L. J. Cappon, 2 vols. (Chapel Hill, 1959), II, 397–402.

77 'It, on the contrary, sometimes increases them, by giving them exercise.' Therefore, 'The increase and dissemination of knowledge, instead of rendering unnecessary the checks of emulation and the balances of rivalry in the orders of society and constitution of government, augment the necessity of both.' 'Discourses,' XIII (*Works*, VI, 274–6).

78 'Discourses,' VIII (*Works*, VI, 256–9). Thus, Adams remarks, the Revolution of 1688 was almost spoilt when James II was seized.

79 'Discourses,' XXXI, XX, VII and XXIII (*Works*, VI, 394 ff., 323, 254, 341).

80 Letter to Thomas Jefferson, July 29, 1791, *Works*, VIII, 507; John R. Howe, Jr., *The changing political thought of John Adams* (Princeton, N.J., 1966), 178, 182–8.

81 Letters to John Taylor, April 1814, *Works*, VI, 473–4.

82 *Ibid.*; see also 429, 455, 469. For Adams, as for Hobbes and Locke, the principle of consent is essential to government; for Aristotle, it is a kind of test, to show the goodness of a constitution, but the

essence of a constitution is the rule or regime it tries to impose: *Politics* 1270b20, 1272b30, 1296b15, 1309b15.

83 Howe, *Political thought*, 180–2.

84 *Federalist*, No. 39. In No. 68, Hamilton was obliged to refute the charge that the Presidency was a monarchical institution.

85 Letter to Adams, November 13, 1787, quoted in Dumas Malone, *Jefferson and his time* (Boston, 1948–), II, 165.

86 Thach, *Creation of Presidency*, 85–7.

87 Letter to James A. Bayard, April 1802, *Works*, VIII, 597. Bower Aly, *The rhetoric of Alexander Hamilton* (New York, 1941), contends that Hamilton's rhetoric was properly adapted to his audience in 1788. However true this was then, it was certainly false thereafter. Donald F. Swanson, *The origins of Hamilton's fiscal policies* (Gainesville, Fl., 1963), 76 ff., suggests that Hamilton scored rhetorical success in the 1790s by producing the illusion that his financial system was drawn up on orthodox English lines. Although this may have boosted Hamilton's standing in financial circles, it was not well calculated to endear him to most Americans. Good politics demands more than good economics. (Cf. Swanson, *Origins*, 83 n. 16).

Chapter 3. The confidence of unchallenged Federalism

1 See Madison's speeches of September 4 and 5, 1787, in *The records of the federal convention of 1787*, ed. Max Farrand, 4 vols. (New Haven, Conn., 1966), II, 500, 513. Edward Channing, 'Washington and parties, 1789–1797,' *Massachusetts Historical Society Proceedings*, 47 (1913), 35–52, takes note of some of the difficulties facing Washington's administration because of the absence of party.

2 *Federalist*, No. 26.

3 The more usual portrait of Federalism as a reactionary appeal to the stability of an organic society is drawn mainly from materials that appeared after 1795 at the earliest, as in the case of James M. Banner, *To the Hartford convention: the Federalists and the origins of party politics in Massachusetts, 1789–1815* (New York, 1967). Thus, Banner accurately reports that Federalists of the old school – the 'politicians' – were deeply committed to effective government as an 'essential guarantor of public order and happiness' (pp. 127, 147), whereas Massachusetts Federalism in the years before the Hartford Convention 'gained inspiration from the native revolution of 1776,' with its 'conspiratorial explanation' of government (pp. xi, 22–52).

4 Something of this relationship, as it existed in the early 1780s, in the precursors of the nationalist (Federalist) movement of the late 1780s, can be seen in Merrill Jensen, 'The idea of a national government during the American Revolution,' *Political Science Quarterly*, 58 (1943), 366–78, and *The new nation* (New York, 1950), 43–84; and E. James Ferguson, 'The nationalists of 1781–1783 and the economic interpretation of the Constitution,' *Journal of*

American History, 56 (1969), 241–61, and *The power of the purse* (Chapel Hill, N.C., 1961).

5 [John Jay], *The Charge of Chief Justice Jay to the Grand Juries on the Eastern Circuit* (Portsmouth, New Hampshire, [1790]), 14.

6 Edward Gray, *An Oration Delivered July 5, 1790* (Boston, 1790), 12.

7 Letter to Henry Lee, May 8, 1825, *The Writings of Thomas Jefferson*, ed. A. A. Lipscomb and A. E. Bergh, 20 vols. (Washington, D.C., 1903–5), XVI, 118.

8 Josiah Bridge, *A Sermon...May 27, 1789, Being the Day of General Election* (Boston, 1789), 51.

9 Timothy Dwight, *A Sermon...7th of July, 1795...Connecticut Society of Cincinnati...* (New Haven, Conn., 1795) and Nathan Strong, *A Sermon...May 13th, 1790* (Hartford, Conn., 1790), 14–15.

10 Israel Evans, *A Sermon, Delivered at Concord...New Hampshire, at the Annual Election...* (Concord, N.H., 1791), 24, 31–2.

11 'Hermes' [Caesar Rodney], *The Oracle of Liberty, and Mode of Establishing a Free Government* (Philadelphia, [1791]), 8, 23.

12 *An Oration, Delivered at Worcester, on the Fourth of July, 1791* (Worcester, Mass., 1791), 4–16. James Truslow Adams, *New England in the Republic, 1776–1852* (Boston, 1927), 193, notes the 'three generations from shirt sleeves to shirt sleeves' tradition in New England in the 1790s.

13 'An American' [Noah Webster], *The Revolution in France* (New York, 1794), 61–2.

14 William Linn, *The Blessings of America. A Sermon...on the Fourth of July, 1791...at the Request of the Tammany Society, or Columbian Order* (New York, 1791), 17.

15 Thomas Hobbes, *Leviathan*, ed. C. B. Macpherson (Harmondsworth, Mdx., 1968), 188 (Chap. 13, last paragraph).

16 William Hillhouse, Jr., *A Dissertation, in Answer to a late LECTURE on the Political State of America...January 12th, 1789* (New Haven, [1789]), 5.

17 Bridge, *Sermon*,7; see Leo Strauss, *Natural right and history* (Chicago, 1953), 184, and above, p. 22.

18 In a letter published in the *Royal Danish America Gazette*, October 17, 1772, *The Papers of Alexander Hamilton*, ed. H. C. Syrett and J. E. Cooke (New York, 1961–), I, 34–8.

19 Hillhouse, *Dissertation*, 18.

20 [John Quincy Adams], 'Publicola,' II, in *The Writings of John Quincy Adams*, ed. W. C. Ford, 7 vols. (New York, 1913–17), I, 72.

21 Hillhouse, *Dissertation*, 3–4.

22 William King Atkinson, *An Oration; Delivered at Dover, New Hampshire, on the Fourth of July, 1791* (Dover, N.H., 1791), 18.

23 Gordon Wood, *The creation of the American Republic, 1776–1787* (Chapel Hill, N.C., 1969), especially Chaps. 2, 3, 10, 13 and 15. The Federalists' substitution of economic virtues for republican virtues made their system less open-ended and indeterminate than Wood suggests (pp. 604–15).

24 *Papers*, I, 67; compare *Federalist*, No. 26.

25 *Second Treatise*, V (Section 34).
26 *Democracy in America*, Vol. II, Part II, Chap. 11. It is not surprising that *Robinson Crusoe* was a best-seller in America, with no fewer than thirty-three editions (many abridged, two in German) from 1787 through 1800: almost three times as many as any other novel (there were twelve editions of *Tom Jones* in this period). (Information derived from Shipton's index of *Early American Imprints*.) On Defoe and the Protestant ethic, see Thomas S. Schrock, 'Considering Crusoe,' *Interpretation*, 1 (1970), 76–106, 169–232.
27 Hillhouse, *Dissertation*, 3–4. See also [Zephaniah Swift], *The Security of the Rights of Citizens in the State of Connecticut Considered* (Hartford, Conn., 1792), 24.
28 *An Oration, Delivered July 4th, 1789...* (Boston, 1789), 12.
29 *An Oration on the Political Situation of the United States of America, in the Year 1789*, in *The Miscellaneous Works of Colonel Humphreys* (New York, 1790), 343. Humphreys himself promoted American prosperity by introducing merino sheep into New England, when he was returning to America in 1802, on the ship *Perseverance*.
30 Hillhouse, *Dissertation*, 18–19.
31 Isaac Keith, *The Friendly Influence of Religion and Virtue on the Prosperity of a Nation* (Charleston, S.C., 1789), 3.
32 Humphreys, *Oration*, 334–5.
33 Keith, *Friendly Influence*, 13.
34 *The Writings of Laco* (Boston, 1789), 14–15. These articles first appeared in the *Massachusetts Centinel* in February and March, 1789.
35 Letter to Henry Knox, April 7, 1790, *American Historical Association Report*, 1896 (1897), 781.
36 *An oration, Delivered to the Society of the Cincinnati, in...Massachusetts, July 4, 1789* (Boston, 1789), 16.
37 Israel Evans, *A Sermon, Delivered at Concord...New Hampshire, at the Annual Election...* (Concord, N.H., 1791), 32–3.
38 *Oration*, 16–18.
39 Perry Miller, 'The moral and psychological roots of American resistance' in *The reinterpretation of the American Revolution*, ed. J. P. Greene (New York, 1968), 256–68.
40 *Oration*, 9.
41 *Oration*, 3. See also William Jay, *The life of John Jay: with selections from his correspondence and miscellaneous papers*, 2 vols. (New York, 1833), II, 292–3.
42 Ferguson, *Power of the purse*, Chap. 8.
43 Letter to Henry Knox, April 7, 1790 (cited above, note 35).
44 Letter to Washington, July 3, 1787, *Works*, VIII, 175.
45 *Federalist*, No. 26.
46 *Oration*, 336, 343, 346.
47 Louis-Guillaume Otto to Armand Marc, August 12, 1790, 'A French Diplomat's View of Congress, 1790,' tr. M. M. O'Dwyer, *William and Mary Quarterly*, third series, 21 (1964), 442.
48 Whitwell, *Oration*, 7–8, 10.

49 *Charge to Grand Juries* (above, note 5), 13–14. In his *Federalist* papers, Jay apparently attempted to transcend the limits of a rhetoric of self-interest. He depended on a set of nationalistic sentiments to take precedence over the interestedness of Americans, in the same way as John Adams expected the universal ambition for distinction to predominate. Patriotism or nationalism was to be based on Americans' gratitude to Providence for the blessings of America. The deficiency of this notion would seem to be shown by the miscarriage of Hamilton's proposal of Christian Constitutional Society clubs. Gerald Stourzh, *Alexander Hamilton and the idea of republican government* (Stanford, Calif., 1970), 107, 125.

50 Letter to George Washington, September 21, 1788, *Life of Jay*, II, 195.

51 Letter to Thomas Jefferson, July 14, 1786, *ibid.* II, 189.

52 Letter to George Washington, August 15, 1786, *ibid.* I, 247.

53 *An Oration Delivered July 5, 1790* (Boston, 1790), 9–15.

54 Atkinson, *Oration*, 13–14.

55 Bangs, *Oration*, 4–0.

56 *An Oration... July 4th, 1793, at... Boston* (Boston, 1793).

57 *Gratulatory Address... July 5th, 1790...* (Boston, 1790), 10–11.

58 See above, p. 29.

59 *Letters on the Opposition to the New Constitution in Virginia* (Richmond, Va., 1789), 17, 47. Reprinted from the *Virginia Independent Chronicle*, December 1788 to July 1789.

60 *Writings of Laco*, 14–15.

61 Letter to Jefferson, October 27, 1786, *Life of Jay*, II, 190.

62 Hillhouse, *Dissertation*, 19.

63 Linn, *Blessings of America*, 30.

64 Evans, *Sermon*, 11.

65 *An Oration... July 4th 1791... Published at the Request of the Pennsylvania Society of the Cincinnati* (Philadelphia, 1791), 20.

66 Hillhouse, *Dissertation*, 19.

67 *Oration*, 12. It was an accepted axiom in eighteenth-century political economy that a rapidly growing population was a concomitant of national wealth. But there was disagreement about the correct means of encouraging population in America. William Barton, in his *Observations on the Progress of Population* (Philadelphia, 1791; reprinted in *Transactions of the American Philosophical Society* [1793], 25–62) followed Jefferson's *Notes on Virginia* by emphasizing the growth in population apart from immigration; and agricultural life was alleged to be most conducive to this growth. Until ideological factors intervened, Federalists were more keen to encourage population by immigration; see 'A Proprietor of Lands on the Sioto,' *Address to the Inhabitants of Alexandria, and other Sea-Ports in the United States of America* (n.p., 1790), 13, as well as the writings discussed in the text. See also Stourzh, *Hamilton*, 123.

68 *Oration*, 343–5.

69 'To the State Societies of the Cincinnati,' *Proceedings of the Cincinnati, By Their Delegates in General Meeting Convened at Philadelphia, May 1790* (New York, 1790), 5.

70 *Gratulatory Address*, 14.

71 Bangs, *Oration*, 15–16.

72 *Blessings of America*, 7, 20–1, 30.

73 *Oration*, 16–17.

74 Thomas Crafts, Jr., *An Oration...July 4th, 1791...* (Boston, 1791), 13.

75 *Oration*, 20–2.

76 Robert Montford, *To the Planters, Tradesmen, Shopkeepers, and Other Voters of Chatham County* (Broadside, Savannah, Ga., 1789).

77 [William Pitt Beers] ('A Citizen of Connecticut'), *An Address to the Legislature and People of the State of Connecticut...* (New Haven, Conn., 1791), 30.

78 *Observations on the Present State of Landed Property in America* (New York? 1792), 1.

79 See Noah Webster, Jr., 'The Farmer's Catechism,' *The Little Reader's Assistant* (2nd ed., Hartford, Conn., 1791), 129–30.

80 Letter to Henry Knox, April 7, 1790 (cited above, note 35).

81 *Works*, III, 310. (The Report, prepared for the House of Representatives, was published in Philadelphia.)

82 *Federalist*, No. 10. In their electioneering, Federalists could appeal to the tendency of their policies to enrich all 'the various classes of the community.' 'A Federalist,' *To the Independent Electors of Pennsylvania* (Broadside, Philadelphia, 1792).

83 On the partial success of this rhetoric, consider the note by Julian P. Boyd, *The Papers of Thomas Jefferson* (Princeton, 1950–), XIX, 123.

84 *An Enquiry Into the Principles on which a Commercial System for the United States of America Should be Founded, &c.* (Philadelphia, 1787), 9, 45.

85 *An Address to an Assembly of the Friends of American Manufacturers* (Philadelphia, 1787), 7–8.

86 *Ibid.* 8, 12, 29–30; in [Coxe], *Reflexions on the State of the Union* (Philadelphia, 1792), 38, the 'virtue and fortitude, which qualify a nation for republican government' are identified with the zealous establishment of public credit.

87 [Coxe] ('An American Citizen'), *An Examination of the Constitution for the United States...* (Philadelphia, 1788), 16.

88 [Coxe] ('A Citizen of the United States'), *Observations on the Agriculture, Manufactures and Commerce of the United States* (New York, 1789), 7, 6, 18–19.

89 *The Works of Alexander Hamilton*, ed. H. C. Lodge, 8 vols. (New York, 1886), III, 297, 306, 295, 310, 317, 324, 352–3, 356.

90 Even today we are reminded of this state of affairs by the phenomenon of the American suburb: see Daniel Elazar, 'Are we a nation of cities?' *A nation of cities*, ed. R. A. Goldwin (Chicago, 1968), 125; cf. William Hazlitt, 'Merry England,' *Essays and Characters*, ed. S. Williams (London, Thomas Nelson & Sons Ltd., n.d.), 64.

91 *Works*, III, 327, 362–3, 351–2, 359, 361. In his draft of Washington's Farewell Address of 1796, Hamilton referred to the first importance of agriculture, but also suggested the establishment of boards to promote both agriculture and manufactures, considering both of them as objects of 'public patronage and care.' *Ibid.* VII, 170–2.

92 *Reflexions*, 7–11, 35. See also Adams, *New England in the Republic*, 195.

93 *Works*, III, 336–7, 346–8.

94 'First Report on Public Credit,' January 14, 1790, *Works*, II, 52–63. (The federal government's issue of paper money, expressly forbidden to the states, was not deemed constitutional until 1871.) Coxe estimated that the public certificates raised the quantity of circulating medium from £3 million to £18 million. *Reflexions*, 8.

95 Hillhouse, *Dissertation*, 19.

96 *A Discourse, Delivered at Ashburnham, July 4th, 1796, at the Request of the Militia Officers...* (Leominster, Mass., 1796).

97 *A Sermon on Temporal and Spiritual Salvation* (Philadelphia, 1790).

98 *Blessings of America*, 18. Linn adapted Psalms lxxviii. 55. 'It was the Lord who conducted to this place the original settlers, supported them under all their difficulties, *cast out the heathen before them, and divided them an inheritance by line, and made them to dwell in their tents.*' (*Ibid.* 24.)

99 *A Sermon...Massachusetts...May 25, 1791* (Boston, 1791), 5–7, 33.

100 John Woodhull, *A Sermon, For the Day of Publick Thanksgiving, Appointed by the President, On Account of the Establishment of the New Constitution, &c., November 26, 1789* (Trenton, N.J., 1790), 23–4. See also Chandler Robbins, *Sermon*, 31–2.

101 Atkinson, *Oration*, 19.

102 *Friendly Influence*, 3–23.

103 *Oration*, 11–12.

104 *Oration*, 5, 9, 20, 25.

105 In addition to the sentiments of Franco-American solidarity noticed above, see Evans, *Sermon*, 32; Gray, *Oration*, 16; Atkinson, *Oration*, 16–17; Crafts, *Oration*, 13–14; Porter, *Oration*, 15–17; Linn, *Blessings of America*, 18–21, 30–4; Woodhull, *Sermon*, 13; [Swift], *Security*, 31–3; and Jay to Washington, September 23, 1791, *Life of Jay*, II, 206. See also Joseph Dorfman, *The economic mind in American civilization*, 4 vols. (New York, 1946–59), I, 286; and Benjamin W. Labaree, *Patriots and partisans: the merchants of Newburyport, 1764–1815* (Cambridge, Mass., 1962), 107–10.

Chapter 4. The Federalist practice of politics and the origins of the Republican party, 1789–92

1 William Maclay, *Sketches of debate in the first Senate of the United States, in 1789–90–91*, ed. G. W. Harris (Harrisburg, Pa., 1880), 38–43.

2 John C. Miller, *The Federalist era* (New York, 1960), 9–10, 77 (cf. 99).

3 Letters of December 8 and 12, *The papers of Thomas Jefferson*, ed.
   J. P. Boyd (Princeton, 1950–), XIV, 339, 352.
4 Letter to Samuel Powel, February 5, 1789, *The writings of George
   Washington*, ed. J. C. Fitzpatrick, 39 vols. (Washington, D.C.,
   1931–44), XXX, 195.
5 Letter to George Richards Minot, April 4, 1789, *Works of Fisher
   Ames*, ed. S. Ames, 2 vols. (Boston, 1854), I, 32–3.
6 John R. Howe, Jr., *The changing political thought of John Adams*
   (Princeton, N.J., 1966), 178–9; James H. Hutson, 'John Adams'
   title campaign,' *New England Quarterly*, 41 (1968), 35.
7 *The writings of James Madison*, ed. G. Hunt, 9 vols. (New York,
   1900–10), V, 355 n., 369 n. and 372 n.
8 Letter to Minot, May 27, 1789, *Works*, I, 46.
9 William Smith to Gabriel Manigault, June 7, 1789, 'South Carolina
   Federalist Correspondence 1789–1797', ed. U. B. Phillips, *American Historical Review*, 14 (1909), 776–90.
10 William Rogers, *An Oration, Delivered July 4, 1789 . . .* (Philadelphia,
   1789), 10.
11 [Edward Church] ('A Gentleman'), *The Dangerous Vice* ———
   (Boston, 1789), 12–13.
12 Howe, *Political thought of Adams*, 207; Alexander DeConde, *The
   quasi war* (New York, 1966), 260, 267.
13 Letter to Joseph Winniston, June 20, 1790, *The papers of John Steele*,
   ed. H. M. Wagstaff, 2 vols. (Raleigh, N.C., 1924), I, 64–5.
14 Who was in one way or another the important broker in the deal
   that he thought he was. See Kenneth R. Bowling, 'Dinner at
   Jefferson's: a note on Jacob E. Cooke's 'The Compromise of 1790',
   and the rebuttal by Cooke, *William and Mary Quarterly*, third series,
   28 (1971), 629–48. Cooke shows that the two issues could have been
   resolved independently of each other, and therefore without
   Jefferson's interference. But Bowling suggests that residence
   might have continued to be a political football if it had not been
   agreed to tie its settlement to assumption. This suggestion seems
   reasonable. Perhaps it was the more partisan and less compromis-
   ing character of national politics after 1791, remarked by neither
   Bowling nor Cooke, that actually guaranteed the 'Compromise of
   1790,' contrary to the expectations of all the architects of that
   compromise. After 1791, party solidarity did not leave much space
   for the kinds of maneuvers that would have been necessary to
   rejuggle the residence coalition.
15 Louis-Guillaume Otto to Armand Marc, July 12, 1790, 'A French
   Diplomat's View of Congress, 1790,' tr. M. M. O'Dwyer, *William
   and Mary Quarterly*, third series, 21 (1964), 438–9.
16 Letter to Thomas Dwight, June 11, 1790, *Works*, I, 79; and Letter
   to Minot, June 23, 1790, *ibid.* 83. For Ames, assumption was the
   great measure, as part of Hamilton's fiscal system; residence the
   little one.
17 *Federalist*, No. 10; *Annals of the Congress of the United States*, 42 vols.
   (Washington, D.C., 1834–56), I, 280–1. Even Tench Coxe, who had

not been a Patriot in the Revolutionary conflict, expressed anonymous support for the threat of such retaliation: *A Brief Examination of Lord Sheffield's Observations on the Commerce of the United States of America* (Philadelphia, 1791), 48. On Madison's disappointment with Congressional proceedings see Richard Allen Rutland, *The ordeal of the Constitution: the Antifederalists and the ratification struggle of 1787–1788* (Norman, Okla., 1966), 283, 310.

18 Letters to Minot, May 16 and July 2, 1789, *Works*, I, 38–9, 59; *Annals of Congress*, I, 253–4.

19 Lee to Madison, April 3, 1790, *Writings of Madison*, VI, 10 n.; Monroe to Madison, July 2, 1790, *The writings of James Monroe*, ed. S. M. Hamilton, 9 vols. (New York, 1898–1903), I, 207.

20 Alfred F. Young, *The Democratic Republicans of New York* (Chapel Hill, N.C., 1967), 345–7; Miller, *Federalist era*, 48; Otto to Marc, May 20, 1790, *loc. cit.* 429; Lance Gilbert Banning, 'The quarrel with Federalism: a study in the origins and character of Republican thought' (Ph.D. thesis, Washington University, 1972), 238–9, 249. Assumption was made more acceptable in New York by an understanding that New York's debt to the Union would be ignored (Young, *Democratic Republicans*, 175–6). It was generally favored by South Carolina interests in the first place. In Virginia, Monroe judged that 'a satisfactory adjustment' of the residence affair would make assumption 'more palatable.' Letter to James Madison, July 25, 1790, *Writings of Monroe*, I, 215.

21 Joseph S. Davis, *Essays on the earlier history of American corporations*, 2 vols. (Cambridge, Mass., 1917), I, 286. Bray Hammond, *Banks and politics in America* (Princeton, N.J., 1957), 149, remarks that at the end of the eighteenth century 'Philadelphia was a city of great wealth, but New York was a city of enterprise.' E. James Ferguson, *The power of the purse* (Chapel Hill, N.C., 1961), 258, refers to New York City as 'the national center of speculation.'

22 With symbolic propriety, only after the new government removed from New York to its temporary residence in Philadelphia – equally a financial center, but also the home of the American Philosophical Society, and the birthplace of the Declaration of Independence – did the political divisions become party divisions. See the comparable findings of Mary P. Ryan, 'Party formation in the United States Congress, 1789 to 1796,' *William and Mary Quarterly*, third series, 28 (1791), 538–9; and H. James Henderson, 'Quantitative approaches to party formation in the United States Congress,' *ibid.* 30 (1973), 316.

23 Vernon G. Setser, *The commercial reciprocity policy of the United States 1774–1829* (Philadelphia, 1937), 99–100.

24 This and the next paragraph have been shaped by my reading of Charles R. Ritcheson, *Aftermath of the Revolution; British policy toward the United States 1783–1795* (Dallas, Tex., 1969), Chap. 1; Samuel Flagg Bemis, *Jay's Treaty* (rev. ed. New Haven, Conn., 1962), Chap. 2 and pp. 260, 271–2; Alexander DeConde, *Entangling alliance: politics and diplomacy under George Washington* (Durham,

N.C., 1958), Chap. 5; Felix Gilbert, *To the farewell address: ideas of early American foreign policy* (Princeton, N.J., 1961), Chap. 3; Jerald A. Combs, *The Jay Treaty* (Berkeley, Calif., 1970), Chaps. 1–2; Paul A. Varg, *Foreign policies of the founding fathers* (Ann Arbor, Mich., 1963), Chaps. 5–7; Albert Hall Bowman, *The struggle for neutrality: Franco-American diplomacy during the Federalist era* (Knoxville, Tenn., 1974), Chaps. 1–2; Gilbert L. Lycan, *Alexander Hamilton and American foreign policy: a design for greatness* (Norman, Okla., 1970); Setser, *Commercial reciprocity*, 101–22.

25 See Ames to Minot, May 29, 1787, *Works*, I, 49–50. Ames says that Madison, though perspicuous, influential and respectable, is 'too much attached to his theories, for a politician... He adopts his maxims as he finds them in books, and with too little regard to the actual state of things.' Of course, there are books that force 'the actual state of things' upon their readers, and Federalists were no less theoretical than Republicans, they only held different theories.

26 Banning, 'Quarrel,' 207, 247–8.

27 Letter to James Madison, February 27, 1790, *Letters of Benjamin Rush*, ed. L. H. Butterfield, 2 vols. (Princeton, N.J., 1951), I, 539; Letter to John Adams, April 13, 1790, *ibid.* 569. See also Harry Marlin Tinkcom, *The Republicans and Federalists in Pennsylvania, 1790–1801* (Philadelphia, 1950), 28–30.

28 Young, *Democratic Republicans*, 180.

29 Claude M. Newlin, *The life and writings of Hugh Henry Brackenridge* (Princeton, N.J., 1932), 125–9; Letter to Tench Coxe, September 1794, *ibid.* 163. Thomas P. Abernethy, *The South in the new nation 1789–1819* (Baton Rouge, La., 1961), 218, points out that 'the rum distillers of Massachusetts bore the brunt of the tax.'

30 *American State Papers, Finance* (Washington, D.C., 1832–4), I, 90–1; *Annals of Congress*, II, 1867; see also Delbert H. Gilpatrick, *Jeffersonian Democracy in North Carolina* (New York, 1931), 48–9.

31 Albert J. Beveridge, *John Marshall*, 4 vols. (Boston, 1916–19), II, 69–70.

32 Curtis P. Nettels, 'The American merchant and the Constitution,' *Publications of the Colonial Society of Massachusetts*, 34 (1938), 35.

33 'A Citizen of Philadelphia,' *A Plea for the Poor Soldiers* (New Haven, Conn., 1790); *Letters on the Opposition to the New Constitution in Virginia* (Richmond, Va., 1789), 15. See also Samuel Stillman, *An Oration, Delivered July 4th, 1789...* (Boston, 1789), 11; James Wilson, *A Charge Delivered...to the Grand Jury...Richmond...the 23rd Day of May, 1791* (Richmond, Va., 1791), 29; and Harry Ammon, 'The formation of the Republican party in Virginia, 1789–1796,' *Journal of Southern History*, 19 (1953), 289 n. 16. There were those who complained that Hamilton's funding, far from being an inequitable windfall to the present creditors, had actually been too hard on them, because of the lowering of the rates of interest payable; e.g. *The Memorial of the Publick Creditors, Citizens of the State of New Jersey* (Trenton, 1790); and *The Memorial of the*

Public Creditors Who Are Citizens of the Commonwealth of Pennsylvania (Philadelphia, 1790). Republicans claimed that this adjustment proved that a strict adherence to the letter of the law was not an advantage of Hamilton's plan; he justified it by pointing to the greater security of funded paper. *Works*, VIII, 410.

34 'First Report on the Public Credit,' January 14, 1790, *The Works of Alexander Hamilton*, ed. H. C. Lodge, 8 vols. (New York, 1886), II, 57–63.

35 Otto to Marc, January 12, 1790, *loc. cit.* 414.

36 Douglas S. Freeman, *George Washington*, 7 vols. (New York, 1948–54; vol. 7 [by J. A. Carroll and M. W. Ashworth], 1957), VI, between pp. 77 and 78; 286–7; letter to Moustier, December 3, 1790, *Papers of Jefferson*, XVIII, 119; C. Gore to R. King, October 23, 1790, *The life and correspondence of Rufus King*, ed. C. R. King, 6 vols. (New York, 1894–1900), I, 393–4; Young, *Democratic Republicans*, 186; Gilpatrick, *Jeffersonian Democracy*, 52; *To the Free Electors of the City of New York...* (Broadside, 1790); O. G. Libby, 'Political factions in Washington's administrations,' *The Quarterly Journal of the University of North Dakota*, 3 (1913), 300–1; Tinkcom, *Republicans and Federalists*, 47.

37 *Annals of Congress*, II, 1956. See above, Chapter 1, n. 19.

38 *The letters of Richard Henry Lee*, ed. J. C. Ballagh, 2 vols. (New York, 1911–14), II, 541–2; Noble E. Cunningham, Jr., *The Jeffersonian Republicans: the formation of party organization, 1789–1801* (Chapel Hill, N.C., 1957), 8–9.

39 An imaginative account of the political aspects of this journey is offered by Young, *Democratic Republicans*, 196–201.

40 Letter to Colonel Monroe, July 10, 1791, *The writings of Thomas Jefferson*, ed. A. A. Lipscomb and A. E. Bergh, 20 vols. (Washington, D.C., 1903–5), VIII, 208.

41 *Memoirs of the administrations of Washington and John Adams*, ed. G. Gibbs, 2 vols. (New York, 1846), I, 68–9.

42 Letters to Dwight, October 30, 1791, and to Minot, November 30, 1791 (a 'Dear Sir' letter, meant to be read by others), *Works*, I, 100–3.

43 *Annals of Congress*, III, 179–80.

44 Letter to Archibald Stuart, December 23, 1791, *Writings*, VIII, 276. Jefferson's introduction of 1818 to the *Anas* paints a misleading picture of his discovery of Federalist monarchism in early 1790. (See Dumas Malone, *Jefferson and his time* [Boston, 1948–], II, 338; Young, *Democratic Republicans*, 165; and Leonard D. White, *The Federalists* [New York, 1948], 223 n. 3.) His chronology was more accurate in his letter to A. H. Rowan, September 26, 1798, *Writings*, X, 60: 'The system of alarm and jealousy which has been so powerfully played off in England has been mimicked here, not entirely without success. The most long sighted politician could not, *seven years ago*, have imagined that the people of this wide extended country could have been enveloped in such delusion, and made so much afraid of themselves and their own power as to surrender it spontaneously to those who are manoeuvring them

into a form of government, the principle branches of which may be beyond their control.' (Emphasis mine.)

45 Carl E. Prince, *New Jersey's Jeffersonian Republicans* (Chapel Hill, N.C., 1967), 11; William A. Robinson, *Jeffersonian Democracy in New England* (New Haven, Conn., 1916), 7–9. See also John H. Wolfe, *Jeffersonian Democracy in South Carolina* (Chapel Hill, N.C., 1940), 67–70; Gilpatrick, *Jeffersonian Democracy in North Carolina*, 54–62; Lisle A. Rose, *Prologue to democracy: the Federalists in the South, 1789–1800* (Lexington, Ky., 1968), 27–35; Tinkcom, *Republicans and Federalists*, 52–55; Raymond Walters, Jr., *Alexander James Dallas* (Philadelphia, 1943), 35–43; and Alfred F. Young, 'The Mechanics and the Jeffersonians: New York, 1789–1801,' *Labor History*, 5 (1964), 194. Ammon, 'Republican party,' and Young, 'Mechanics,' 195, and *Democratic Republicans*, stress the importance of foreign policy issues in the alteration of 'the republican interest' into a more widespread 'republican movement' in Virginia and New York. However, Young also notices the significance of Robert R. Livingston's opposition to Hamilton's program. The delay of partisan activity in Virginia was probably influenced by the Virginia Republican leaders' lengthy attempts to secure Washington's allegiance. When it did come, there was no difficulty (*pace* Ammon) inherent in the fiscal issue which prevented its being used there, as is clear from the publications of John Taylor in 1793 and 1794. (Approved by Jefferson and Madison; see Cunningham, *Republicans: party organization*, 54–7.) Taylor's *Examination of the Late Proceedings in Congress*... was first published in March 1793, not, as Ammon says, in late 1793.

46 *Annals of Congress*, II, 1867; III, 531.

47 *Works*, VIII, 250–64.

48 *The papers of Alexander Hamilton*, ed. H. C. Syrett and J. E. Cooke (New York, 1961–), XI, 559.

49 *The Politicks and Views of a Certain Party Displayed* (n.p., 1792), 28–9.

50 *Works*, VIII, 280–1.

51 Cunningham, *Republicans: party organization*, 45–9; Young, *Democratic Republicans*, 330.

52 Letters to Thomas Jefferson, December 8, 1788, and March 29, 1789, *Writings of Madison*, V, 310, 334.

53 J. A. Carroll, 'American newspapers and editorial opinion, 1789–93,' in Freeman, *Washington*, VI, 393–413, from which much of the above account is gathered.

54 Cunningham, *Republicans: party organization*, 29–31, 35–45.

55 Henry McGilbert Wagstaff, *Federalism in North Carolina, the James Sprunt Historical Publications*, 9 (Chapel Hill, N.C., 1910), 24.

56 Letter to Thomas Dwight, December 31, 1792, *Works*, I, 126; see also Monroe to Jefferson, July 17, 1792, *Writings of Monroe*, I, 239.

57 Letter to T. M. Randolph, November 16, 1792, *Writings*, VIII, 439–40. Jefferson's report was a little rosy, for seven of the thirteen (not eleven) Congressmen-elect in Pennsylvania seem to have been blessed with nomination by both party tickets, and the other six

were three from each ticket. Tinkcom, *Republicans and Federalists*, 65–6.

58 Letter to Thomas Pinckney, December 3, 1792, *Writings*, VIII, 443–4.

59 Banning, 'Quarrel,' 280–1; Donald H. Stewart, 'Jeffersonian journalism: newspaper propaganda and the development of the Democratic-Republican party, 1791–1801' (Ph.D. thesis, Columbia University, 1950), 1,109–10, judging by the reiteration by Republican editors and the intensity of reaction by Federalists, suggests that 'the three most deadly weapons' in the Republican armory were the charges of monarchism, excessive government spending and British influence in the Washington and Adams administrations.

60 Letter to T. M. Randolph, January 7, 1793, *Writings*, IX, 13.

61 'The Union,' *Writings*, VI, 104.

62 Letter to Madison, April 21, 1790, *The letters and papers of Edmund Pendleton*, ed. D. J. Mays, 2 vols. (Charlottesville, Va., 1967), II, 565–7; see also letter to Harry Innes, August 11, 1790, *ibid.* 571.

63 Letter to N. Lewis, February 9, quoted in Malone, *Jefferson*, II, 328; on February 4 he had warned Robert R. Livingston in New York that there was 'a vast mass of discontent gathered in the South, and how and when it will break God knows.' Letter to Livingston, *The writings of Thomas Jefferson*, ed. P. L. Ford, 10 vols. (New York, 1892–9), V, 277.

64 The interpretation of Richard E. Ellis, *The Jeffersonian crisis* (Oxford, 1971), suggests that the defusing motive is likely, considering the division of the Republican party itself into moderates and extremists. Ellis quotes (p. 234) the letter to Thomas Cooper, July 9, 1807 (*Writings*, ed. Ford, IX, 102), in which Jefferson said he 'had always expected that when the Republicans should have put down all things under their feet, they would schismatize among themselves. I have always expected, too, that whatever names the parties might bear, the real division would be into moderate and ardent republicanism.' But the schisms of the Republican party were local phenomena, and Jefferson strove with some success to keep them local. As Ellis notes (p. 103), Jefferson 'was never prepared to purge' the radicals from the party. Jefferson maintained an intransigent neutrality with regard to the local schisms, in order to maintain the national ascendancy of the Republicans over the defeated Federalists. And most of the participants in both sides of the schism were – unlike John Randolph – prudent enough to claim their loyalty to Jefferson (see Noble E. Cunningham, Jr., *The Jeffersonian Republicans in power: party organization, 1801–1809* (Chapel Hill, N.C., 1963), 226, 235, 300, 304). In his letter to Cooper, following the remarks quoted by Ellis, Jefferson continued, 'In this division there is no great evil,' for what was at stake was 'one shade only, instead of another, of republicanism.' The divisions within the Republicans were not as serious as the division between the Republicans and the Federalist 'apostasy' (*loc. cit.*). The moderates and extremists of each of the

8

rival parties in the 1790s shared their moderate and extreme temperaments with their respective opposites; they were no less opposite for that. (Cooper himself – though a moderate in the Pennsylvania schism, who was eventually driven from state politics to the chair of chemistry in Carlisle [now Dickinson] College – had radical credentials as good as his opponents': his radical philosophy had made him unacceptable to the Royal Society, he had begun correspondence between the Manchester Constitutional Society and the Jacobins in France, he had been vilified by Burke in the House of Commons and he had been convicted under the Federalists' Sedition Act.) The moderation of some Republicans consisted not in their lukewarm convictions, but in the prudent means they adopted to ensure the ascendancy of their beliefs.

65 *Federalist*, No. 1.
66 Aristotle, *Nicomachean ethics*, VI, vii.
67 Letter to Thomas Dwight, January 23, 1792, *Works*, I, 111.
68 *Essays*, I, 307–8.
69 Hamilton to Washington, August 18, 1792, *Works*, II, 262.
70 *An Oration... July 4th, 1792... Boston...* (Boston, 1792), 11–16.
71 Davis, *Essays*, II, 31; see also James Truslow Adams, *New England in the Republic 1776–1852* (Boston, 1927), 202–3; and Douglass C. North, *Growth and welfare in the American past: a new economic history* (Englewood Cliffs, N.J., 1966), 63, 69.
72 *Essays*, II, 286. Jefferson himself, although differing on the source, testified to the ubiquity of the speculative temper, which he claimed had 'even disarmed the hand of the tailor of his needle and thread.' Letter to Gouverneur Morris, August 30, 1791, *Writings*, VIII, 240–1.

Chapter 5. The idealism of the Republican challenge

1 Julian P. Boyd, 'Thomas Jefferson's "Empire of Liberty",' in *Thomas Jefferson: a profile*, ed. M. D. Peterson (New York, 1967), 184.
2 'A Full Vindication of the Measures of the Congress, &c.' (1774), *The papers of Alexander Hamilton*, ed. H. C. Syrett and J. E. Cooke (New York, 1961–), I, 67.
3 *The Antifederalist papers*, ed. M. Borden (Michigan State University Press, 1965), 36; see also Cecelia M. Kenyon, 'The political thought of the Antifederalists,' introduction to *The Antifederalists* (New York, 1966), xxxix–xlii.
4 *The states rights debate*, ed. A. T. Mason (2nd ed., New York, 1972), 106.
5 *Antifederalist papers*, ed. Borden, 36–8.
6 Charles C. Thach, Jr., *The creation of the Presidency 1775–1789* (Baltimore, Md., 1969; first ed. 1923), 34–43, 53–4, 88, 176.
7 See letter to Richard Henry Lee, December 3, 1787, *The writings of Samuel Adams*, ed. H. A. Cushing, 4 vols. (New York, 1904–8), IV, 323–6; 'Dissent of the Antifederalist minority' (of Pennsylvania), December 18, 1787, *States rights*, ed. Mason, 141; Philip A.

Crowl, 'Anti-Federalism in Maryland, 1787–1788,' *William and Mary Quarterly*, third series, 4 (1947), 464; *The papers of George Mason*, ed. R. A. Rutland, 3 vols. (Chapel Hill, N.C., 1970), III, 1,059–63; Letter to Patrick Henry, September 14, 1789, *The letters of Richard Henry Lee*, ed. J. C. Ballagh, 2 vols. (New York, 1911–14), II, 502; Richard Allen Rutland, *The ordeal of the Constitution: the Antifederalists and the ratification struggle of 1787–1788* (Norman, Okla., 1966), 29–30; and Jackson Turner Main, *The Antifederalists: critics of the Constitution 1781–1788* (Chapel Hill, N.C., 1961), 129.

8 *Federalist*, No. 10; see also No. 3.

9 *Loc. cit.*

10 *Op. cit.* 39.

11 Gordon S. Wood, *The creation of the American Republic, 1776–1787* (Chapel Hill, N.C., 1969), 520; Rutland, *Ordeal*, 312, 314; Lance Gilbert Banning, 'The quarrel with Federalism: a study in the origins and character of Republican thought' (Ph.D. thesis, Washington University, St. Louis, Mo., 1972), 181–92, suggests that Antifederalists can be understood as spokesmen for the old English opposition fear of corrupting power, but he neglects the basis of Antifederalists' fears of government, in their benign judgement of the people. If this judgement is not seen as an important part of Antifederalism, it is difficult to see why Antifederalist fears should be considered as 'the seeds from which opposition to Hamilton eventually grew' (Banning, p. 194.) They could just as well be seen as the seeds of opposition to Jefferson. Opposition ideology was protean; it supported (without being definitive and characteristic of) Revolutionary Patriots, Federalists of the 1780s, Antifederalists, Jeffersonian Republicans, Old Republicans and Federalists after the Revolution of 1800. The connection between Antifederalism and Jeffersonian Republicanism was less flexible than that.

12 *Antifederalist papers*, ed. Borden, 180.

13 *States rights*, ed. Mason, 145.

14 *Ibid.* 106; see also R. H. Lee to George Mason, October 1, 1787, *Papers of Mason*, III, 996; Kenyon, 'Political thought of Antifederalists,' xiii, xliv–vi, lxii–v; and Main, *Antifederalists*, xiii–xiv, 117–27.

15 Letter of Monsieur d'Ivernois, February 6, 1795, *The writings of Thomas Jefferson*, ed. A. A. Lipscomb and A. E. Bergh, 20 vols. (Washington, 1903–5), IX, 299–300.

16 No. 51. Today political scientists talk less happily about 'electoral disaggregation.'

17 'Notes on Professor Ebelings's Letter of July 30, 1795,' *Writings*, ed. Ford, VII, 48.

18 Letter to Nathaniel Niles, March 22, 1801, *Writings*, X, 232–3.

19 Letter to General Warren, March 21, 1801, *ibid.* 231.

20 Letter to James Madison, September 8, 1793, *ibid.* IX, 228.

21 Quoted in Gerald Stourzh, *Alexander Hamilton and the idea of Republican government* (Stanford, Calif., 1970), 116.

22 (And – occasionally – when criticizing the Constitution's lack of a bill of rights.) Kenyon, 'Political thought of Antifederalists,' xcii–iv.

Even then, the notion was never far away; for example, when R. H. Lee contemplated 'the Commercial plunder of the South,' he spoke of 'the encroachments of power upon the indispensable rights of human nature.' Letter to George Mason, October 1, 1787, *Papers of Mason*, III, 996.

23 Kenyon, 'Political thought of Antifederalists,' cxii; see also Main, *Antifederalists*, 184–6. Kenyon suggests that the Jacksonian notion of the simplicity of government was an attempt to solve this Antifederalist problem (*ibid.* cxiii). But this notion first emerged with the Republicans, in the 1790s. See Marvin Meyers, *The Jacksonian persuasion* (New York, 1960), 28–9; and Rutland, *Ordeal*, 123.

The hypothesis propounded by Lee Benson, *Turner and Beard* (Glencoe, Ill., 1960), 215–28, that the struggles of the 1780s and 1790s were fundamentally between 'agrarian-minded' and 'commercial-minded' Americans, makes too little allowance for these differences between Republicanism and Antifederalism.

24 'The Farmer Refuted,' February 1775, *The papers of Alexander Hamilton*, ed. H. C. Syrett and J. E. Cooke (New York, 1961–), I, 95.

25 *Political Inquiries* (Wilmington, Del., 1791), i–viii, 47, 107, 9–10.

26 *Ibid.* 79.

27 'Common Sense,' *The complete writings of Thomas Paine*, ed. P. S. Foner, 2 vols. (New York, 1945), I, 4, 6. On Coram, see John A. Munroe, *Federalist Delaware* (New Brunswick, N.J., 1954), 188–92.

28 Cecelia M. Kenyon, 'Where Paine went wrong,' *American Political Science Review*, 45 (1931), 1,089.

29 *Ibid.* 1,092–5.

30 *The Rights of Man*, ed. H. Collins (Harmondsworth, Mdx., 1969), 116.

31 *Ibid.* 233.

32 'Common Sense,' *loc. cit.*

33 *Ibid.* 7, 28.

34 *Rights of Man*, 203, 199.

35 Speech in the Virginia ratifying convention, June 11, 1788, *Papers of Mason*, III, 1,059.

36 *Federalist*, No. 51.

37 *Ibid.* Nos. 35 and 36 (Hamilton); No. 57 (Madison).

38 *Op. cit.* 4 (original emphasis).

39 Quoted in Albert Hall Bowman, *The struggle for neutrality: Franco-American diplomacy during the Federalist era* (Knoxville, Tenn., 1974), 118 n. 38.

40 Joseph Priestley, *Letters to the Right Honourable Edmund Burke, Occasioned by his Reflections on the Revolution in France, &c.* (Birmingham, 1791; reprinted in New York, 1791), iv.

41 *Ibid.* viii, 2, 22 (cf. 140–52). (Paine alleged that the King had become a mere executive official, on the model of the American President, by the new French Constitution.)

42 *Rights of Man*, 65, 113; *The writings of John Quincy Adams*, ed. W. C. Ford, 7 vols. (New York, 1913–17), I, 71–5; Noble E. Cunningham,

Jr., *The Jeffersonian Republicans: the formation of party organization, 1789–1801* (Chapel Hill, N.C., 1957), 12.

43 *Letter from Mr. Paine to Mr. Secretary Dundas* (New York, 1792), 6–7; Paine ignored the fact that Yorktown had been a (monarchical) French victory as much as an American one, and credited America's independence to its 'Representative system of Government, though since better organized.'

44 *Rights of Man*, 250, 184–6, 234.

45 *Op. cit.* 4–5.

46 Letter to James Madison, January 30, 1787, *The papers of Thomas Jefferson*, ed. J. P. Boyd (Princeton, 1950–), XI, 93.

47 *Rights of Man*, 187, 136, 166, 230, 186, 203, 187, 80, 88 (original emphasis).

48 First Inaugural Address, March 4, 1801, *Writings*, III, 320–1. See Lynton K. Caldwell, *The administrative theories of Hamilton and Jefferson* (Chicago, 1944), 133–4.

49 *Rights of Man*, 148, 230, 136, 92, 140, 190, 220, 166.

50 Letter to Barlow, June 20, 1792, *Writings*, VIII, 382–3.

51 *The works of Joel Barlow*, 2 vols. (Gainesville, Fla.; 1970), I, 120, 173, 222, 246–7, 266–8, 275, 282–4, 289–307, 377.

52 Anthony, Earl of Shaftesbury, *Characteristicks*, 3 vols. (n.p., 1714), I, 88–102.

53 Gottfried Wilhelm Leibniz, *Judgement of the Works of the Earl of Shaftesbury* (1712), in *The political writings of Leibniz*, tr. P. Riley (Cambridge, 1972), 195–8. See also the summaries of Ernest Tuveson, 'The origins of the "Moral Sense",' *Huntington Library Quarterly*, 11 (1948), 241–59; Daniel Walker Howe, *The Unitarian conscience: Harvard moral philosophy, 1805–61* (Cambridge, Mass., 1970), 45–8; Yehoshua Arieli, *Individualism and nationalism in American ideology* (Cambridge, Mass., 1964), 99–108; Isaac Kramnick, *Bolingbroke and his circle* (Cambridge, Mass., 1968), 88–95; and Harvey C. Mansfield, Jr., *Statesmanship and party government: a study of Burke and Bolingbroke* (Chicago, 1965), 54–8, 75. Wilson Carey McWilliams, in his study of *The idea of fraternity in America* (Berkeley, Calif., 1973), underestimates the extent to which fraternity can be a truly modern idea, built on Hobbesian grounds, though in opposition to Hobbes as well as to traditional ideas of fraternity.

Reliance on something like the eighteenth-century version of the moral sense seems to persist even today as the resort of the idealistic positivist; see A. J. Ayer, 'Love among the logical positivists', (London) *Sunday Times*, April 9, 1972, p. 16.

54 Letter to Doctor John Manners, June 12, 1817, *Writings*, XV, 124; see also Jefferson to John Adams, October 14, 1816, *ibid.* 76–7.

55 Bernard W. Sheehan, 'Paradise and the noble savage in Jeffersonian thought,' *William and Mary Quarterly*, third series, 26 (1969), 352–3.

56 *Notes on the State of Virginia* (London, 1787), VI, 99–107; XI, 150–1; Letter to James Madison, January 30, 1787, *Papers of Jefferson*, XI,

93; Letters to Thomas Law and to John Adams, June 13, 1814, and to Samuel Kercheval, July 12, 1816, *Writings*, xiv, 141–2; xv, 40.

57 Above, p. 23.

58 Letters to Benjamin Rush, April 21, 1803; to John Manners, June 12, 1817; to Dupont de Nemours, April 24, 1816; to John Adams, October 14, 1816; and to John Holmes, April 22, 1820 – *Writings*, x, 382, 385; xv, 124; xiv, 490; xv, 76–7, 249; *Notes on Virginia*, xi, 151. In Jefferson's notable dialogue between Head and Heart (Letter to Maria Cosway, October 1786, *Papers*, x, 443–53), Heart does indeed hold sway, as it claims (p. 450), over the 'sphere of morals'; Head may talk (pp. 448–9) in a genuinely Epicurean vein, but acknowledges (p. 445) that 'publick utility' is one of its chief objects.

In contrast to Jefferson, Nathaniel Chipman, a Federalist, said that the moral sense was 'not to be understood any thing like a moral instinct' (*Sketches of the Principles of Government* [Rutland, Vt; 1793], 51–2), and the Rev. Simon Finley Williams remarked: 'As reason is that which dignifies the nature of man above the brutal herd and feathered tribe, 'tis also a distinguishing trait in his character, that he is as far superior for sociability than they, as reason exceeds instinct. The powers of sympathy within us create the most pleasing as well as the most painful sensations.' Without this rational mutual attraction, men 'would enjoy no more good from society than the beasts of the field, no more pleasure from the claims of friendship than the fowls of heaven.' (*An Oration, Delivered on the Fourth of July, 1796... at Meredith Bridge* [Dover, N.H., 1796], 4–5.)

59 Letter to Mr. Lithson, January 4, 1805, *Writings*, xi, 55; Merrill Peterson, *Thomas Jefferson and the new nation* (New York, 1970), 941. J. W. Cooke, 'Jefferson on Liberty,' *Journal of the History of Ideas*, 34 (1973), 573–4, notices the relationship in Jefferson's mind between liberty, property and virtue, and the importance of a median amount of property to combat the 'dangerous allurements of luxury, dissipation and vice.'

60 Stourzh, *Hamilton*, 191–5; see also *Papers of Mason*, iii, 1,258–9; and Henry Nash Smith, *Virgin land: the American West as symbol and myth* (New York, 1957), 21–2, 304. Nash teaches (p. 89) that the Leatherstocking story, which flourished on the agrarian ideal, was transmuted into the modern detective story when nature was no longer believed to be so benign. See Leo Strauss, *Natural right and history* (Chicago, 1953), 181 n. 18.

61 *Notes on Virginia*, xiv, 248; xvii, 269; Joseph Dorfman, *The economic mind in American civilization*, 4 vols. (New York, 1946–59), i, 435. Tocqueville was to suggest that moderately wealthy Americans did not avoid but embraced both the hopes of the poor and the fears of the rich.

62 *Discourses*, i, 4–6.

63 *Notes on Virginia*, xiii, 212, 209.

64 Kenyon, 'political thought of Antifederalists,' lvi–xi, lxxxiii–v.
65 Dumas Malone, *Jefferson and his time* (Boston, 1948–), II, 172–3;
   Rutland, *Ordeal*, 272–8.
66 Letter to James Madison, March 15, 1789, *Papers of Jefferson*, XIV,
   661.
67 *Writings*, VIII, 12–13.
68 Bernard Bailyn, 'Boyd's Jefferson: notes for a sketch,' *New England
   Quarterly*, 33 (1960), 380–400; cf. Gilbert Chinard, *Thomas Jefferson:
   the apostle of Americanism* (Boston, 1929), 213.
69 *Writings*, VIII, 36; see also letters to James Monroe, June 20, 1790,
   and to Dr. Gilmer, June 27, 1790, anticipating and outlining the
   residence-assumption deal (*ibid.* 43–4, 53).
70 Letter to Mason, February 4, 1791, *Papers of Mason*, III, 1,224.
   Mason had predicted in the Philadelphia and Richmond Conventions in 1787 and 1788 that funding would lead to the 'pestilent
   practice of stock-jobbing' (*ibid.* 1,088–9).
71 Letter to Jefferson, January 10, 1791, *Papers of Mason*, III, 1,218.
72 Monroe told Jefferson that his preface to the *Rights of Man* had
   made his opinions as well known as if he had published a volume.
   Letter to Jefferson, July 25, 1791, *The writings of James Monroe*, ed.
   S. M. Hamilton, 9 vols. (New York, 1898–1903), I, 226.
73 *Writings*, XVIII, 186–7.
74 *Ibid.*
75 Letter to Colonel Innes, March 13, 1791, *ibid.* VIII, 145–6. See also
   letters to James Monroe, July 10, 1791; to Edward Rutledge,
   August 25, 1791; and to Gouverneur Morris, August 30, 1791; *ibid.*
   208, 232–4, 240–1. Jefferson began his suspicious *Anas* in August
   1791.
76 *Anas*, February 29, 1792, *ibid.* I, 290–2 (original emphasis). Before
   February 1791, Jefferson himself had outlined a plan for the
   federal subsidy of American fisheries; 'Report on Cod and Whale
   Fisheries,' February 1, 1791, *ibid.* III, 120–44. This plan, however,
   was a part of Jeffersonian foreign policy, seeking commercial
   retaliation against Britain. Samuel Flagg Bemis, *Jay's Treaty*, rev.
   ed. (New Haven, Conn., 1962), 111; Malone, *Jefferson*, II, 334; Julian
   P. Boyd, *Papers of Jefferson*, XIX, 140–72.
77 *Anas*, March 7, 1792, *Writings*, I, 293; Letter to Colonel Nicholas
   Lewis, April 12, 1792, *ibid.* VIII, 324–5.
78 Letter to the President of the United States, May 3, 1792, *ibid.* VIII,
   341–9.
79 Letters to Madison, June 4, 1792, and to Lafayette, June 16, 1792,
   ibid. 366, 380–2.
80 *Anas*, July 10, 1792, and October 1, 1792, and Letter to the President of the United States, September 9, 1792, *ibid.* I, 309–12, 318;
   VIII, 394–408. Washington's sanction would have had national
   significance, but it was particularly important for the Republicans
   in Virginia. As late as June 1792, Monroe advised Jefferson that,
   although there was opposition to the government's fiscal policies
   in Virginia, and 'the general sentiment of the people' there was

antimonarchical, they did not yet seem 'even to suspect' the insidious manner in which monarchism was being advanced through government corruption. (Letter to Jefferson, June 17, 1792, *Writings*, I, 231–2.) Monroe's advice is confirmed by John Mercer's *Oration on the 4th of July, 1792, Before the President, Professors, and Masters of William and Mary College* (Richmond, Va., [1792]). The Paine–'Publicola' controversy was not yet connected with federal policy by many Virginians.

81 Rutland, *Ordeal*, 31–2.

82 *Anas*, May 23, 1793, *Writings*, I, 353.

83 Letter from Henry Lee, January 21, 1795, *Life and correspondence of James Iredell*, ed. G. J. McRee, 2 vols. (New York, 1857–8), II, 436.

84 Above, p. 27.

85 'Consolidation,' December 5, 1791, *The writings of James Madison*, ed. G. Hunt, 9 vols. (New York, 1900–10), VI, 67–9 (original emphasis). Neal Reimer, 'James Madison's theory of the self-destructive features of republican government', *Ethics*, 65 (1954), 37, recognizes that partisan solidarity is at odds with Madison's Federalist large republic theory.

86 Cf. letter to Jefferson, October 24, 1787, *Papers of Jefferson*, XII, 278.

87 'Public Opinion,' December 19, 1791, *Writings*, VI, 70 (original emphasis).

88 *Rights of Man*, Part 2, chap. 3, 197–206.

89 January 2, 1792, *Writings*, VI, 80–2.

90 January 23, 1792, *ibid.* 86 (original emphasis).

91 *Ibid.* 87–91.

92 *Federalist*, Nos. 10, 49–51. On the other hand, 'The Antifederalists wanted a more rigorous system of separation of powers, more numerous and more effective checks and balances.' Kenyon, 'Political Thought of Antifederalists', lxxvi–x.

93 February 6, 1792, *Writings*, VI, 91–3.

94 *Ibid.* 93–5.

95 Letter to Jefferson, October 17, 1788, *Papers of Jefferson*, XIV, 20 (above, p. 27).

96 March 5, 22 and 29, 1792, *Writings*, VI, 96–103.

97 April 2, 1792, *ibid.* 104–5 (original emphasis).

98 September 26, 1792, *Writings*, VI, 106–19.

99 *Federalist*, No. 10.

100 *Writings*, VI, 113–18. Jefferson used the same words – 'a government...addressed to the reason of the people and not to their weaknesses' – to describe the party division to his son-in-law in January 1793 (quoted above, p. 81).

101 *Ibid.* 119. Madison noted here that it was 'now well understood that there are peculiarities' in the American 'political situation' that might temporarily favor the anti-republicans – an allusion to Washington's decision to continue as President but to refuse to lend his aura to the Republicans, as Jefferson had learned in July.

102 Letter to William Eustis, the Republican governor-elect of Massachusetts, May 22, 1823, *Writings*, IX, 136; see also letter to

Jefferson, May 27, 1823, *ibid.* 140. William N. Chambers, *Political parties in a new nation: the American experience, 1776–1809* (New York, 1963), 92, mistakes Madison's intention as a 'balance' of the two parties, rather than an overbalance of the morally superior Republicans.

103 Letter to Henry Lee, June 25, 1824, *ibid.* 190.

104 December 20, 1792, *Writings,* VI, 120–3 (original emphasis).

105 Leonard D. White, *The Federalists* (New York, 1948), 225.

106 Banning, 'Quarrel,' 290–9, concerned to place Logan within the paradigm of opposition rhetoric, fails to notice this basis of Logan's politics in human nature. If, as Banning claims (pp. 295 ff.), 'Logan's pamphlets of 1791 and 1792 can...be studied as a record of the transformation of a Federalist of 1787 into a Republican stalwart,' it would be well to pay attention to Logan's thoughts on human nature, since these clarify the principles and the origins of the Republicans' departures from Federalism and appeals to Antifederalist logic.

107 *Letters Addressed to the Yeomanry...* (Philadelphia, 1791), 3–7, 9–14, 19, 23–4, 27, 32, 35, 38, 43.

108 *Ibid.* 34–6.

109 Davis, *Essays,* I, 428–34.

110 *Of Commerce and Luxury* (Philadelphia, 1791), iii–iv. I have not found any English editions of this work.

111 *Ibid.* 1, 7, 9, 11–18, 22, 24, 33, 35–6.

112 Rush claimed authorship of the work in a letter to Madison, April 10, 1790, *Letters,* I, 543. In this same letter, Rush repeated his strong support of the federal government, and his equally strong disgust with the corrupting tendencies of 'the Secretary's report' (on public credit).

113 *Information to Europeans...* (Philadelphia, 1790), 3–4, 6–11, 14.

114 Letter to John Adams, July 21, 1789, *Letters,* I, 522–3; *Information to Europeans,* 11; 'Commonplace Book,' 1791, *The autobiography of Benjamin Rush,* ed. G. W. Corner (Princeton, 1948), 197–200.

115 Letter to Jeremy Belknap, June 21, 1792, *Letters,* I, 620–1.

116 It should be noted that he fought this battle with Republican techniques, too. On the rival theories of the proper treatment of yellow fever, see Martin S. Pernick, 'Politics, parties, and pestilence,' *William and Mary Quarterly,* third series, 29 (1972), 559–86. Republicans blamed the disease on local conditions; Federalists blamed it on foreign importations. Pernick suggests that both parties were right in part.

117 Letter from Rush, September 24, 1792, 'Some papers of Aaron Burr,' ed. W. C. Ford, *Proceedings of the American Antiquarian Society,* 29 (1919), 97 (original emphasis).

118 Rutland, *Ordeal,* 81–2.

119 Letter to Richard Henry Lee, April 22, 1789, *Writings of Samuel Adams,* IV, 327; *Life and correspondence of Rufus King,* ed. C. R. King, 6 vols. (New York, 1894–1900), I, 318–19.

120 Rutland, *Ordeal,* 105–7.

121 (Boston, 1791), v–vi, 12, 42–3.
122 *The Path to Riches* (Boston, 1792), 46, 7, 5, 8, 68, 6, 40, 36–8, 73, 57.
123 See E. James Ferguson, *The power of the purse* (Chapel Hill, N.C., 1961), 70–1, 174.
124 *The Federalist era* (New York, 1960), 174 n. 48.
125 Alfred F. Young, 'The Mechanics and the Jeffersonians: New York, 1789–1801,' *Labor History*, 5 (1964), 194, quoting a letter from Alexander Macomb to William Constable, February 21, 1792.
126 Benjamin W. Labaree, *Patriots and partisans: the merchants of Newburyport, 1764–1815* (Cambridge, Mass., 1962), 140.
127 Lisle A. Rose, *Prologue to democracy: the Federalists in the South, 1789–1800* (Lexington, Ky., 1968), 70–1.
128 Richard J. Purcell, *Connecticut in transition: 1775–1818* (Middletown, Conn., 1963; first published 1918), 208.
129 David Hackett Fischer, *The revolution of American conservatism: the Federalist party in the era of Jeffersonian democracy* (New York, 1965), 203–18. Regarding the political implications of this sociological fact, see Henry Adams, *History of the United States of America during the first administration of Thomas Jefferson*, 2 vols. (New York, 1891), I, 264–5.
130 'Publicola,' IV, *The writings of John Quincy Adams*, ed. W. C. Ford, 7 vols. (New York, 1913–17), I, 81.
131 As expressed by a follower of Beard, Wilfred E. Binkley, *American political parties* (4th ed., New York, 1962), 87.

Chapter 6. Principles and rhetoric in the critical elections of 1793–1800

1 Ames to Minot, February 20, 1793, *Works of Fisher Ames*, ed. S. Ames, 2 vols. (Boston, 1854), I, 128; Jefferson, *Anas*, August 3, 1793, *The writings of Thomas Jefferson*, ed. A. A. Lipscomb and A. E. Bergh, 20 vols. (Washington, D.C., 1903–5), I, 383 (original emphasis).
2 C. Gore to R. King, Boston, March 10, 1793, *Life and correspondence of Rufus King*, ed. C. R. King, 6 vols. (New York, 1894–1900), I, 483.
3 *Anas*, March 2, 1793, *Writings*, I, 345–6.
4 For fuller information on the Giles Resolutions, see Dumas Malone, *Jefferson and his time* (Boston, 1948–), III, 14–36; and Noble E. Cunningham, *The Jeffersonian Republicans: the formation of party organization, 1789–1801* (Chapel Hill, N.C., 1963), 51–4.
5 [John Taylor], *An Examination of the Late Proceedings in Congress, Respecting the Official Conduct of the Secretary of the Treasury* [Richmond, Va., 1793] ('United States, 8th March, 1793'), 3–7, 11–13, 27–8.
6 *Journal of the First Session of the Senate of the United States of America* (Washington, D.C., 1820), 502; *Life and correspondence of King*, I, 513.
7 Letter to ———, March 18, 1793, *The papers of Thomas Jefferson*, ed. J. P. Boyd (Princeton, N.J., 1950–), IX, 45.

8 Theodore Dwight, *An Oration ... Cincinnati ... Connecticut ... 4th July, 1792* (Hartford, Conn., 1792), 11, 15, 17, 18; Joseph Blake, Jr., *An Oration ... July 4th, 1792 ... Boston ...* (Boston, 1792), 14.

9 *A Letter from M. Condorcet ... With A Letter from Thomas Paine to the People of France ...* (New York, 1793), 13; Charles D. Hazen, *Contemporary American opinion of the French Revolution* (Baltimore, Md., 1897), 254–9.

10 Charles Crawford, *Observations Upon the Revolution in France* (Boston, 1793), 35.

11 William Stuart, *An Oration ... before the Uranian Society in the City of New York ... 12th March, 1793* (New York, 1794), 19–21.

12 [Hugh Henry Brackenridge], 'Louis Capet lost his Caput,' *National Gazette*, April 20, 1793, in *The life and writings of Hugh Henry Brackenridge*, ed. C. M. Newlin (Princeton, N.J., 1932), 131; Joel Barlow, *A Letter to the National Convention of France, on the Defects in the Constitution of 1791 ...* (London, 1792; reprinted New York, 1793), in *The works of Joel Barlow*, 2 vols. (Gainesville, Fla., 1970), I, 35.

13 *Life and correspondence of King*, I, 440–8; see also [Hamilton], 'Americanus,' *The works of Alexander Hamilton*, ed. H. C. Lodge, 8 vols. (New York, 1886), IV, 261–82.

14 John T. Morse, Jr., *John Quincy Adams* (Boston, 1899), 19.

15 *The writings of John Quincy Adams*, ed. W. C. Ford, 7 vols. (New York, 1913–17), I, 135–46 (reprinted from *Columbian Centinel*, April 24 to May 11, 1793).

16 *The Letters of Pacificus*, appended to *The Federalist* (Hallowell, 1852), 405–31.

17 *Writings*, III, 226–43 (April 28, 1793); see also Brackenridge's unsigned letter 'To the President of the United States,' *National Gazette*, May 15, 1793, in *Life and writings*, 131–2: 'there is an implied obligation to assist the *weak* against the *strong*, the *oppressed* against the *oppressor*, on the same principle as in the case of an individual in a state of nature, who sees another attempt an unjust force upon a third, and ought to interfere to preserve right.' Brackenridge, a Westerner, suggested helping France by making 'a push' toward Canada.

18 Unlike Adams ('Publicola,' x, in *Writings of John Quincy Adams*, I, 105), Hamilton did not avail himself of Rousseau's opinion that making war was properly an action of the executive.

19 *A Sermon, Massachusetts, May 29, 1793 ... Election* (Boston, 1793), 14–15, 28–9.

20 *A Sermon, Delivered at Worcester, on the Eleventh of June 1793 Before the ... Free and Accepted Masons of the Commonwealth of Massachusetts* (Worcester, 1793), 8, 15–16, 20.

21 [Brackenridge], '*To the President of the United States,*' *loc. cit.*

22 John Quincy Adams, *An Oration ... July 4th, 1793, at ... Boston ...* (London, 1793 [reprinted from Boston edition]), 15–16.

23 *An Oration ... in the Baptist Meeting-House ... July 4th, 1793* [Providence, R.I., 1793], 14, 19.

24 *A Sermon...New York, July 4th, 1793...at the Request of the Tammany Society, or Columbian Order* (New York [1793]), 32.

25 'Oration by Citizen Brackenridge...,' *A Political Miscellany* (New York, 1793), 28.

26 'Extracts from a Speech, Made by Maximilien Robertspierre [*sic*], in the National Convention, on the Tenth of May 1793,' *ibid.* 12–13. (See also Maximilien Robespierre, *Report upon the Principles of Political Morality* [Philadelphia, 1794], 2–5.)

27 'Extract from an Oration...Elihu Palmer, citizen of Pennsylvania...,' *Political Miscellany*, 23–4.

28 Samuel Deane, *An Oration, Delivered in Portland, July 4th, 1793...* (Portland, Maine, 1793), 11–12.

29 Elias Boudinot, *An Oration...Elizabeth-Town, New Jersey,...Society of the Cincinnati, on the Fourth of July, M.DCC.XCIII.* (Elizabeth-Town, N.J., 1793), 22.

30 Alexander MacWhorter, *A Festival Discourse...* (Newark, N.J., 1793), 13.

31 Elisha Lee, *An Oration...Lenox, the 4th July, 1793...* (Stockbridge, Mass., 1793), 12–13, 6, 14–15.

32 Letter to William Short, January 3, 1793, *Writings*, IX, 11; and *Anas*, February 7, 1793, *ibid.* I, 331.

33 Letter to Edmund Randolph, June 2, 1793, *ibid.* IX, 108–9.

34 Albert Hall Bowman, *The struggle for neutrality: Franco-American diplomacy during the Federalist era* (Knoxville, Tenn., 1974), Chap. 3.

35 Letter to Jefferson, August 21, 1793, *The writings of James Monroe*, ed. S. M. Hamilton, 9 vols. (New York, 1898–1903), I, 271–2.

36 Conference with Washington, *Anas*, August 6, 1793, *Writings*, I, 385–6.

37 Letter to Madison, August 11, 1793, quoted in Cunningham, *Republicans: party organization*, 55–6; Bowman, *Struggle*, Chap. 4.

38 [Alexander Graydon], *Memoirs of a Life, Chiefly Passed in Pennsylvania, within the Last Sixty Years* (Edinburgh, 1822; first published 1811), 383; Ames to Dwight, August 1793, *Works*, I, 229.

39 *Second Treatise*, XII (sections 144–8) (cf. XIII [section 153]).

40 *The Letters of Helvidius*, appended to *The Federalist* (Hallowell, 1852), 434–8, 455–6, 450. (The 'Helvidius' essays also appear in Madison's *Writings*, VI, 138–88). In 1794 James Thomson Callender's *Political Progress of Britain*, detailing the underside of the British Empire, was reprinted in Philadelphia, from the Edinburgh and London edition of 1792, with the addition of approving remarks from Jefferson (p. 3).

41 *Staunton, September 3d, 1793. Considering it the duty of the people of this district...* [Broadside, Staunton, Va., 1793].

42 Monroe to John Taylor, August 29, 1793, 'Letters of James Monroe,' ed. W. C. Ford, *Proceedings of the Massachusetts Historical Society*, 42 (1909), 321.

43 'Caroline Resolves Concerning Relations with France, September 10, 1793,' *The letters and papers of Edmund Pendleton*, ed.

D. J. Mays, 2 vols. (Charlottesville, Va., 1967), II, 608–10, 612 ed. n. (my emphasis).

44 Letter to Washington, September 11, 1793, *ibid.* 613.

45 Ames to Dwight, August 1793, *Works*, II, 129. John Trumbull complained that the partisan warfare in America 'blighted' artistic enterprise. *The autobiography of Colonel John Trumbull*, ed. T. Sizer (New Haven, Conn., 1953), 173. On the peculiar 'violence of parties' in America in the 1790s, see D. M. Erskine to Thomas Erskine, December 11, 1798, and January 1, 1799, 'Letters from America, 1798–9,' ed. P. H. Menk, *William and Mary Quarterly*, third series, 6 (1949), 259, 277–8.

46 Samuel Latham Mitchill, *An Oration, Pronounced before the Society of Black Friars, at their Anniversary Festival...New York...the 11th of November, 1793* (New York, 1793), 30. Mitchill spoke 'under the full conviction, that the genuine and candid sentiments now communicated are *right*' (original emphasis). He called upon Americans to 'reclaim' the wayward 'with gentle management if thou canst; if not...rising terrible in thy anger, thou shalt reduce them to an observance of order, or send them howling from the land!'

47 'Defense of the President's Neutrality Proclamation' [May, 1793], *The Papers of Alexander Hamilton*, ed. H. C. Syrett and J. E. Cooke (New York, 1961–), XIV, 502.

48 Letter to Madison, June 29, 1793, *Writings of Jefferson*, IX, 148. Not all 'monocrats' sided with Britain. The Rev. James Wilson was not so very exceptional when he praised Hamilton and the cause of domestic manufactures, but thought Britain's 'perseverance in her present system must inevitably involve her Arts and Commerce, her manufactures and national glory, in the common vortex of ruin'; Britain's only hope was republicanism. *An Oration Delivered before the Providence Association of Mechanics and Manufacturers, at their Annual Election, April 14, 1974* (Providence, R.I., 1794), 15–16, 25.

49 'The reason for Jefferson's retirement was no doubt stated by the astute French Minister, Fauchet, to his government: 'Il s'est retiré prudemment pour n'être point forcé à figurer malgré lui dans scènes dont tôt ou tard on dévoilera le secret.''' Moncure Daniel Conway, *Omitted Chapters of History, Disclosed in the Life and Papers of Edmund Randolph* (New York, 1888), 211.

50 *Loc. cit.* 457.

51 'Report on the privileges and restrictions on the commerce of the United States in foreign countries. December 16, 1793.' *Writings*, III, 262, 276.

52 Jerald A. Combs, *The Jay Treaty* (Berkeley, Calif., 1970), 116.

53 Letter to Jefferson, March 3, 1794, *Writings of Monroe*, I, 281–2; Cunningham, *Republicans: party organization*, 70.

54 Vernon G. Setser, *The commercial reciprocity policy of the United States 1794–1829* (Philadelphia, 1937), 109–16.

55 Jefferson, 'Report on Commerce,' *loc. cit.* 279.

56 *The Speeches of Mr. Smith...in the House of Representatives, in*

January, 1794, on... Commercial Regulations... (Philadelphia, 1794), 31–3, 72–4 (original emphasis). Summarized in Smith's *Address... to his Constituents* (Philadelphia, 1794).

57 James Madison, *Speech, in the House of Representatives... January 14, 1794... in Support of His Propositions for the Promotion of the Commerce of the United States, and in Reply to William Smith, of South-Carolina* (New York, 1794), 11–15.

58 Charles R. Ritcheson, *Aftermath of the Revolution; British policy toward the United States 1783–1795* (Dallas, Tex., 1969), Chap. 15.

59 Letter to Madison, April 3, 1794, *Writings*, IX, 282–3.

60 [William Findley] ('A Citizen'), *A Review of the Revenue System Adopted by the First Congress under the Federal Constitution...* (Philadelphia, 1794), 1–3, 48, 52, 63, 69, 73, 100–3, 113–15, 125–9.

61 *Discourses*, I, 7; III, 1. Machiavelli's notion of the original reign of terror resembles the Federalists' Hobbesian theory of the state of nature.

62 [John Taylor], *An Enquiry into the Principles and Tendency of Certain Public Measures* (Philadelphia, 1794), 1, 3, 7–10, 29–40, 52–5, 64, 58, 62. A more concise (also anonymous) statement of Taylor's position was *A Definition of Parties... Political Effects of the Paper System Considered* (Philadelphia, 1794).

63 Samuel Flagg Bemis, *Jay's Treaty* (rev. ed., New Haven, Conn., 1962), 271.

64 Letter to Jefferson, May 26, 1794, *Writings of Monroe*, I, 297.

65 Letter to Christopher Gore, May 2, 1794, *Works*, I, 142.

66 Letter to John Jay, June 4, 1794, *Papers*, XVI, 456–7.

67 Democratic Society of the City of New York, *ADDRESS to the REPUBLICAN CITIZENS of the UNITED STATES* (New York, 1794), 1. See also Archibald Buchanan, *An Oration... the Republican Society of Baltimore, on the Fourth of July,* [*1794*] (Baltimore, Md., 1795), 25–39.

68 *Oration... on the Fourth of July, 1794... American Revolution Society... and... State Society of Cincinnati* (Charleston, S.C., [1794]), 5.

69 See William Jones, *An Oration... at Concord, the Fourth of July, 1794* (Concord, Mass., 1794), 18–19; John Phillips, *An Oration... July 4th, 1794... Boston...* (Boston, 1794), 13–17; Elijah Waterman, *An Oration... the Society of Cincinnati, Hartford, July 4, 1794* (Hartford, Conn., 1794), 9–13; and Samuel Stillman, *Thoughts on the French Revolution* (Boston, 1795), 26.

70 Jefferson, 'Report on Commerce', *Writings*, III, 274–5; 'Federalist,' V (from *Boston Centinel*, August 8, 1795), in *The Treaty – Its Merits and Demerits Fairly Discussed and Displayed* [Boston, 1796], 109; Benjamin W. Labaree, *Patriots and partisans: the merchants of Newburyport, 1764–1815* (Cambridge, Mass., 1962), 111.

71 *To the Freeholders of the District of Fairfax, Loudon, and Prince William* [Richmond? 1794], 4–6. (Probably published in December; cf. Cunningham, *Republicans: party organization*, 74.)

72 Letters to Christopher Gore, November 18 and December 17, 1794; and to Dwight, December 27, 1794, *Works*, I, 152, 157–8.

73 Letter to Murray, December 16, 1794, *The life and correspondence of James McHenry*, ed. B. C. Steiner (Cleveland, Ohio, 1907), 156.
74 Letter to Madison, December 28, 1794, *Writings*, IX, 296; see also Alfred F. Young, *The Democratic Republicans of New York* (Chapel Hill, N.C., 1967), 419–25; and Leland D. Baldwin, *Whiskey rebels* (rev. ed., Pittsburgh, Pa., 1968), 270.
75 Letter to Thomas Dwight, February 3, 1795, *Works*, I, 166.
76 *Fellow Citizens: The Approach of every important Election...* (Broadside, Albany, N.Y., 1795).
77 [James Madison], *Political Observations* ([Philadelphia], 1795), 3–15. (Dated April 20, 1795; circulated throughout the country by John Beckley: Cunningham, *Republicans: party organization*, 102.)
78 [James Sullivan] ('Citoyen de Novion'), *The Altar of Baal Thrown Down: Or, The French Nation Defended, against the Pulpit Slander of David Osgood, A.M.* (Boston, 1795), 10.
79 Phineas Hedges, *An Oration...Republican Society of Ulster County, and other Citizens... Montgomery...4th of July, 1795* (Goshen, N.Y., 1795), 11–12.
80 Barnabas Bidwell, *An Oration...in Stockbridge, July 1795* (Stockbridge, Mass., 1795), 6, 20.
81 William Hunter, *An Oration...in Newport, July 4, A.D. 1795...* (Newport, R.I., 1795), 14–20. See also Elijah Kellogg, *An Oration...at Portland, July 4, 1795...* (Newburyport, Mass., [1795]), 9–14; and Jonathan Maxcy, *An Oration...in Providence, July 4, A.D. 1795...* (Providence, R.I., 1795), 8–18.
82 Kellogg, *Oration*, 22.
83 Hamilton, 'Report on the Public Credit, January 16, 1795,' *Works*, III, 37–42; 'The Federalist,' IV, in *The American Remembrancer; or, An Impartial Collection of Essays, Resolves, Speeches, &c. Relative, or Having Affinity, to the Treaty with Great Britain*, 3 vols. (Philadelphia, 1795–1796), II, 220.
84 [Eleazer Oswald], *Letters of Franklin, on the Conduct of the Executive, and the Treaty...* (Philadelphia, 1795), 18; 'Caius,' 'Address to the President of the United States,' July 21, 1795, *American Remembrancer*, I, 112; 'A Political Watchman,' 'Observations on the Disposition of Administration to France and England,' *ibid.* II, 203.
85 [Hamilton], *A Defence of the Treaty of Amity, Commerce, and Navigation...as it has appeared in the papers under the signature of Camillus* (New York, 1795), in *Works of Hamilton*, V, 273; [William Loughton Smith] ('A Citizen of South-Carolina'), *A Candid Examination of the Objections to the Treaty...* (Charleston, S.C., 1795), 16, 25, 32–3.
86 Bemis, *Jay's Treaty*, 369; Ritcheson, *Aftermath*, 319–32.
87 [Albert Gallatin] ('A Citizen of Pennsylvania'), *An Examination of the Conduct of the Executive of the United States, Towards the French Republic...* (Philadelphia, 1797) ('written last summer'), 2, 8, 19, 21.
88 'Speech of Mr. J. Thompson, at...Petersburg...August 1, 1795...', *American Remembrancer*, I, 22–6; 'Atticus,' V, *ibid.* II, 225–8; [Edmund Randolph], *Political Truth* (Philadelphia, 1796), 4, 9–11, 14–15, 43.

89 Combs, *Jay Treaty*, 168–9.
90 [Alexander James Dallas], *Features of Mr. Jay's Treaty* (Philadelphia, 1795), 37 (original emphasis); [Oswald], *op. cit.* 22, 38.
91 'Atticus,' VI, *American Remembrancer*, III, 67–8; 'A Republican,' 'Remarks on some of the probable consequences of Mr. Jay's Treaty,' *ibid.* II, 209; [Robert R. Livingston] ('Cato'), *Examination of the Treaty of Amity, Commerce, and Navigation*... (New York, 1795), 85–6; Joseph Fenwick to his cousin, August 20, 1795, 'Letters... 1787–95,' ed. R. K. MacMaster, *Maryland Historical Magazine*, 60 (1965), 55.
92 'Atticus,' VI, *loc. cit.* (original emphasis).
93 [Oswald], *op. cit.* 34.
94 'Strictures on the President's Circular Answer,' *American Remembrancer*, II, 147 ff.
95 [Oswald], *op. cit.* 45–6, 22; [Dallas], *op. cit.* 23–4.
96 'Atticus,' VII, *American Remembrancer*, III, 72. See also *An Address, and Instructions from the People of Spotsylvania County, To James Madison, Esquire* [Broadside, Fredricksburg, 1795]; and *To the Speaker and Members of the House of Representatives*...; *The Representation and Petition of the Subscribers, Inhabitants of the State of———, and Citizens of the United States* [Broadside, Philadelphia? 1795], and *To...Selectmen... Lynnfield* (Salem, Mass. 1796), both circular petitions, seeking to prompt the House of Representatives to do something to maintain American rights against the Treaty.
97 Letter to Edward Rutledge, November 30, 1795, *Writings*, IX, 314.
98 *Annals of the Congress of the United States*, 42 vols. (Washington, D.C., 1834–56), V, 1,291, 1,295; Lisle A. Rose, *Prologue to democracy: the Federalists in the South, 1789–1800* (Lexington, Ky., 1968), 141.
99 Malone, *Jefferson*, III, 259; Young, *Democratic Republicans*, 559 and 'The Mechanics and the Jeffersonians: New York 1789–1801,' *Labor History*, 5 (1964), 198; Cunningham, *Republicans: party organization*, 117; Theodore Sedgwick to R. King, March 12, 1797, *Life and correspondence of King*, II, 159; Letter to Colonel Bell, May 18, 1797, *Writings of Jefferson*, IX, 386; Labaree, *Patriots*, 112; Rose, *Prologue*, 112–14, 128–30.
100 Letter to Colonel James Monroe, July 10, 1796, *Writings*, IX, 348–9; see also letter to James Sullivan, February 9, 1797, *ibid.* 378.
101 *An Argument Respecting the Constitutionality of the Carriage Tax*... (Richmond, [1795]).
102 Malone, *Jefferson*, III, 275.
103 (Philadelphia, 1796); Federalist policies had convinced Paine that the American Constitution was less laudable than he had previously thought – in fact it 'is a copy, though not quite so base as the original, of the form of the British Government...' (*Letter*, in *The Complete Writings of Thomas Paine*, ed. P. S. Foner, 2 vols. [New York, 1945], II, 693.
104 *An Oration, Delivered...on the Fourth of July, A.D. 1796*... (Providence, R.I., 1796), 6–7, 10–16.

105 *An Oration, Delivered July 4th, A.D. 1796...in Newport...*(Warren, R.I., 1796), 20–2.

106 Solomon Sibley, *An Oration Delivered at Mendon, July 4th, 1796...*(Boston, 1796), 7–10; [The Rev.] John Taylor, *An Oration, Delivered...at Deerfield, on the Fourth of July, 1796* (Greenfield, Mass., 1796), 7–14; Samuel Worcester, *An Oration...New Ipswich ...July 4, 1796* (Amherst, N.H., 1796), 8–9, 28; William Loughton Smith, *An Oration, Delivered...Before the Inhabitants of Charleston, South Carolina, on the Fourth of July, 1796* (Charleston, S.C., [1796]), 2–3, 31–2.

107 *An Address to the Citizens of the District of York, in Virginia* (Philadelphia, 1797] (dated Rosewell [Gloucester County], August 5, 1796), 19–21.

108 Albert Gallatin, *A Sketch of the Finances of the United States* (New York, 1796), 100–17, 131, 144–9, 168; Malone, *Jefferson*, III, 255.

109 *Annals of Congress*, VI, 2874.

110 Letter to Jefferson, July 17, 1792, *Writings of Monroe*, I, 238.

111 Letter to William B. Giles, December 31, 1795, *Writings*, IX, 314–18, on Edmund Randolph's trimming. On the partisan usage, 'betweenite' (as opposed to 'moderate'), in these years, see Manning J. Dauer, *The Adams Federalists* (Baltimore, Md., 1953), 276.

112 Letter to Madison, July 5, 1796, *Writings of Monroe*, III, 25.

113 Letter to Madison, December, 17, 1796, *Writings of Jefferson*, IX, 352.

114 Letter to Edward Rutledge, December 27, 1796, *ibid.* 354; see also Rush to Jefferson, January 4, 1797, *Letters of Benjamin Rush*, ed. L. H. Butterfield, 2 vols. (Princeton, 1951), II, 784–5; Jefferson's reply to Rush, January 22, 1797, *Writings*, IX, 373–4; and letter to Thomas Mann Randolph, November 28, 1797, *ibid.* XVI, 201. The French government tended to agree with Jefferson that he would not be able to calm French anger; Malone, *Jefferson*, III, 289–90.

115 *President II: Being Observations of the Late Official Address of George Washington: Designed to Promote the Interest of a Certain Candidate for the Executive, and to Explode the Pretensions of Others. Addressed to the People of the United States* (Philadelphia and Newark, 1796), 4, 8, 12–16.

116 [William Loughton Smith], *The Pretentions of Thomas Jefferson to the Presidency Examined; and the Charges against John Adams Refuted. Part I* (United States [Philadelphia], October 1796), 19–30; *Part II* (United States, November 1796), 39–42 ('Vindication of Mr. Adams's Defence of the American Constitutions,' by 'Union' [William Vans Murray]). Answered by [Tench Coxe], *The Federalist* (Philadelphia, November 1796), who declined to impugn the Bank, funding, the excise and neutrality, but 'felt serious anxieties' at the doctrine of hereditary power visible in Adams' *Defence* and in the 'Discourses on Davila' (which were not positively identified as Adams' work until 1800: Jefferson, *Anas*, March 11, 1800, *Writings*, I, 435).

117 Robert Goodloe Harper to Ralph Izard, November 4, 1796, 'South Carolina Federalist Correspondence 1789–1797,' ed. U. B.

Phillips, *American Historical Review*, 14 (1909), 782–4; Theodore Sedgwick to R. King, March 12, 1797, *Life and correspondence of King*, II, 156–9; Letters to John Adams, March 5, 1797, and April 1, 1797, *Men and times of the Revolution; or memoirs of Elkanah Watson...*, ed. W. C. Watson (2nd ed., New York, 1861), 398–9; Jefferson to Madison, January 1, 1797, *Writings of Jefferson*, IX, 359.

118 Ellis (*Jeffersonian crisis*, 273) cites this flirtation between Adams and the Republicans in support of his minimization of the differences between the moderates of both parties. But Stephen G. Kurtz (*The Presidency of John Adams* [Philadelphia, 1957], 209–38 [pp. 218–38 are cited by Ellis]) has carefully shown how full-fledged partisan motives figured in the jockeying for position by the new President and Vice-President. And when it became clear that the proposed *entente* was not judged conducive to Republican policies, the same Republicans – leaders and followers – who had considered the idea found no difficulty in returning to the campaign version of Adams' politics as irredeemably anti-republican. Adams, who stood to gain by involving Republicans in his administration, was too proud to press on with this policy after he had received cold rebuffs for his attempts to recruit Jefferson or Madison as Ambassador to France. (Perhaps he abandoned this attempt because Hamilton favored it: Hamilton to McHenry, April ?, 1797, *Life and correspondence of McHenry*, 212–13.) The vestiges of the policy are evident in Adams' appointment of Benjamin Rush to a Treasury job, on the assumption that 'His talents might be enlisted by due Notice being taken of him' (Pickering to Adams, *Letters of Rush*, II, 1,210). It was Rush who in 1805 approached Adams' son about offers of a foreign mission, and John Quincy Adams was appointed minister to Russia in 1809 by President Madison. (John T. Morse, Jr., *John Quincy Adams* [Boston, 1899], 68.) Thus the policy which John Adams had tried unsuccessfully in 1797 was used successfully by Jefferson and Madison.

119 Letter to Madison, January 22, 1797, *Writings of Jefferson*, IX, 367–8.

120 Letters to Christopher Gore, December 17, 1796, and to Thomas Dwight, January 5, 1797, *Works*, I, 211, 213.

121 Letters to Phillip Mazzei, April 24, 1796, and Colonel Arthur Campbell, September 1, 1797, *Writings*, IX, 335–6, 419–21; Gallatin to James Nicholson, May 26, 1797, in Henry Adams, *The life of Albert Gallatin* (Philadelphia, 1879), 183.

122 Letter to Colonel Aaron Burr, June 17, 1797, *Writings*, IX, 402–3.

123 *Ibid.*

124 Letter to St. George Tucker, August 28, 1797, *ibid.* 419.

125 John Miller Russell, *An Oration, Pronounced at Charlestown, July 1797* (Charlestown, Mass., 1797), 13–15. The second edition (Philadelphia, 1797) of this speech carried an Advertisement in which William Cobbett praised Russell's 'CLASSICAL ORATION' for its 'true Demosthenean fire.'

126 Samuel F. Dickinson, *An Oration...at Belcherstown, July 4th, 1797* (Northampton, Mass., 1797), 8, 16.

127 Isaac Lewis, *The Political Advantages of Godliness. A Sermon ... Connecticut ... Election, May 11, 1797* (Hartford, Conn., 1797), 8–9.
128 John Mellen, *A Sermon ... Massachusetts ... Election, May 31, 1797* (Boston, 1797), 10 (original emphasis).
129 Samuel F. Dickinson, *op. cit.* 9–11, 19–20.
130 Dr. Oliver Fiske, *An Oration, Pronounced at Worcester ... July 4, 1797* (Worcester, Mass., 1797), 4–11.
131 Dr. Samuel Rockwell, *An Oration ... at Salisbury, Fourth July, Ninety-Seven* (Litchfield, Conn., [1797]), 4–14.
132 Fiske, *op. cit.* 14–15; John Callender, *An Oration, Pronounced July 4, 1797, at the Request of the Inhabitants of the Town of Boston ...* (Boston, 1797), 19; Jack Foster, *An Oration, Delivered at New-Salem, July 4th, 1797 ...* (Northampton, Mass., 1797), 16. Ernest Tuveson, in *Redeemer nation* (Chicago, 1968), remarks that Federalists were abler exponents of manifest destiny than Republicans were. But Federalists' nationalistic messianism was less well adapted than Republican evangelism to the needs of American *party* politics – a point overlooked by J. G. A. Pocock in an account of Federalists and Republicans (in *The Machiavellian moment* [Princeton University Press, 1975], chap. 15) which utilizes Tuveson's remark.
133 Elihu Palmer, *An Enquiry Relative to the Moral and Political Improvement of the Human Species. An Oration ... New York on the Fourth of July ...* (New York, 1797), 2, 6–9, 11–15, 34–5. See also [John Dickinson], *The Letters of Fabius, in 1788 ... and in 1797 ...* (Wilmington, Del., 1797), 83–171; Thomas Erskine, *A View of the Causes and Consequences of the Present War with France* (London, 1797), 6 (noticed in a letter to General Gates, May 30, 1797, *Writings of Jefferson*, IX, 391); and James Monroe, *A View of the Conduct of the Executive ...* (London, 1798; first published in Philadelphia, 1797), 71–6.
134 Gallatin to Nicholson, May 26, 1797, in Adams, *Gallatin*, 184.
135 Richard Buel, Jr., *Securing the Revolution: ideology in American politics, 1789–1815* (Ithaca, N.Y., 1972), 147–8.
136 Repeated in letters to Thomas Pinckney, May 29, 1797, and to Peregrine Fitzhugh, Esq., February 28, 1798, *Writings of Jefferson*, IX, 388–91; X, 2.
137 Alexander DeConde, *Entangling alliance: politics and diplomacy under George Washington* (Durham, N.C., 1958), 498.
138 May 16, 1797, *Annals of Congress*, VII, 56.
139 *Ibid.* 12–14.
140 June 3, 1797, *ibid.* 237.
141 December 19, 1797, Adams, *Gallatin*, 188.
142 Letter to Madison, January 3, 1798, *Writings*, IX, 432.
143 Speech of John Nicholas, January 18, 1798, *Annals of Congress*, VII, 849.
144 *The Speech of Albert Gallatin, Delivered in the House of Representatives ... on the first of March, 1798, upon the Foreign Intercourse Bill* [Philadelphia, 1798], 20–26 (also in *Annals of Congress*, VI, 1,118–1,143).

145 Robert Goodloe Harper, *Speech on the Foreign Intercourse Bill...on the 2d of March, 1798. Annexed to Observations on the Dispute Between the United States and France,* fourth American ed. [Boston, April 1798], 109, 139–40 (also in *Annals of Congress,* VI, 1,159–1,200).

146 William Seal Carpenter, 'The separation of powers in the eighteenth century,' *American Political Science Review,* 22 (1928), 34; Edward S. Corwin, 'The progress of political theory between the Declaration of Independence and the meeting of the Philadelphia Convention,' *American Historical Review,* 30 (1925), 511–13; F. William O'Brien, S.J., 'The executive and the separation principle at the Constitutional Convention,' *Maryland Historical Magazine,* 55 (1960), 201–20.

147 Thomas Jefferson, 'The description of a Mould-board of the least resistance, and of the easiest and most certain construction, taken from a letter to Sir John Sinclair, President of the board of agriculture at London,' *Transactions of the American Philosophical Society,* 4 (Philadelphia, 1799), 320–1 (dated March 23, 1798 – before the XYZ publication, but after Adams' message notifying Congress of the failure of negotiations, and recommending military and naval preparedness – and read May 4, 1798).

148 George Logan, *An Address on The Natural and Social Order of the World... Delivered Before the Tammany Society...the 17th of May, 1798* (Philadelphia, [1798]), 3–7, 11.

149 [John Dickinson], *A Cauton; or Reflections on the Present Contest between France and Great Britain* ([Philadelphia], 1798), 6.

150 Letter to Peregrine Fitzhugh, February 23, 1798, *Writings,* x, 4.

151 Thomas Cooper, *Political Arithmetic* [Philadelphia? 1798]; Jefferson caused eight dozen copies of this pamphlet to be circulated in Virginia in 1800 (Cunningham, *Republicans: party organization,* 221).

152 George Clinton, Jr., *An Oration, Delivered on the Fourth of July, 1798... Mechanics and Tradesmen... Democratic Society... Tammany Society... Cooper's Society, and...[other] Citizens* (New York, 1798), 12–13.

153 *Ibid.* 12.

154 Joseph Warren Scott, *An Oration...July 4, 1798...New Brunswick* (New Brunswick, N.J., 1798), 8; see also James Winchester to McHenry, April 18, 1798, *Life and correspondence of McHenry,* 305–6. (Federalists now saw American party divisions as either an effect [Charles H. Atherton, *An Oration...at Amherst...July 4, 1798* (Amherst, Mass., July 1798)], or a cause [Alexander Addison, *An Oration, on the Rise and Progress of the United States of America, to the Present Crisis...* (Philadelphia, 1798)] of French designs on America.)

155 Paul Allen, *An Oration...in Providence...4th Day of September, A.D. 1798* (Providence, R.I., 1798), 16–18.

156 David B. Ogden, *An Oration...on the Fourth of July, 1798* (Newark, N.J., 1798), 3 (cf. 4); John C[otten] Smith, *An Oration...at Sharon...4th of July, 1798* (Litchfield, Conn., 1798).

157 Thomas S. Sparhawk, *An Oration...at Buckston...July 4th*, A.D. *1798* (Boston, 1798), 7–14; Samuel Austin, *An Oration...at Worcester on the Fourth of July, 1798...* (Worcester, Mass., 1798), 14; Samuel Emerson, *An Oration...Fourth of July, 1798...* (Portland, Maine, 1798), 8; see also John Thornton Kirkland, *An Oration...the Society of ΦBK...Harvard College...July 19, 1798* (Boston, 1798), 6–8; Nathaniel Emmons, *A Discourse, Delivered May 9, 1798, the Day of Fasting and Prayer Throughout the United States* (Wrentham, Mass., 1798), 26; Israel B. Woodward, *American Liberty and Independence. A Discourse, Delivered at Watertown, on the Fourth of July, 1798* (Litchfield, Conn., 1798), 4–13; Samuel W. Bridgham, *An Oration...in Providence, on the Fourth of July*, A.D. *1798...*(Providence, R.I., 1798), 6–12; and Humphrey Marshall, *The Aliens: A Patriotic Poem* (Philadelphia, 1798), 12.

158 [James Sullivan] ('An American'), *An Impartial Review of the Causes and Principles of the French Revolution* (Boston, 1798), 66–99.

159 Letter to Timothy Pickering, June 4, 1798, *Works*, I, 226–9.

160 Entries for June 7 and 26, 1798, in Charles Warren, *Jacobin and Junto...the diary of Dr. Nathaniel Ames* (Cambridge, Mass., 1931), 75, 99.

161 Letter to Jefferson, June 1798, *Writings of Monroe*, III, 129–30; Jefferson concurred with this view: Letter to John Taylor, June 4, 1798, *Writings*, XVI, 206–9.

162 Jefferson to Maria Eppes, December 14, 1801, in Noble E. Cunningham, *The Jeffersonian Republicans in power: party organization, 1801–1809* (Chapel Hill, N.C., 1963), 71.

163 Spencer Roane to Monroe, March 24, 1799, in Cunningham, *Republicans: party organization*, 150.

164 Above, page 148.

165 Jefferson to John Taylor, June 4, 1798, *Writings*, XVI, 206–9.

166 *The early Republic, 1789–1828*, ed. N. E. Cunningham, Jr. (New York, 1968), 143–4.

167 Letter to Jefferson, October 17, 1788, *Papers of Jefferson*, XIV, 20.

168 Speech on December 21, 1798, *Debates in the House of Delegates of Virginia, upon Certain Resolutions ... upon ... the Alien and Sedition Laws* (Richmond, Va., 1798), 163–4; see also the speeches by Taylor on December 13 (p. 5), Mercer on December 15 (p. 27) and Barbour on December 17 (pp. 58–9).

169 Cunningham, *Republicans: party organization*, 129; see also Malone, *Jefferson*, III, 423; and Julian P. Boyd, 'Thomas Jefferson's "Empire of Liberty",' in *Thomas Jefferson: a profile*, ed. M. D. Peterson (New York, 1967), 178–94.

170 *Dinwiddie County Resolutions, November 19, 1798* (Richmond *Examiner, December 6, 1798*), *Early Republic*, ed. Cunningham, 63–9; *An Address from Students of the College of William and Mary, June 8, 1798*, ibid. 58–63; George Nicholas, *A Letter from George Nicholas, of Kentucky, to his friend in Virginia* (Lexington, Ky., 1798), 4–12; James Ogilvie, *A Speech Delivered in Essex County in support of a*

Memorial...on the subject of the Alien and Sedition Acts (Richmond, Va., 1798), 10–12.

171 Chilton Williamson, *Vermont in quandary: 1763–1825* (Montpelier, Vt., 1949).

172 James Lyon, *A Republican Magazine: or, Repository of Political Truths* (Fairhaven, Vt., 1798), vol. 1, no. 4, December 15, 1798, p. 192.

173 Gallatin to his wife, December 14, 1798, Adams, *Gallatin*, 224.

174 [Henry Lee] ('A Citizen of Westmoreland County'), *Plain Truth* [Richmond? 1799], 19; Henry McGilbert Wagstaff, *Federalism in North Carolina, the James Sprunt Historical Publications*, 9 (Chapel Hill, N.C., 1910), 30–3, notes the softness of this Federalist comeback.

175 Cunningham, *Republicans: party organization*, 133–4.

176 Harry Marlin Tinkcom, *The Republicans and Federalists in Pennsylvania, 1790–1801* (Philadelphia, 1950), 189 (cf. 159–60).

177 Letter to Oliver Wolcott, October 16, 1798, *Life and letters of George Cabot* (Boston, 1877), 173; Fisher Ames to Pickering, November 22, 1798, *Works*, I, 241; William A. Robinson, *Jeffersonian Democracy in New England* (New Haven, Conn., 1916), 31–2.

178 Gallatin to his wife, January 18, 1799, Adams, *Gallatin*, 226.

179 Gerard H. Clarfield, *Timothy Pickering and American diplomacy 1795–1800* (Columbia, Mo., 1969), 215, concludes that by mid-1798, Pickering was led 'to the ultimate absurdity of believing that there could be no safety for the United States so long as she remained at peace with France.' George Cabot judged that a war would have been popular because of America's 'commercial spirit,' although he added that 'a love of glory and spirit of Patriotism would have grown upon the love of gain.' Letter to Pickering, February 21, 1799, *Life and letters*, 219–20.

180 Tinkcom, *Republicans and Federalists in Pennsylvania*, 215–19. The leader of 'Fries' Rebellion' was a Federalist.

181 Hamilton to Theodore Sedgwick, February 2, 1799, *Works*, VIII, 525–6.

182 'Laocoon,' No. I (first published in the *Boston Gazette*, April 1799), *Works*, II, 112–14.

183 'Laocoon,' No. II, *ibid.* 128.

184 John C. Miller, *The Federalist era* (New York, 1960), 276.

185 Paul Allen, *An Oration...in Providence...4th Day of September*, A.D. *1798* (Providence, R.I., 1798), 11.

186 Woodward, *American Liberty...* (above, note 157), 14.

187 Alexander DeConde, *The quasi war: the political diplomacy of the undeclared war with France 1797–1801* (New York, 1966), 267, 270; Cunningham, *Republicans: party organization*, 230.

188 Kurtz, *Presidency of Adams*, 374–408.

189 Jacob E. Cooke, 'Country above party: John Adams and the 1799 mission to France,' in *Fame and the Founding Fathers*, ed. E. P. Willis (Bethlehem, Pa., 1967), 53–77; Malone, *Jefferson*, III, 430–4; Henry Adams, *History of the United States of America during the first administration of Thomas Jefferson*, 2 vols. (New York, 1892–9), I, 352–62.

190 Jonathan Maxcy, *An Oration... in Providence, on the Fourth of July, 1799* (Providence, R.I., 1799), 5–12.
191 David Daggett, *Sun-Beams May Be Extracted from Cucumbers, But the Process is Tedious. An Oration... the Fourth of July, 1799... New Haven* (New Haven, Conn., 1799).
192 Thomas Beedé, *An Oration... at Roxbury, July 4, 1799...* (Boston, 1799), 6.
193 Amos Stoddard, *An Oration... Portland... Fourth Day of July, 1799* (Portland, Maine, 1799), 4, 26 (original emphasis).
194 *The Writings of James Madison*, ed. G. Hunt, 9 vols. (New York, 1900–10), VI, 338–40.
195 [Henry Lee] ('A Citizen of Westmoreland County'), *Plain Truth* [Richmond? 1799], 34–47; see also 'An Inhabitant of the North-Western Territory,' *Observations on a Letter from George Nicholas, of Kentucky...* (Cincinnati, 1799), 41.
196 Thomas Andros [Andrews], *An Oration, Delivered at Dighton (Massachusetts), July 4th, 1799* (Newbedford [sic], Massachusetts, 1799), 10–15; Samuel Fiske, *An Oration... at Claremont... July 4th, 1799* (Windsor, Vt., 1799), 8.
197 Cunningham, *Republicans: party organization*, 211–12.
198 Letter to Gerry, January 26, 1799, *Writings*, X, 74–9
199 Cunningham, *Republicans: party organization*, 130.
200 Edmund Pendleton, *An Address... to the American Citizens, on the Present State of Our Country* (Boston, 1799); in *Letters and Papers*, II, 658–9.
201 Charles Ambler, *Sectionalism in Virginia from 1776 to 1861* (Chicago, 1909), 77–8.
202 Thomas Cooper, *Political Essays, Originally Inserted in the Northumberland Gazette, with additions* (Northumberland, Pa., 1799), 30–3.
203 *The Substance of Two Speeches of Mr. Gallatin... the 7th and 11th of February, 1799* (Philadelphia, 1799).
204 [John James Beckley] ('Americanus'), *Address to the People of the United States...* (Philadelphia and Newport, 1800), 3. Five thousand copies of this pamphlet were widely circulated (Cunningham, *Republicans: party organization*, 197).
205 [Philip Morin Freneau] ('Robert Slender'), *Letters on Various interesting and important Subjects* (Philadelphia, December 30, 1799), 135 (reprinted from *Aurora*, March–October, 1799).
206 Tinkcom, *Republicans and Federalists*, 215–53; Malone, *Jefferson*, III, 462–3.
207 Cunningham, *Republicans: party organization*, 235–8. There was speculation that the marriage of Theodosia Burr (Aaron Burr's daughter) to a South Carolina politician had something to do with this outcome; Maria Nicholson to Mrs. Gallatin, February 5, 1801, Adams, *Gallatin*, 244–5.
208 Charles Pinckney, *Three Letters, Addressed to the People of the United States...* (Charleston, S.C., 1799).
209 Robinson, *Jeffersonian Democracy in New England*, 87–9.

210 John Smith, *An Oration, Pronounced July 4th, 1799...Suffield...* (Suffield, Conn., 1799), 3–15.
211 Ezekiel Bacon, *An Oration, Delivered at Williamstown, on the 4th of July, 1799* (Bennington, Vt., 1799), 5–6, 9–15.
212 Letter to Timothy Pickering, November 5, 1799, *Works*, I, 263.
213 DeConde, *Quasi war*, 259–60.
214 Oliver Wolcott to Fisher Ames, December 29, 1799, *Memoirs*, II, 316.
215 'Report on the Resolutions,' *Writings of Madison*, VI, 357.
216 Albert Gallatin, *Views on the Public Debt, Receipt & Expenditure of the United States* (New York, 1800), 58–61.
217 DeConde, *Quasi war*, 265–6.
218 Elihu Palmer, *The Political Happiness of Nations, An Oration. Delivered at the City of New York, on the Fourth July...* [New York, 1800], 11.
219 Noah Webster, Jr., *Ten Letters to Joseph Priestly...* (New Haven, Conn., 1800), 9, 29.
220 Letter to Hamilton? [editor's surmise], August 26, 1800, *Works of Ames*, I, 281.
221 Edward Bangs, *An Oration...at Worcester, July 4, 1800* (Worcester, Mass., 1800), 21 (pp. 6–15 present the Federalist 'art of government'; see also above, p. 51).
222 Cunningham, *Republicans: party organization*, 223–7. Cunningham gives a good account of 'Campaign Appeals' in 1800 (pp. 212–29), and I have not discussed any of the interesting literature he treats here. My only quarrels with his treatment are with his failure (p. 214) to connect the charge of monarchism with the fiscal issues (Republicans did make this connection; for example, [James Cheetham], *An Answer to Alexander Hamilton's Letter, Concerning ...John Adams...* [New York, 1800]), and with his assumption (p. 222) that agrarianism could be expected to appeal only to practicing farmers (Philip Freneau's *Letters on various interesting and important Subjects* [Philadelphia, 1799], 18, 135, provides one exceptional case to Cunningham's statement that agrarianism was stressed only in agricultural regions).
    The Reverend William Linn's *Serious Considerations on the Election of a President* (New York, 1800) sparked off the publicity of Jefferson's deism. One of the many Republican replies to Linn was *Series Facts, Opposed to 'Serious Considerations'* (n.p., October 1800), by 'Marcus Brutus,' who included in his response a genealogy of the Federalist policies that Jefferson and the Republicans were opposing: 'the funding system begets and perpetualizes debt; debt begets intrigue, offices, and corruption; those beget taxation; taxation begets the treasury; the treasury begets a swarm of Pickerings and Daytons; Pickerings and Daytons beget a standing army, and a standing army begets monarchy, and monarchy begets an enslaved and impoverished people' (p. 4).
223 *Connecticut Republicanism. An Oration on the Extent and Power of Political Delusion. Delivered in New Haven... September, 1800* ([New Haven?], 1800), ii. Bishop's Republican belief in the 'Chinese

policy' as the model for America was criticized in Federalist terms by [Noah Webster, Jr.], *A Rod for the Fool's Back* (New Haven, Conn., and Bennington, Vt., [1800]), asserting the civilizing and liberalizing power of commerce.

224 (Newark) *Centinel of Freedom*, December 16, 1800, in Cunningham, *Republicans: party organization*, 247.

225 Cunningham, *Republicans: party organization*, 247–8.

226 *Ibid.*; Robinson, *Jeffersonian Democracy in New England*, 33–5.

Chapter 7. Party politics and party government

1 Adams to Cunningham, September 27, 1808, *Correspondence between the Hon. John Adams and the late William Cunningham, Esq., beginning in 1803, and ending in 1812*, ed. E. M. Cunningham (Boston, 1823).

2 Francis Crawford to Ebenezer Foote, March 7, 1801, in Noble E. Cunningham, Jr., *The Jeffersonian Republicans: the formation of party organization, 1789–1801* (Chapel Hill, N.C., 1957), 260.

3 It might be noted that the national party arrangement was often an important influence on local party contests. Benjamin W. Labaree, *Patriots and partisans: the merchants of Newburyport, 1764–1815* (Cambridge, Mass., 1962), 141, notices that Federalists there had even greater strength in local contests than in national ones. If parties were the neutral instruments of politics that they are seen to be by many political scientists and historians, or if national party labels were mere tags in local contests, the phenomenon of one-party states and areas would not be so evident in the United States, because the pressure for a two-party competition at this level would be more effective.

4 William N. Chambers, *Political parties in a new nation: the American experience, 1776–1809* (New York, 1963), 15.

5 Jefferson to Mazzei, April 24, 1796; to James Sullivan, February 9, 1797; and to Thomas Pinckney, May 29, 1797, *The writings of Thomas Jefferson*, ed. A. A. Lipscomb and A. E. Bergh, 20 vols. (Washington, 1903–5), IX, 335–7, 376–9, 388–91; Jefferson to Joel Barlow, May 3, 1802, *The writings of Thomas Jefferson*, ed. P. L. Ford, 10 vols. (New York, 1892–9), IX, 370–2. (Jefferson seems to have drafted a passage on 'the whigs and tories of nature' for his first Inaugural Address, but did not include it in the final version: *Writings*, ed. Ford, VIII, 1 n.) Madison to William Eustis, May 22, 1823, *The writings of James Madison*, ed. G. Hunt, 9 vols. (New York, 1900–10), IX, 135–6; Monroe to Andrew Jackson, *The writings of James Monroe*, ed. S. M. Hamilton, 9 vols. (New York, 1898–1903), V, 342–7.

6 Letter to Timothy Pickering, June 4, 1798, *Works of Fisher Ames*, ed. S. Ames, 2 vols. (Boston, 1854), I, 227–8.

7 *Massachusetts Mercury*, 1800, in William A. Robinson, *Jeffersonian Democracy in New England* (New Haven, Conn., 1916), 53; see also Jedidiah Morse, *A Sermon, Preached at Charlestown, November 29, 1798* (Worcester, Mass., 1799), 12–15.

8 David Ramsay, *An Oration...on the Fourth of July, 1794...American Revolution Society... and... South-Carolina State Society of Cincinnati* (Charleston, S.C. [1794]), 12.

9 David Hackett Fischer, *The revolution of American conservatism: the Federalist party in the era of Jeffersonian Democracy* (New York, 1965), 203–18.

10 Letter to the Count de Moustier, October 9, 1787, *The papers of Thomas Jefferson*, ed. J. P. Boyd (Princeton, 1950–), XII, 225.

11 Letter to Christopher Gore, November 10, 1799, *Works of Fisher Ames*, ed. S. Ames, 2 vols. (Boston, 1854), I, 265–9.

12 'Falkland No. II,' 1801, *ibid.* II, 132; see also [Alexander Graydon], *Memoirs of a Life, Chiefly Passed in Pennsylvania, within the Last Sixty Years* (Edinburgh, 1822; first published 1811), 389; and Dumas Malone, *Jefferson and his time* (Boston, 1948–), III, 289–90.

13 Fischer, *Conservatism*, 172–3 and *passim*; John A. Munroe, *Federalist Delaware* (New Brunswick, N.J., 1954), 235; Shaw Livermore, Jr., *The twilight of Federalism: the disintegration of the Federalist party 1815–1830* (Princeton, N.J., 1962), viii–ix.

14 Stephen G. Kurtz, *The Presidency of John Adams: the collapse of Federalism, 1795–1800* (Philadelphia, 1957), 407, 404.

15 Henry Adams, *The life of Albert Gallatin* (Philadelphia, 1879), 492. See also his *History of the United States during the administrations of Thomas Jefferson and James Madison*, 9 vols. (New York, 1889–91).

16 Monroe to Jefferson, *Writings of Monroe*, III, 269.

17 See Marvin Meyers, *The Jacksonian persuasion* (New York, 1960).

18 On this point, see Chapter 1 above and Staughton Lynd, *Intellectual origins of American radicalism* (London, 1969), 6–8.

19 Jane Austen, *Northanger Abbey*, Chap. XXVIII.

INDEX

235

Cambridge Studies in the History and Theory of Politics

Editors: MAURICE COWLING, G. R. ELTON, E. KEDOURIE, J. G. A. POCOCK, J. R. POLE *and* WALTER ULLMAN

A series in two parts, studies and original texts. The studies are original works on political history and political philosophy while the texts are modern, critical editions of major texts in political thought. The titles include:

TEXTS

LIBERTY, EQUALITY, FRATERNITY, by James Fitzjames Stephen. Edited with an introduction and notes by R. J. White

VLADIMIR AKIMOV ON THE DILEMMAS OF RUSSIAN MARXISM 1895–1903. An English edition of 'A Short History of the Social Democratic Movement in Russia' and 'The Second Congress of the Russian Social Democratic Labour Party', with an introduction and notes by Jonathan Frankel

TWO ENGLISH REPUBLICAN TRACTS: PLATO REDIVIVUS OR, A DIALOGUE CONCERNING GOVERNMENT (c. 1681), by Henry Neville and AN ESSAY UPON THE CONSTITUTION OF THE ROMAN GOVERNMENT (c. 1699), by Walter Moyle. Edited by Caroline Robbins

J. G. HERDER ON SOCIAL AND POLITICAL CULTURE, translated, edited and with an introduction by F. M. Barnard

THE LIMITS OF STATE ACTION, by Wilhelm von Humboldt. Edited with an introduction and notes by J. W. Burrow

KANT'S POLITICAL WRITINGS, edited with an introduction and notes by Hans Reiss; translated by H. B. Nisbet

KARL MARX'S CRITIQUE OF HEGEL'S 'PHILOSOPHY OF RIGHT', edited with an introduction and notes by Joseph O'Malley; translated by Annette Jolin and Joseph O'Malley

LORD SALISBURY ON POLITICS. A SELECTION FROM HIS ARTICLES IN 'THE QUARTERLY REVIEW' 1860–1883, edited by Paul Smith

FRANCOGALLIA, by François Hotman. Latin text edited by Ralph E. Giesey. English translation by J. H. M. Salmon

THE POLITICAL WRITINGS OF LEIBNIZ. Edited and translated by Patrick Riley

TURGOT ON PROGRESS, SOCIOLOGY AND ECONOMICS: A PHILOSOPHICAL REVIEW OF THE SUCCESSIVE ADVANCES OF THE HUMAN MIND ON UNIVERSAL HISTORY. REFLECTIONS ON THE FORMATION AND DISTRIBUTION OF WEALTH, edited, translated and introduced by Ronald L. Meek

TEXTS CONCERNING THE REVOLT OF THE NETHERLANDS, edited and with an introduction by E. H. Kossmann and A. F. Mellink

GEORG WILHELM FRIEDRICH HEGEL: LECTURES ON THE PHILOSOPHY OF WORLD HISTORY: REASON IN HISTORY, translated from the German edition of Johannes Hoffmeister by H. B. Nisbet and with an introduction by Duncan Forbes

A MACHIAVELLIAN TREATISE BY STEPHEN GARDINER, edited and translated by Peter S. Donaldson

STUDIES

REGICIDE AND REVOLUTION: SPEECHES AT THE TRIAL OF LOUIS XVI, edited with an introduction by Michael Walzer; translated by Marian Rothstein

1867: DISRAELI, GLADSTONE AND REVOLUTION: THE PASSING OF THE SECOND REFORM BILL, by Maurice Cowling

THE CONSCIENCE OF THE STATE IN NORTH AMERICA, by E. R. Norman

THE SOCIAL AND POLITICAL THOUGHT OF KARL MARX, by Shlomo Avineri

MEN AND CITIZENS: A STUDY OF ROUSSEAU'S SOCIAL THEORY, by Judith Shklar

IDEALISM, POLITICS AND HISTORY: SOURCES OF HEGELIAN THOUGHT, by George Armstrong Kelly

THE IMPACT OF LABOUR 1920–1924: THE BEGINNING OF MODERN BRITISH POLITICS, by Maurice Cowling

ALIENATION: MARX'S CONCEPTION OF MAN IN CAPITALIST SOCIETY, by Bertell Ollman

THE POLITICS OF REFORM 1884, by Andrew Jones

HEGEL'S THEORY OF THE MODERN STATE, by Shlomo Avineri

JEAN BODIN AND THE RISE OF ABSOLUTIST THEORY, by Julian H. Franklin

THE SOCIAL PROBLEM IN THE PHILOSOPHY OF ROUSSEAU, by John Charvet